Carel de Mallery Sculp.   Phls Galle excud.

STUDIES IN HISTORICAL GEOGRAPHY

Mirrors of the New World

Images and Image-Makers
in the Settlement Process

Mirrors
of the
New World

Images and Image-Makers
in the Settlement Process

J. M. POWELL

DAWSON · ARCHON BOOKS

First published in 1977

© J. M. Powell 1977

Wm Dawson & Son Ltd, Cannon House
Folkestone, Kent, England

Archon Books, The Shoe String Press, Inc
995 Sherman Avenue, Hamden, Connecticut 06514 USA

British Library Cataloguing in Publication Data

Powell, J M
 Mirrors of the New World. — (Studies in historical geography).
 1. America — Colonization 2. America — History
 3. Great Britain — Colonies
 I. Title. II. Series
 970   E18.82   77-30328

ISBN 0-7129-0764-5
ISSN   0308-6607

Archon ISBN 0 208 01654 6

Printed litho in Great Britain
by W & J Mackay Ltd, Chatham

for Liverpool,
where the New World always beckoned

Contents

Illustrations

Endpapers: An engraving by Carel van Mallery (1576–1631) from a drawing depicting an imaginary interpretation of America. Courtesy of the New York Historical Society, New York City

Preface

The primary intention of this book is to outline the characteristics and potential of one type of humanistic perspective in geography. It concentrates upon a selection of case studies derived from the predominantly English-speaking countries of the New World, in order to provide a brief guide to some important facets of settlement evolution which might not be so well treated by the adoption of other perspectives. The first chapter examines the theme of imagery, a major explanatory focus running through the book, and Chapter 2 sketches in some of the relevant European background to New World settlement. Chapter 3 distinguishes the crucial significance of ideas and ideals in the settlement process by analysing certain aspects of the search for Arcady, or the consuming belief in the agrarian ideal, which was very widely pursued throughout the New World over several generations. The theme of Refractions is deliberately placed next, to underline instead, or in addition, the geographical significance of contrasting contemporary viewpoints of the social and physical environments of the New World. On the other hand, although the search for health, the subject of Chapter 5, has some particularly close logical connections with each of the preceding chapters, it could be examined without loss after reading the sixth case study, which is concerned with 'future images' and related appraisals of the social environment contained within the ideas and ideals of utopianism and millenarism. The conclusion attempts to draw out the common anthropocentric thread and suggests opportunities for further study.

This contribution is based essentially on teaching programmes developed at Monash University, Melbourne, over the past ten years. It owes a good deal to the response of many Monash students and also to some graduate and undergraduate classes elsewhere, especially students at the University of Texas at Austin and the universities of Liverpool, England, and Canterbury, New Zealand, with whom I was privileged to work over this period. My own past and present students at Monash will certainly recognize, and I hope forgive, the massive compression represented in this rather simplified synthesis. I must also record my gratitude to several colleagues and scholarly institutions whose advice, example and encouragement proved invaluable, directly and in-directly, during my peripatetic authorship — especially Jim Cameron, Peter Haggett, Les Heathcote, John Hudson, Dennis Jeans, Ron Johnston, Bill Laatsch, Dick Lawton, Malcolm Lewis, David Mercer, Jerry McDonald, Roy Merrens, Bruce Proudfoot, Yi-Fu Tuan, the staffs of the New York Historical Society, the British Museum, British Newspaper Library and La Trobe Library, Melbourne. In addition, the notes and bibliography testify in detail to the influence of a very wide range of individual scholars on this modest production. Parts of Chapters 5 and 6 previously appeared in the *Geographical Review* and the *Australian Geographer* and I am grateful for the permission granted respectively by the American Geographical Society and the Geographical Society of New South Wales which allowed me to make further use of this material. The bulk of the typing was undertaken by Helen MacDonald and Hennie Coram and the illustrations were prepared by my technical colleagues at Monash under the direction of Jack Missen, Gary Swinton and Hervé Alleaume.

Once again, my greatest debt has been to my wife, Suzie, and our children, Melita and Stephen, for their continuing extraordinary patience.

J. M. Powell
Monash, April 1977

I know I have the best of time and space, and was never measured and never will be measured.

(Walt Whitman)

1

Introduction

In 1954 a distinguished American historian denounced the failure of his profession 'to take an analytical view of the one factor which is present in all history — namely, the human factor'. The historian was David M. Potter, and his particular mission at that time was to bring some of the principles and practice of modern social science into the definition and exploration of the emergence of national characteristics which were distinctively American.[1] In company with the sociologists H. Gerth and C. Wright Mills,[2] for example, Potter believed that the 'structural and historical features of modern society must be connected with the most intimate features of man's self', and he argued that the historian's analysis of the human factor had to be made at two levels — 'both in its singular manifestation, where it involves the individual man, or in its group manifestation, where it involves society'.[3]

The present work is addressed primarily to students of human geography and is designed to suggest that, despite significant philosophical and methodological reorientations which have enriched the discipline during recent years, there may still be abundant scope for the vigorous promotion of a humanistic perspective with the potential to broaden the choice of content foci and to complement, clarify or challenge some of the dominant modes of explanation now in vogue. This volume is historically orientated, but it is not an 'historical geography' in any commonly accepted sense. It is certainly intended, however, to emphasize the point that several workers in that branch of the subject have already made notable contributions towards the elucidation of humanistic styles of analysis which could have wider application, and to suggest that other historical geographers might be convinced of the special relevance of Potter's injunction for their own brand of scholarship — even to the extent of casting off the old inhibitions and traditional predilections which they have long embraced. The book is, accordingly, built very simply upon successive points of interest, synthesis and information which have been selected to provide an outline of some of the problems and prospects of a humanistic approach towards the interpretation of geographical change. It is far from exhaustive, even in terms of this limited objective. Similarly, no effort has been made to provide a detailed connected narrative, yet the series of studies is to some degree thematically unified by the fact that each selection is concerned with vital settlement processes in North America, Australia and New Zealand, principally in the nineteenth century.

Human Nature in Geography

> A man consists of what I may call an Old World of personal consciousness and, beyond a dividing sea, a series of New Worlds — the not too distant Virginias and Carolinas of the personal subconscious and the vegetative soul; the Far West of the collective unconscious, with its flora of symbols, its tribes of aboriginal archetypes; and, across another, vaster ocean, at the antipodes of everyday consciousness, the world of Visionary Experience . . . Some people never consciously discover their antipodes. Others make an occasional landing. Yet others (but they are few) find it easy to go and come as they please.[4]

It would be illogical and misleading to concede even the very title 'human geography' to any field of teaching and research which is not founded in some large measure upon an understanding of what Huxley described as the distinctive geography of the mind. This is simply to suggest that for the field as a whole the particular but quite partial controls of geometry and the cash register deserve special rather than overriding attention, and that an understanding of man himself should provide the essential nucleus, the basal root of the subject. In 'reality' the earth's surface is a vast mosaic of *terrae incognitae*, of irreducibly unique private images which may be inchoate, fantastic, diffuse, irrational and extremely difficult, even for the individuals holding those images, to comprehend. Certain public images which are conscious and communicable in every respect provide the necessary 'universe of discourse' within which most human activity takes place, and above all, 'each culture screens perception of the milieu in harmony with its particular style and techniques'.[5] If the surface of the earth is shaped 'by refraction through cultural and personal lenses of custom and fancy', then the chief concern of human geography should indeed be the investigation of the ways in which men can be seen to be 'creating order and organizing space, time and causality in accordance with our apperceptions and predilections'.[6] The study of the roles of images and image-makers in rapidly emerging New World societies during the nineteenth century illustrates and emphasizes this crucial humanistic argument.

This book is addressed principally to university students, not to the *cognoscenti* of the subject. It is therefore aimed at providing a concise guide to some established and developing viewpoints and deliberately includes only the minimum of original work. My debt to a wide range of scholars in North America, Australia, New Zealand and Europe will soon become apparent, but the provocative essays of John Kirtland Wright[7] should be noted here for their distinctive contribution towards the development of humanistic perspectives within geography. In 1947 — preceding, for example, David Potter's appeal for a reorientation in historiography — Wright demonstrated the urgent need for a thorough analysis of *geosophy*, which he defined as 'the study of geographical knowledge from any or all points of view'.[8] His idea was that contributions to this new and relatively more introspective branch of the subject might be addressed to three major areas of enquiry. The first of these was 'the geosophy of scientific geography', including the history and methodology of the discipline and comparative biographical studies of the careers of individual geographers in so far as they influenced the development of the subject. The second was concerned with geographical conceptions, scientific and otherwise, including their interaction with certain human behaviours and motivations, and the examination of particular categories of geographical knowledge in relation to 'the changing tides of doctrine and opinion'. He entitled the third area 'aesthetic geosophy', by which he meant the analysis of the expression of geographical conceptions in literature and art. Each of these loosely defined fields subsequently attracted scholarly attention, but until very recently,[9] few geographers managed to achieve the degree of introspection or the depth of philosophical penetration which was apparently required; in addition, throughout the discipline and especially in historical–cultural approaches, the term 'geosophy' came to be more narrowly identified with studies of perception and associated environmental behaviour.

For the modern reader the major strength of Wright's 1947 essay is surely his demonstration of the need for more probing analyses of image-making and his suggestion that this type of humanistic approach could contribute effectively towards the neglected field of geographical epistemology. He discussed, for example, the significance of *pro-*

motional imagining, aesthetic imagining and *intuitive imagining.* The first of these processes, according to Wright, was almost entirely subjective, since it was dominated by emotions which could lead the imagination to produce illusory or deceptive ideas which would conform more closely with what the individual preferred. He also emphasized the existence of 'realistic subjectivity' in these same processes, whereby passionate devotion to a cause might result in an equally committed quest for realistic ideas which could be useful in advancing or defending that cause. Aesthetic imagining was described as a subspecies of promotional imagining, in which the desires to enjoy the very process of imagining and to give satisfaction to others by comunicating the results in written or graphic form were the dominant personal interests to be promoted. The purpose of intuitive imagining was said to be more objective because the leading intention was to secure realistic conceptions. Subjectivity nevertheless enters this process to the extent that it makes use of one's personal impressions of selected facts instead of impersonally considering and weighing all the evidence. Wright argued, therefore, that much of the accumulated wisdom of the world, including geographical knowledge, has not been acquired from the rigorous application of scientific research, but through the insight and imagination of philosophers, statesmen, prophets, artists and scientists.

There is an obvious connection between Wright's original appeal and the approach nominated in the title of this book. The selection of motivating images discussed in the following chapters is certainly closely associated with his call for a detailed study of 'geosophy', but that term has acquired some ambiguities and will not be used here. My intention — as far as space allows — is to examine the origins, nature and function of each communicable image or set of images within its relevant social setting; accordingly, a prominent and distinguishing characteristic of the book is the frequent casting of specific groups and individuals as principal geographical agents. Before we proceed to the main body of the text, however, some of the problems and prospects of alternative approaches and definitions must be briefly outlined.

'Eiconics': the Study of Images

The psychologists' traditional interest in images was supplanted after the last world war by the growth of research into the stimulus–response reflex, but in the later 1960s a powerful counter-thrust demonstrated the validity of a 'centralist' position in which the conscious and purposeful observer was taken as the starting point. Imagery was welcomed back to the fold and is now a most virile, if contentious, branch of the discipline. This is especially true of recent cognitive approaches, in which the study of imagery as a fundamental process ranges from the brief image or *icon* which serves as the source of storage in short-term memory, to global behaviour changes, or personality transformations, including hallucinatory imagery under the influence of drugs or hypnosis. These approaches also consider the role of the image in verbal learning as well as its relationship to the basic sensory and cognitive aspects of perception.[10] During the same period, students of the 'behaviouralist' school gained strength within human geography and in common with the succeeding wave of 'perception' specialists, whose work was not always simply or adequately distinguished from that of the behavioural camp, they used the word 'image' very freely to suit their own purposes. In fact the term became very common in the humanities and social sciences generally, yet its meaning was seldom discussed at length.

This neglect is particularly unfortunate, not least because Kenneth Boulding had produced a lucid and valuable interpretation of the meaning and function of images as early as 1956, and although this work has been repeatedly cited, there is some reason to doubt that its provocative message was always thoroughly digested.[11] The following brief synopsis may serve to guide readers through those sections of *The Image* which are most relevant to the present argument; others will prefer to examine Boulding's excellent contribution for themselves.

For Boulding the image was the subjective knowledge structure of an individual or organization, and the centre-piece of his enquiry into 'an organic theory of knowledge' (p.16). His argument was that the image is built from messages or information derived from the enveloping social and physical milieu over the entire life-history of the individual experiencing that milieu. If it is well-defined or comfortably established, the image is 'resistant' to change: there is a tendency to reject messages which conflict with its accepted picture or pictures of the world. Messages may also clarify, confirm, or introduce serious uncertainty into an image which for some reason is fundamentally less secure, and the repetition, revision and re-statement of 'hostile' or 'reinforcing' messages may enhance their strength, and improve their potential for influencing the character of the image. Boulding's major proposition was of course that behaviour depends upon the image. He also contended that 'the development of images is part of the culture or the subculture in which they are developed, and it depends upon all the elements of that culture or subculture' (p.16). The importance of the latter statement for this book is that we must be concerned with understanding complex societies which were characterized by a large European immigrant component, and by imported beliefs and misconceptions about the New World. And these rapidly evolving societies were striving to come to terms with their strange environments, gradually modifying their images of those environments as they themselves changed and learned more about their new situations.

Boulding suggested that the human image had ten principal features. In its *spatial* aspect it was concerned with picturing the individual's location in the physical world around him, whereas the *personal* aspect provided a picture of that individual located in a world of other people, roles and organizations, and the *temporal* characteristics showed the individual in the stream of time, and varied, for example, from culture to culture according to differing notions of time. The *relational* aspect concerned the individual's picture of the universe as a system of laws and regularities, and would also vary between and within cultures, even between individuals to some extent. The image was also divided into *conscious, subconscious and unconscious sectors*, so that a type of 'scanning' mechanism was required to distinguish them; it also possessed dimensions of *certainty or uncertainty, clarity or vagueness, even ambivalence*. There were in addition aspects of *reality or unreality* — according, that is, to the degree of correspondence between the image itself and some 'real' world which was 'outside' or 'beyond' it — and, related to this, the image also incorporated a *public/private scale*, determined by the extent to which it was peculiar to the individual or shared with others. Above all, there was the crucial component of *value*, which referred to the ordering of the various parts of the image along a better/worse scale. Finally, associated with this, but of less importance, there was the *affectional component*, in which the various items making up the rest of the image are imbued with feeling, or affect. Boulding's concluding statement on the proposed new field of 'eiconics' must have struck a responsive chord amongst those seeking alternative and enduring, non-positivistic methodologies for the social sciences: 'It leads in the direction of a broad, eclectic, organic, yet humble epistemology looking for processes of organization rather than specific tests of validity and finding these processes in many areas of life and experience: in art, religion, and in the common experiences of life, as well as in science' (p.175).

The image is entirely the property of the individual. Exercising due restraint, however, it is permissible and useful to extend our interpretation by analogy and metaphor to the examination of the activities of groups, organizations and whole societies. Then, while maintaining key individuals in strong focus, we may also identify certain 'public images' which have influenced environmental appraisal and behaviour, and so elucidate a type of human geography which properly reflects the ideas, ideals and institutions of society.

Boulding elaborated his attractive thesis in a series of bold forays into such diverse fields as history, sociology, administration, biology, politics and economics. Most students of the behavioural and perception schools within human geography should still find the bulk of his succinct but thorough exposition perfectly acceptable — although the type of content and macroscopic level of analysis in which they have normally been engaged does not encourage or sustain the exhaustive treatment which this approach obviously requires. There is now a well-supported argument that images of the past and particularly of the future, as well as images of the present, are profoundly influential.

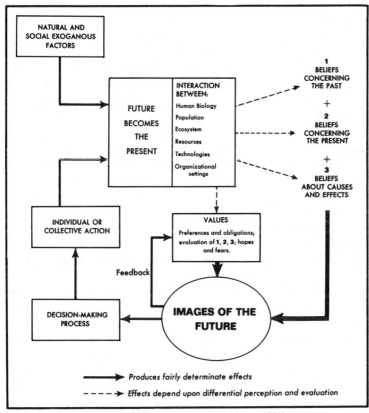

Fig 1   Images of the future. (Adapted from Bell and Mau, 1971)

These 'temporal' viewpoints were clearly identified but not fully developed in Boulding's treatise, and were very well publicized in Polak's (1961) *The Image of the Future*, subtitled *Enlightening the Past, Orientating the Present, Forecasting the Future*, and more recently by Bell and Mau.[12] The latter define images of the future as expectations 'about the state of things to come at some future time', and these expectations are described as ranges of 'differentially probable possibilities' rather than as single points along a continuum (p.23). So they argue that decision-making is largely a future-orientated process which can be represented as a 'spiral of progressive interaction between information and action': that is, a type of feedback cycle based upon the key elements of motivated individuals (alone or in groups), their images of the future and their resultant behaviours, all forming a dynamic system which brings the future into being in the present (Figure 1).

Bell and Mau acknowledge their debt to the 'dialectical sociology' of Georges Gurvitch, who attempted 'a view of society as a whole in all its effervescent and vividly dynamic aspects', delving beneath the 'crust of tradition and organization' to discover the 'well-springs of revolutions, of rapid change, the irrational roots of behaviour, *the creative acts and attitudes*' which provide the social scientist with challenge and excitement (my emphasis).[13] Following Gurvitch's lead, Bell and Mau have successfully experimented with an approach which emphasizes 'initiative, novelty, spontaneity, self-modification, creativity, goal-seeking, and self-determination, by thinking of social change as a complex cybernetic system'.[14] Present structures — the limits or capacities of human biology, population characteristics and distribution, resource endowment, various organizational settings (religious, educational, political, economic and familial), technological abilities and so on — help to shape beliefs about the past and present, including ideas about social causation and the mixture of social values. Beliefs and values help to shape images of the future, and these in turn interact with values to order the images along a scale of preferences. So the emerging future becomes the present, which includes unintended as well as intended consequences. The new condition is differentially perceived and given meaning, and the cycle continues as 'an unending spiral of the creation of society' (p.28).

Bell and Mau therefore prefer to emphasize man's capacity to rearrange his natural and social environments. They reject the idea of man as a mere creature of his surroundings even more completely, perhaps, than Boulding himself rejected it. And it is highly significant that their philosophy and methodology should spring from and be directed towards the analysis of social change in 'developing' or 'modernizing' nations, especially since the Second World War, for in some respects the same adjectives might usefully be applied to the societies of North America, Australia and New Zealand before 1914. The working model proposed by these authors does appear to have important potential for identifying a number of the most dynamic forces which were at work during a vital period of growth in these New World countries. The tasks specified by the model are obviously highly relevant to such matters of central concern throughout the field of human geography as settlement, land use and other patterns of distribution whose profound transformations have commonly been precipitated, accompanied or reflected by social change. It is clear that the examination of specific images of the future, as well as the consideration of image-making processes in general, must be one of the special objectives of any humanistic approach towards geographical change.

Further qualifications might be added to Boulding's guide. For most forms of historical–cultural analysis in human geography, including the case studies discussed in the following chapters, the formidable list of attributes and functional elements drawn up in *The Image* might be usefully shortened to include just three interlocking components — attitudes, values and information. Complex problems of definition are involved here, but it is reasonably safe and sufficient to say that an attitude essentially connotes a disposition and that it incorporates three connected features, the 'cognitive', 'affective' and 'behavioural' characteristics, which influence the response towards objects and situations. The cognitive element concerns awareness, knowledge, beliefs, ideas; the affective component, which monopolizes the attention of many workers in this area, refers to feelings — likes, dislikes, fears; and these are influenced by, and in turn also influence, behaviour. Values or value orientations are relatively more stable or resistant functional elements which may be said to give a 'ranking' to the range of attitudes identifiable for an individual or group, and changes in these orientations should introduce a number of profound modifications in behavioural dispositions. This may be seen, for instance, in the 'assimilation' of certain ethnic minorities and their assumption of new life styles. The information component may be loosely described as the amount, content and quality of the messages entering the image, which admittedly does some violence to Boulding's interpretation. Alternatively, this term could refer to the basic 'factual' details of the mental picture itself — providing, in the latter case, that a more restricted definition of 'attitude' is accepted, as it appears to have been during the urban geographers' early enthusiasm for the 'reconstruction' of 'mental maps', in which the potentials for a productive fusion with broader attitudinal studies were not always perceived or explored.

Even in the most humanistic investigations in cultural–historical geography it is not always possible, nor indeed is it often profitable, to insist upon rigid definitions. Although the insights into imagery obtained directly or indirectly from modern social science have proved to be especially valuable in these areas, two qualifications must be clearly established. First, the more specialized literature does not appear to have resolved the confusion of terminology to the extent of encouraging the already harassed student of historical and geographical 'synthesizing' to plump for specific methodologies.[15] Second, the types of image-making with which human geographers are usually concerned cannot be understood without proper consideration of the broader setting of human communicative behaviour. This provides our next introductory theme.

Communication and Interaction

Human relationships exist and develop through the mechanism of communication, a mechanism which includes all the symbols of the mind, together with the means of conveying these symbols through space and preserving them through time. A new epoch in communication and in the whole system of society was introduced in the early nineteenth century and continued during the invasion of the New World by European immigrants. This revolutionary change followed massive innovations in four major areas of communication: expressiveness, or the improved competency to convey a range of ideas and feelings; the relative permanence of the record, which in a sense helped to overcome time; speed, or the overcoming of space; and diffusion, or improved access to all classes of society.[16] The greatest advances were made in the last two areas, but it is not easy to separate them from the others. The enlargement of the vocabulary and the development of publishing, photography and library technologies supported significant advances in scientific thinking, for example, and inevitably, all of these improvements in the mechanisms of communication extended public consciousness far beyond the confines of the local group.

The analysis of the act of communication itself is customarily broken down into a few fundamental questions: Who/Says What/In Which Channel/To Whom/With What Effect? Similarly, there is a fair measure of agreement upon the societal functions performed by the communication process. It assists the search or surveillance of the environment, disclosing opportunities and threats which affect the value position of the individual, group or community as a whole. It also illustrates or provides for some correlation of the various components of society interpreting or responding to their environment, and it is clearly essential for the transmission of the social inheritance.[17] Communication is therefore a thoroughly social affair, and its various systems make social life possible. It is surprisingly neglected in the study of human geography.

Man is the only living creature with the creative capacity to live simultaneously in two realms of experience, the symbolic and the physical. Our basic 'perceptual receptors' concentrate upon the raw data of the physical world — the sight, sound, touch, smell and taste of things — but the composite assumptions and hunches about the real essence of a person, object or event make up our sense of the symbolic. And the 'facts' are drawn or selected from each realm of experience by

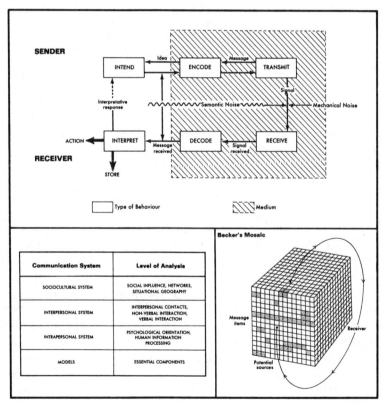

Fig 2   Some aspects of the communication process. (Sources: after Mares, 1966 and Mortensen, 1972).

the proactive human participant, who locates them in some wider frame or image which assists interpretation. Communication may therefore be intrapersonal, since an individual may assign significance to messages without the presence of another person, or interpersonal, where it takes place between two or more parties (see Fig. 2). It also involves co-orientation, where the process requires the maintenance of a shared frame of reference, and it is obviously contextual, for it cannot be understood if divorced from its physical and socio-cultural setting. How did the immigrants to America, Australia or New Zealand learn about their new environments; why, when, how and to what extent did they modify or reject their original images? The 'reality' of each of those environments was in large measure socially constructed, especially in so far as it was the arena for social interaction, a repository of dreams and nightmares, failures and successes, for their predecessors and contemporaries. It was also a fundamental ingredient of their own present and future, a vital part of their very identity. Naturally, few transactions between the settler and his physical environment, and none between himself and the rest of society, could ever have taken place within a vacuum; whatever his personal circumstances, he could not escape belonging to various information-sharing networks, various communication systems.

There were (and still are) many new immigrants in these countries who frequently suffered the experience of coping with the most complex of communicative events, be it a novel idea or news of some specific event, primarily because of their unfamiliarity with the working of the particular communication system in which they found themselves. The communication model which may best describe this situation is 'Becker's Mosaic' (see Fig. 2). This model is represented as a constantly-changing cube of information layers, in which each section is a potential source of information, but those shaded are 'unavailable' for use for several social and other reasons. The path taken through the cube by the searcher or receiver of the information might result in his gaining only a partial message.[18] Certainly the mosaic helps to account for variations in exposure to messages by its emphasis upon the complications introduced by a constantly changing social milieu. In some circumstances (or locations in the mosaic) receivers may be inundated with relevant information; in others they may encounter only a few isolated items. Certain individuals may be better attuned than others to receive information, according to the different kinds of relationships they have established at various levels; yet again, some of these relationships may be confined to special situations, not to recurrent events. And if we consider the changing personal circumstances of the receiver himself (holding the social milieu constant), another, 'internal' mosaic might be placed alongside the first. This is an extreme example, but it suggests the utility of clearly-defined public images in conditions of pronounced geographical and social mobility and the opportunities therein for a special class of communication experts who were major actors in the New World settlement process. The contributions of this group, which we will now call the *promoters*, are encountered in several of the following chapters.

An elementary modification of the more traditional schematic representation of communication processes is also illustrated in Fig. 2, in which some emphasis is placed upon the so-called 'behavioural setting' of each of the main processes and upon the relationship established from the outset between the receiver and sender, affecting all subsequent transactions. The diagram restates the familiar precept that communication involves sending something/to someone/through a particular medium/for a particular purpose. Each sector merits careful attention in its own right, as well as for its contribution as a unit within the entire system. For such themes as the analysis of the promotion of specific locations or types of environment, or the adoption/rejection of innovations, the separation of the intentive behaviour of the sender and the interpretative behaviour of the receiver offers a useful reminder of the complexities of these processes which the older models still ignore. 'Mechanical noise' may result from outside interference affecting the physical clarity of the signal — competing arguments pointing to other types of decision, for example, or the deliberate blocking, interrupting or blurring activities of counter-promotional activity, such as anti-emigration propaganda — or interference within the system arising from faults in the receiving or transmitting mechanisms, including inadequate performances for whatever reason from the groups or individuals involved in the transaction. 'Semantic noise' is usually taken to refer to any kind of alteration made to the original message by the fallibility of the actual medium of communication; in most of our examples this medium is language, but maps, drawings, engravings, paintings and even photographs are also significant. The most obvious example of semantic noise is the employment of botanical and topographical terms borrowed from a European background but often irrelevant and dangerously misleading in the New World context.

It is impossible to achieve a comprehensive understanding of the evolution of settlement and the transformation of regional landscapes over large areas of the globe without careful examination of the central processes of image-making, which in the context of human geography may be loosely described as the subjective, socially-based processes of environmental appraisal. Other types of approach could of course be sustained by the general humanistic perspective adopted here; similarly, it must be emphasized that this exploration of images and image-making is offered simply as a complement, not as an alternative, to existing modes of analysis.[19] Yet the New World, always full of dreams awaiting the conjurers, does appear to illustrate the working of these selected processes particularly well. Within that vast theatre of settlement activity, the examples discussed in the following chapters have been deliberately drawn from the predominantly English-speaking countries of North America, Australia and New Zealand, with which my own activities in teaching and research have been largely concerned. Finally — allowing again for some freedom of interpretation — the book as a whole may find some acceptance as a brief exploration in one type of *dialectical* human geography, in so far as it is based primarily upon the investigation of some dominant values and attitudes in contemporary societies. And no attempt is made to disguise a personal conviction that the humanistic philosophy on which this modest sortie is based might usefully be applied to other areas of explanation in geography.

2

Prelude: Land and Society in Europe

The essence of the geographer's interest in the remarkable period of change from the late eighteenth century until the First World War is plain enough. There was, for example, a massive relocation of European people — approximately 35 millions moved to North America alone between 1815 and 1914 — together with their learned and inherited environmental attitudes, farming skills and preferences, and so on. There was also considerable relocation within each of the New World territories as the settlement frontiers expanded and contracted. In addition, these processes were in various ways regionally and locally selective with respect to both the exporting and the receiving areas, depending especially upon economic, social and political conditions, the efficiency and orientation of promotional activities, and the real or perceived advantages and disadvantages of the physical environments of respective 'old' and 'new' territories which were being held up for comparison. The present chapter sketches some of the European background which is essential to an understanding of this theme of relocation. It begins by attempting to highlight the seemingly limitless potential of the newly discovered territories to provide a rich supply of speculative environmental theories and social concepts which were useful to the Europeans. Then follows a more specific examination of selected aspects of social change and agrarian idealism in a few major areas; the descriptions in this second section are very broadly indicative of significant conditions throughout Northern and Western Europe, a region which supplied the great bulk of New World immigration during the period under review.

Le Triomphe Du Nouveau Monde[1]

Learning in the ancient world was essentially an amalgam of poetry and myth, theological speculation and rudimentary science. The world-view of the medieval European was largely derived from Greek, Roman and Arab scholarship, which was often imperfectly understood and frequently clouded or distorted by Christian conceptions and preferences. So the forfeited Eden was said to be located in the unknown East, while the 'Fortunate Islands' of classical lore and the Celtic 'Otherworld' or promised land were somewhere in the Western ocean. A rich collection of imaginary islands was scattered around the great limbo of the Atlantic; each island was the precious sanctuary of a culture hero or venerated spirit being, the haunt or refuge of some bizarre or terrifying beast, the base of some powerful satanic influence. For the farthest West of that great ocean European symbolisms drawn from the rising and setting of the sun suggested a happy land in which departed souls would find eternal rest, while the Irish tradition drew a much bolder picture of the land of 'Tir-nan-Og' — a country of perpetual youth, without sickness, grief or death. Over several centuries adventurers, missionaries, hermits, merchants and fishermen provided additional material which maintained and reinvigorated all such hopes, fears and speculations, and the work of Columbus and that of his contemporaries and successors eventually encouraged a much wider public to examine the implications of these portentous 'discoveries'.[2]

During the sixteenth and seventeenth centuries there was increasing interest throughout Europe in the character and origins of the strange environments and native societies in these extensive new lands. Why had God chosen to conceal them from the rest of the world for so long? Were the indigenes specially-created 'pre-Adamites', or were they descendants of the refugees from some lost Atlantis, or of the ancient Egyptians, Ethiopians, Greeks or Phoenicians; might they be the survivors of those Canaanites who had fled before Joshua, or the remnants of Israel's lost tribes? And what, indeed, was to be made of the stories of vast deserts, swamps, mountains, frozen wastes, and such astonishing flora and fauna; of amazons and albinos; of pygmies, Patagonian giants and dog-faced men? Europe's leading scholars were drawn inexorably towards the investigation of these perplexing topics, and by the mid eighteenth century their bookish interpretations incorporated or were challenged by the data accumulated by actual experience on the various settlement frontiers of the Americas.

So the inhabitants of the Old World were gradually persuaded to reject most of the wilder fantasies which had crowded their earlier visions of the new territories. During the latter part of the eighteenth century, particularly in pre-revolutionary France, there was a profound modification in what might be called the European image of the New

World. Despite considerable repression and heavy censorship, French society in the eighteenth century was exceptional for its literature of ideas. The many gifted writers of the day learned to out-manoeuvre the authorities by wit and allegory as much as by the use of surreptitious publication, and their works were eagerly sought by the educated public. The transformation of the dominant French image of the New World must of course be seen against this unique background, yet a short description of some of the processes involved in this transformation may also serve as a more general introduction to the type of humanistic perspective favoured in this book.

The semantic confusion inherent in the epithet 'New World' may have encouraged an overlapping of the notion of a newly created world with that of a newly discovered world. The Comte de Buffon's monumental *Histoire naturelle* (1749–89) gave scientific respectability to the idea of the geological and biological youth of the Americas: in a volume published in 1761 he suggested that the animal species were less vigorous, smaller and less varied than those of the Old World, and that these differences were caused by the cooler and more humid climate to be expected from a continent which had emerged more recently from under the sea. The native peoples provided Buffon with another index — the Indian was 'a mere animal of the first rank' — and it was claimed that European domestic animals positively degenerated after their introduction. Nature was still totally wretched: America had scarcely completed its emergence from the great flood, or floods, and for the most part this newest of worlds was dominated by insects and reptiles.

> In these melancholy regions nature remains concealed under her old garment and never exhibits herself in fresh attire. Being neither cherished nor cultivated by man she never opens her fruitful and beneficent womb . . . In this abandoned condition everything languishes, corrupts, and proves abortive. The air and the earth, overloaded with humid and noxious vapours, are unable to purify themselves, or to profit by the influence of the sun, who darts in vain his most enlivening rays upon this frigid mass.[3]

In the same year there appeared a successful French translation of the *Travels* of Swedish naturalist Peter Kalm. The original work was based upon extensive personal field work in the British and French colonies, and since the author was an accomplished scientist his comments upon the marked 'degeneration' of the settlers and their livestock, together with his suggestion that climate might be the prime factor for this deterioration, had to be taken seriously.[4] The Abbé Corneille de Pauw was rather more direct than Kalm in his criticisms. In his *Recherches philosophiques* (1768), de Pauw stated categorically that the climate of the New World was so unfavourable to all forms of life that both animals and men, whether native or European, inevitably degenerated; above all, each generation of settlers born in the American colonies would therefore become progressively more inferior — physically, morally and intellectually inferior — to their European forebears. Similar claims were made in the Abbé Raynal's *Histoire philosophique et politique*, which ran to thirty-seven editions between 1772 and 1820.

It is important to stress that these arguments rested heavily upon the classical principles of environmental determinism, especially the dominating concept of pervasive climatic influences which had been vigorously restated in Montesquieu's *Esprit des lois* (1748). Indeed, for most of the eighteenth-century readers of Buffon, Kalm, de Pauw and Raynal, the logical basis of their major criticisms was not doubted: since the American climate was so different from that of Europe, it followed that the progress of civilization in the two continents must also differ profoundly.[5] The sharp contrasts in mean temperatures between some European and North American locations situated along similar latitudes were offered as additional support, and the naive but widespread belief in America's geological 'youth' served to explain, encourage and emphasize further disclosures of real or imagined environmental differences. It is equally important to note that de Pauw and Raynal, and also, in their own ways, such leading thinkers as Voltaire and Montesquieu, were for a time steadfastly opposed to the idea of emigration and colonial settlement. There was already, in fact, a significant degree of prejudice throughout France against colonialism, which was due in part to the failure of that country's colonial ventures, in part to the supposed introduction of syphilis from America, and also to the inflationary situation which had developed after the importation of large quantities of gold. The 'degeneration' hypothesis was accordingly very rapidly diffused.

A counter-current to this notion developed from French observation of the remarkable progress of the British colonies in North America, and particularly from the publicity given by the *Philosophes* to the ideals of economic, political and religious freedom which were pursued with some vigour in Pennsylvania and elsewhere. The arguments stemming from this quarter gained strength after the middle of the century and were particularly well-nourished by the traditional hostility between Britain and France, by confident predictions of the imminent separation of the British colonies from the mother country, and by the international acclaim received by Benjamin Franklin and other leading American thinkers.

With notable success, Franklin's own prodigious efforts came to be directed towards convincing prominent French intellectuals that the picture of the degenerate American was manifestly inaccurate and that conditions in his country actually presented a clear and practical confirmation of the wisdom of several of their own theories. The system proposed by the *Physiocrats*, for example, argued that land was the only true source of wealth, that the key to national prosperity was therefore the advancement of agriculture, and that the majority of the people should live in farming communities. Franklin attempted to demonstrate that the population of the maligned American colonies had virtually no urban component, yet was doubling every twenty years, supported almost entirely by an agricultural economy. Similarly, the French philosophical faith in the 'social utility' of knowledge was shown to correspond very well with the utilitarian emphasis engendered by the conditions of frontier life. By the early 1770s the Physiocrats' picture had relatively easily been overlaid with the moralistic portrait favoured by a number of Rousseauists who were inclined towards the idea of the archetypal American as the supreme embodiment of the simple and virtuous rural man.

In summary, it can be said that for the educated minority in France, there was obviously no single, composite picture of the New World during these years: there was, rather, a complex suite of coexisting, blurred and conflicting visions which had been produced by and for influential groups and individuals. The debate on America was indeed part of a series of debates which had dominated European thought for many years, and the discovery and early exploitation of the new continent clearly served a very useful function for the intellectuals of the Old World. Whether by attack or defence, their analysis of America provided the safest of opportunities for criticising any aspect of the European economy, society or government. Deterministic environmental beliefs and an abiding ignorance of actual conditions in the colonies fuelled the early part of the debate. Reorientation towards more favourable interpretations of America followed the entry of a highly gifted and committed New World spokesman, Franklin, who skilfully exploited his own prestige and that of his major contacts in France.[6]

This necessarily superficial sketch of a familiar but exceedingly complex subject may be permitted if it is accepted as a convenient device to illustrate the significance of the study of image-making as a basic operational procedure in servicing the humanistic perspective. The example was concerned with a number of important concepts of America which were held in France during a specific period. *It points to*

*some of the ways in which men invest the social and physical environment with
meaning, even in the complete absence of direct and personal experience: images or
mental pictures of the environment are thereby created and communicated, making
sense of the world and the place of the individual or group within it.*

European concepts of the newly discovered lands and of the
achievements of the young colonies continued to reflect the needs,
problems, aspirations and capacities of the Europeans themselves. But
ideas of the relative abundance of resources in the New World came to
dominate or support a rich variety of more specific images in the old and
new territories alike. The 'abundance' theme has been stressed by
Potter[7] and others, and it does not require detailed separate treatment
here; at this stage of our exploration, however, it is essential to
acknowledge its clear and powerful influence. After the first few decades
of the nineteenth century there was sufficient development in the New
World to confound most of the critics and to attract a number of
futuristic statements from the most influential media of the day. The
grand destiny of the New World countries was said to be assured by
their bountiful resources. Even the proud and insular British were
moved to similar pronouncements, though there were, inevitably, some
important qualifications. So the *Illustrated London News* of 22 December
1849 reflected that 'men of our blood and language have permeated
with our intelligence, our industry, and our enterprise, the remotest
ends of the earth', that British sons have established 'new empires, at
present as brilliant, and promising in the future to be more brilliant,
than our own'. Though the Anglo-Saxon race 'may continue to rule the
world', its central power base would soon move from Britain to North
America with the realization of the massive potential of that richly-
endowed continent.

An empire twenty, thirty, or fifty times as extensive, and as rich as ours, has
already risen on the other side of the Atlantic, to entice to its bosom the best
blood which remains to us. The young, the hardy, the persevering of our
country, and of all the countries of Europe, that groan under the weight of
debt, of difficulty, and of a surplus population, and that cannot say to their
sons, as the New World does, that every man is a man, welcome, for the sake
of his manhood, to the great feast of Nature, where there is enough and to
spare for the meanest, are daily invited to leave the shores of effete Europe,
and settle in more vigorous America. The growth of the United States is, in
reality, the downfall of Great Britain. All the unhappy circumstances that are
of prejudice to us, are of benefit to them. With us, the mouths that clamour to
be fed are causes of decay. With them, every additional mouth is an
additional pair of hands, and every additional pair of hands is an increase in
wealth, power and influence. Let us pour our millions into the great valley of
the Mississippi, and it will hold and feed them all, were their numbers
quadrupled. Such is our great rival in the West.

This was indeed a prophetic vision, especially since Britain herself —
though not without pain — had been experiencing rapid industrialization and urbanization, with accelerating technological
advances and an associated expansion of foreign trade. Yet the same
perceptive observer noted the competitor in the antipodes — 'another
rival almost equally formidable, equally splendid, fed in the same
manner from our entrails, and rising daily upon our fall'. The great
colossus of the Southern Hemisphere, still imperfectly known, was
throwing off the convict legacy and building a new society.

> Who shall fix the bounds of the future prosperity of the great Australian
> continent? While in this old country the pauper vegetates or dies, accursed of
> the land that produced him, in that new country the pauper becomes a
> labourer; he no longer vegetates, but lives; and if he lives long enough, he
> may become a patriarch, sitting under the shade of his own fig-tree, and
> counting by thousands and tens of thousands his flocks and herds — a new
> Job in a land of plenty. Fertile soil, delicious climate, elbow room, and
> Freedom from taxation — these are the blessings of the Australian. The
> Englishman enjoys the first two in an imperfect manner; the last are aliens —
> he knows them not, and will never know them while England holds her place
> among the nations.

The ties between the Old World and the New World were obviously
particularly strong during the nineteenth century: there developed a
complicated matrix of interrelationships which seemed to include
virtually every major facet of life and economy, and those aspects of
geographical change with which we will be concerned must be set
within this wider frame of reference. The significance of the interaction
between the primary units involved in the building of the matrix was
highlighted by Walter Prescott Webb in 1952. Webb entitled these
units the *Metropolis* of Western Europe, Scandinavia and the British
Isles, and the *Great Frontier* of the Americas, South Africa, Australia
and New Zealand. His famous portrayal of the two as dramatic
characters was produced more than a century after the similar
observations noted above and it illustrates still further the importance
which must be attached to the abundance theme.

> Let us so consider the drama by imagining the stage of the Western World set
> for the long historical interplay, with the Metropolis and the frontier in the
> leading roles. From the right side comes the Metropolis clad in the culture of
> an old civilization, rich in ideas and institutions, equipped with experience in
> government and skilled in all the known arts, accompanied by a host of
> attendants; but with all this, the Metropolis is poor in worldly goods, a little
> threadbare of garment and extremely short of food, a condition shared
> generously with the supporting cast. From the opposite side appears a rude
> figure, lacking in all the refinements, ignorant of government and law, shy on
> arts and letters, and almost devoid of attendants. The contrast is heightened

because the frontier comes laden with what the Metropolis lacks, and craves more than anything else to have, and that is a burden of wealth, or of the stuff that wealth is made of, in such quantity and variety as the Metropolis never hoped to see.[8]

Webb's controversial works still provide the boldest extension of the original 'frontier hypothesis' by which Frederick Jackson Turner attempted to link Westward settlement, and especially agrarianism, with the development of distinctively American characteristics.[9] Even more than Turner, however, Webb was inclined towards a brand of environmental determinism which is not readily accepted by modern social scientists. Abundance cannot be treated as if it were bred by the new environments themselves by some type of spontaneous generation; it was created by culture, and specifically by technology, out of those new environments. Expanding this argument, it could be said that most societies have in fact experienced innumerable frontiers (scientific, social, political, technological and others) and that it is not always useful or possible to define them spatially though they may be associated, of course, with various changes in spatial organization. The term 'frontier', then, is used in its widest sense in this book; similarly, 'abundance' is recognized as the differentially perceived availability of great resource potential. Indeed, the historical pursuit of that potential may be defined most profitably in terms of the viewpoints of the actors involved, individually and collectively.

Social Change and Agrarian Ideals

Land remained the prime source of wealth in every European country throughout the eighteenth century and, despite increasing urbanization and industrialization, most Europeans continued to gain their livelihood from agricultural employment. Their images of the New World were in part determined by the kinds of lives they saw and experienced in Europe. Their reflections on individual perfectibility, on personal dignity and independence, were inevitably based in important measure upon their perception of the intimate and deeply rooted relationship between land and life. Throughout the eighteenth century and during the early part of the nineteenth century there was a growing realization that the equation in Europe had perhaps been manipulated by a small section of the population for its own gain. The balance might be redressed in the Old World by political action; where the New World was concerned, the advantages of its great clean slate slowly became apparent and served very well indeed to emphasize the ills of

Europe, while at the same time suggesting opportunities for some experimentation with new equations to express a happier relationship between land and society.

As in so many other aspects of life, the pace of change in the rural sector varied considerably within that great reservoir of potential New World immigrants. A bold division may be drawn between 'moderniz-ing' Western Europe and the relatively stagnant economies of the East and South, the most obvious boundaries being formed by the river Elbe in Germany, the Pyrennees and the river Po, placing Northern Italy in the more developed sector. In response to marked population growth, Britain, the Netherlands, Northern Italy and parts of France and Germany successfully experimented with more flexible crop rotations, new and improved crop strains and livestock breeds, and the clearing and reclamation of 'waste' lands previously underused. Far less was achieved elsewhere, principally because of the greater obstacles imposed by the physical environment, general ignorance and apathy, and the resistance of great landowners who feared that the new ideas would lead to the removal of the peasants' traditionally bonded relationship with the land. Agricultural techniques and the organi-zation of rural society in Eastern and Southern Europe, and over most of Russia, remained stable or reverted to more primitive forms.[10]

In Britain the 'improvers' were essentially the wealthier farmers. In France the initiative derived from the efforts of the national government, commercially-minded noblemen and the Physiocrats, who were committed to the idea that the soil was the true source of all wealth. There was far more resistance to innovation in France, however, for a number of social and political reasons, and the strongest support for traditional practices came from the smaller or middle-range proprietor, the *laboureur*. The *laboureur* survived well enough, but the 'yeoman', his counterpart (in a general sense only) across the Channel, was said to be one of the chief casualties in the far more sweeping changes which were then transforming Britain's agricultural landscape. Certainly, the claim was frequently made by authoritative con-temporary observers that the rapid enclosure of the common lands was accelerating the consolidation of very large estates, leading to the extinction of the previously highly-regarded and relatively populous intermediate class. A major result of the 'agricultural revolution' in Britain was indeed said to be the replacement of the original social structures by a more simple division based on small numbers of large landlords and very well-to-do farmers of tenant or independent status, and a host of dependent farm labourers.

But in fact, to return to the continental scale, a similar fundamental regionalization may be applied to the theme of land ownership. East of the Elbe vast estates were held by the nobles, who depended upon their exploitation of armies of serfs. With the exception of Denmark, where serfdom remained prevalent until the end of the eighteenth century, properties were much smaller North and West of the Elbe, and the middle and lower classes had more freedom — this was generally true of Scandinavia, South West Germany, Switzerland, the Netherlands, Northern Italy and most of France. Serfdom was actually being extended at the expense of the small independent cultivator in East Prussia, Poland and Russia, and in the last two areas especially, the territories held by individual lords were so great that landed wealth was often more accurately assessed in terms of the amount of labour controlled. Britain offers the most crucial exception to this regionalization. The estates of many of the landed magnates in Britain were almost Russian or Eastern European in terms of the sheer scale of the operations conducted on them; in addition, however, they were frequently far more productive and their owners were exceedingly wealthy by any European standard. In Ireland, another notable exception to the rule, absentee British landlords imposed crippling burdens upon the peasantry and the farming system was peculiarly primitive. And in real terms, the Irish peasants and labourers, like the rural proletariat of Sicily or Southern Spain, can scarcely have been very much better placed than the serfs of Eastern Europe and Russia.

Obviously, ideas as well as people crossed the world during the great international migrations and those ideas did not necessarily require a massive transplanting of people. The Old World and the New were always bound together: observing and recording each other, held together in close mutual tension in so many ways. It should be useful, maintaining this book's declared eclecticism, to examine briefly some aspects of this actual and potential interaction during the eighteenth and early nineteenth centuries. There follows, therefore, some discussion of general developments and prominent ideas concerning land and society in a selection of those European countries which were to play vital roles in these migrations.

The Image of America in France

Contrary to most popular belief, perhaps, in some respects the French rather than the British have been the people with whom Americans have had their longest and closest contact.[11] Moreover the French have always been more centrally placed than the British in the complex of Western culture. What, then, was the French image of America in the eighteenth and early nineteenth centuries?

Undoubtedly, French concepts of America continued to defend and affirm locally-produced ideological and political viewpoints, as described earlier. Consequently, the image or images of America provided an important element in the ideas leading up to the French Revolution. For, as the eighteenth century wore on and America's own revolution was successfully reconnoitred, an old argument solidified: certain key doctrines of the century were apparently achieving their first realization in the United States. And for leading French liberals, the greater their faith in these doctrines, the greater the tendency to exaggerate what had been achieved in practical terms in the new nation — 'It was a projection of French aspirations upon a scene which was both accommodating and distant enough to blur the inconsistencies and contradictions.'[12] France's 'Americanists' became the apostles of a political and ideological credo, and the United States was their model.

During the 1780s the agrarianism and ruralism of the Physiocrats gradually declined as an ingredient in the image of America, which then became based upon two distinct concepts. The first favoured a Rousseauan emphasis, arguing that the young American nation had united its simplicity, virtue, equality and liberty with a standard of enlightenment more characteristic of a mature people. The second was the Progressionists' contention that America was the forerunner of a new age in which man would advance to perfection. As events in France moved towards revolution, the image of America was very quickly transformed from a philosophical symbol to a political slogan; in the process, America also came to be seen as a peaceful asylum for troubled Europeans.

So the French image of America was essentially a symptom of France's own maladies. This was particularly well displayed in the influential writings of Michel-Guillaume St. Jean de Crèvecoeur, who returned to France in 1781 after a period of farming in New York State. His account of his experiences was published in English in 1782 under the title *Letters from an American Farmer*; a subsequent French edition incorporated the talents of leading Americanists, and the result was a deliberate transformation of the original book into one more suited to French tastes and aspirations. The image of America presented in *Lettres d'un cultivateur americain* (1784) actually projected all the aspirations of the troubled Europeans: the Physiocrats' stress on the agricultural economy; Rousseau's call for a 'return to nature' and the elevation of equality, simplicity and virtue; the demands for political reform from Condorcet and other Progressionists; Voltaire's arguments for liberty, tolerance and humanitarianism; and the basic promise of hope and boundless opportunity for the Old World's weary citizens.

America, Crèvecoeur said, was a 'new birth', a 'second generation' of man under a new sun and in a new world free from the errors, the prejudices, and the ignorance of the Old World. The new nation had been founded in 'an age of enlightenment' by courageous and enlightened men fleeing the fanaticism and catastrophes of Europe. Here the energy of men's minds, long confined by poverty, ignorance, and oppression, could at last exert itself and find fulfillment . . . All this was promised of a new society in which all men lived in liberty and equality, and in which the simple antique virtue of the Golden Age was at last renewed.[13]

France did not experience the population pressures of several other European countries, and the French emigrated in smaller numbers than did their European neighbours. But their views of the New World were highly influential. Certainly, the image of America held by Frenchmen was useful not only in their own country: it also provided good support and handsome rhetoric for the images of environment and society which were then emerging in America itself, as will be shown later. A similar claim may be made for our next case study, although it differs markedly from the French example in terms of its narrow scope and relatively introverted character.

Images of the Peasant in Germany

In simple geographical terms the German people were obviously centrally placed to observe changes in Europe's social fabric and agricultural landscape, and the important changes in German attitudes towards the rural proletariat in the late eighteenth century provide an instructive guide for the investigation of subsequent styles of image-making in and for the New World.[14]

A new and more positive attitude towards the peasant and his way of life was developed in Germany (more accurately, the German States) at this time, and this greatly assisted in the moves leading to the abolition of serfdom in the early decades of the nineteenth century. It would be unwise, as was seen earlier with regard to French notions of the New World, to attempt to separate the creation or evocation of more favourable images from the enveloping intellectual climate of the time: in this case, the interweaving of economic, political and religious ideas built a sound foundation for the new image.

Germany's doctrinaire Physiocrats (as in France) exceeded the more sober economists in proclaiming the unique social significance of agriculture — it was said to be important for the kind of man it developed, as well as for the essential goods it produced. It was indeed responsible for the very existence and continuity of society, and the preservation of legal and political processes: the best guarantor of social integrity, through the specific influences it 'exerted' on human beings. Agriculture had to be seen as the moral foundation and training ground of all forms of virtue and utility, the very basis of civilized life; the suggestion of masculinity, of the raw strength and stamina imparted to agriculturalists, also meant that the peasants were occasionally referred to as the best and strongest soldiers. According to Gagliardo this type of eulogy was frequently countered by reports of the prevalence of superstition, ignorance and laziness amongst the German peasantry, and these same arguments often appeared as part of an alternative propaganda which emphasized that the prevailing system did not bring out the better latent qualities — that it was, in fact, subduing those finer characteristics.[15]

Another observation made by Gagliardo on this period of changing attitudes concerns the celebration in poetry and romantic literature of the piety of the German peasant. This piety was supposedly derived from the nature of the peasant's occupation: the vagaries of the weather and the general uncertainty of agricultural operations were said to foster true humility and a profound sense of dependence upon environmental conditions manufactured by God alone. Inevitably, in these respects especially, the peasant was contrasted with the effete townsman. In addition, this type of argument was employed against the prophets of the Enlightenment, whose bitter attacks on the Bible and religious dogma were perceived in some quarters as the cause of an alarming disturbance running through the social system. The townsman in his artificial or 'built' environment was more easily seduced by the Enlightenment's abstractions than was the peasant who inhabited the 'real' world and feared his God. Closely related to this contention was the proposition that the peasant's special type of empirical knowledge was simply fundamentally different from the more respected or orthodox types: his 'natural wisdom' required no books, because it was fixed in custom, in the teachings of tradition. So the Physiocrat Johann Heinrich Merck, in 1778, offered the tale of the senior politician who decided to relinquish his books and pens and city life, and to become a peasant on a small farm. Enjoying all the advantages of happy family life and outdoor pursuits, the reformed politician also proved to himself and others in the tale that small-scale, independent farming was the best course for any thinking man who wished to throw off the chains of uniformity to see what his own patience and understanding might accomplish.

As Gagliardo demonstrates, these opinions did succeed in establishing a new image of the small farmer and thereby assisted the political economists by creating a more favourable climate for agricultural reform. Increasingly, the German farmer was vaguely conceived as a 'natural man' whose good instincts should be left to themselves for the benefit of society as a whole, the social and legal status of the peasant was undoubtedly improved, and the remaining enclaves of serfdom were abolished. Most importantly, a romantic mystique began to surround country life and the peasant, and this became a prominent influence in German thought during the many tensions and dissatisfactions of the nineteenth century.

What was desired but could not be achieved in Germany might be attainable in North America or some other part of the New World. But in addition, the arguments used in the development of distinctive rural ideologies in North America and Australia with which we will be concerned showed some interesting comparisons with the German experience. Above all, for these same countries as for Germany before the middle of the nineteenth century, the political utility of the agrarian rhetoric should not be understated.

Emigration Impulses in Scandinavia and the British Isles

One of the key requirements for the analysis of widespread emigration during the century after the Battle of Waterloo is the identification of the degree and rate of regional economic growth in the exporting and receiving areas. The pace of development in the United States was of course the major phenomenon of the age, but Australia and New Zealand, Brazil and Canada, South and East Africa, all experienced pronounced growth; similarly, it is vital to note that expansion in England, France, Northern Italy, West Germany, Sweden, the Netherlands and Bohemia-Moravia also exerted a remarkable attractive power over population movements within Europe. At any time, the chief controls over the flows into these areas were the rate of capital migration, the absorptive capacity of the underdeveloped region, the industrial potential of specific growth areas and the state of the business cycles in the two countries involved in the exchange.[16] And there are strong indications that demographic change and economic conditions in the countries of origin were more significant than the 'pull' factors of the destinations.

For our present purposes the important points are that emigration to the New World was a special element in the spectrum of increased spatial mobility experienced over most of Europe, and that the temporal variability and geographical selectivity of overseas emigration were not simply reflecting the variety of concepts of the New World held by Europeans: they were also based upon local perceptions of conditions in the source area and, presumably, local evaluations of potential European destinations. The mixed European inheritance was a crucial dynamic feature in environmental appraisal and settlement adaptation in the New World and, to introduce our later discussion, some of the complexities of the changing tempo of emigration must now be sketched.

There were three distinct waves of emigration to the United States in the nineteenth century.[17] The first began in the 1830s and continued until 1860, with a peak during the period 1847–54; Hansen entitled this the 'Celtic' period, since most of the emigrants originated in Ireland, Wales and the Scottish Highlands, with large numbers also from regions anciently Celtic in Norway, Holland, Belgium and the Upper Rhine district. Between 1860 and 1890 English farming families and agricultural labourers predominated, and German and Scandinavian emigration was also very strong. For Hansen this was the 'Germanic' or 'Teutonic' phase, marked by the comparative homogeneity of cultures and land systems. Two distinct source regions dominated the third period, from 1890 to 1914: the Mediterranean countries, and the Slavic area of the Russian Empire, including especially the Finns, Latvians, Lithuanians, Poles and Ukrainians. Our present brief discussion is focussed upon the first two waves.

The Scandinavian Exodus

The excellence and long continuity of the detailed official records in Scandinavia has encouraged many emigration analysts to use the examples of Norway and Sweden as model cases. Both countries experienced a series of rapid surges in population growth during the nineteenth century, with peaks in the 1820s, 1850s, and the late 1870s and 1880s.[18] The severe pressures exerted by each of these surges acted upon a relatively prosperous rural economy in which the traditional freehold occupied pride of place both socially and economically. Despite rapid clearing activities, an enclosure movement, the introduction of the potato and the general modernization of agricultural techniques, there were also deeply entrenched attitudes which encouraged the vigorous rejection of any attempt to subdivide the original family freeholds and the mounting pressures of increasing population dimmed the hopes of the landless majority. With the retention of ancient inheritance practices, younger children now felt increasingly disadvantaged by the amount and form of compensation received from the individual heirs, since new farms and alternative employment opportunities were more difficult to obtain. But under these same circumstances, the honoured family freehold was itself eventually threatened by the heavy financial encumbrances carried by the title-holder.

Emigration from Scandinavia in the early nineteenth century involved relatively few people but their reasons for departure were significant. Ideological discontent was a major propellant — with hostility towards the intellectuals' domination of the established Lutheran church and public resentment over military service, high taxation, undemocratic political representation and heavy bureaucratization. A much stronger exodus occurred in the late 1860s and early 1870s, following over-speculation in agricultural lands, crop failures and local famine in 1867–9. These were the great years of an 'America fever' generated by the American Federal and State governments, private land and emigration agents, steamship companies and emigrants' letters home. In the 1870s, Sweden's 'surplus' rural population was to some extent taken up by the process of industrialization and urbanization,

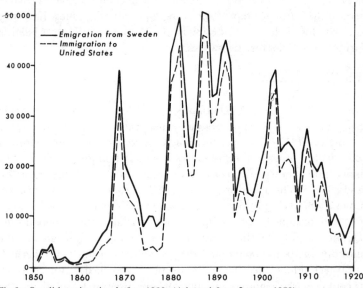

Fig 3   Swedish emigration before 1920. (Adapted from Janson, 1970)

and in any event the prospective emigrant was not encouraged by the American crisis of 1873 and its aftermath. The European agricultural depression of the 1880s was scarcely assisted by the successful expansion of the New World's agricultural frontiers, and a new Swedish exodus was registered in those years. Another ebb was recorded in the last decade of the century, associated with the American crisis of 1893.

The variation shown in the highly simplified graph of Swedish emigration (Fig. 3) is therefore ample proof of the overriding significance of comparative economic conditions. But we also require to know why the United States was preferred over other New World locations, and why Swedish immigration was concentrated into certain regions in that country. Swedish images of America clearly exhibited locational discretion, dependent at least in part upon non-economic factors.

The Irish and America

In Ireland, similar demographic pressures acted in a different social setting and upon an economy much poorer than that of Scandinavia.[19] Between the mid eighteenth and mid nineteenth centuries the Irish population grew no more quickly than those of several other European countries, but there was general underemployment and wretched poverty, and the small tenants had little incentive to make deep-seated improvements on land which so many of them rented from absentee English landlords. Industrialization in Ulster offered an escape for some, and seasonal employment in England and Scotland helped many more to survive. For the landlords, more efficient estate management usually appeared to demand the severe rationalization of their properties, including eviction and amalgamation. America provided a welcome solution for all concerned and between 1815 and 1845 approximately 850,000 Irishmen crossed the Atlantic. The floodgates were opened, however, with the onset of the potato famine: between 1846 and 1854 almost a million and a quarter of Ireland's population left for America. By the end of that period the Irish had contributed twenty-five percent of all European immigrants in the United States, and they far exceeded that proportion in some regions. The dream of America had wide appeal for the Irish, but the emigration response varied immensely from place to place within Ireland, reflecting especially the abilities of families and individuals to finance their own passages or to have them arranged in some way. The distribution of plain need was a rather less important control.

British Motivations

Industrialization commenced early in Britain, particularly in textiles, and by the middle of the nineteenth century fifty percent of the population was located in urban areas, with the rural sectors of several large regions starting a long decline. Between 1850 and 1910 the British population increased from twenty-two to forty-two millions, despite a slowing-down of industrial expansion in and after the 1880s, and a protracted but irregular exodus to several competing emigration fields provided the essential safety-valve. General labourers and farm workers emigrated in disproportionately large numbers, whereas skilled workers were far less in evidence than their contemporary strength in the British workforce might suggest. The United States was normally the most important destination, but the Australian colonies were very prominent during the gold-mining boom of the 1850s and again during the 1870s and 1880s; similarly, Canada was a major recipient in the 1880s and in the early years of the twentieth century, and after the First World War Australia and Canada each moved ahead of the United States.[20]

Erickson claims that economic ambitions were paramount in the motives of many British emigrants.[21] This was especially true, she says, of farmers and farmers' sons who had moved from pockets of stagnant and falling population in which their perceived range of opportunity was restricted. Emigrants of this type sampled by Erickson took capital with them when they crossed the Atlantic, and there was a general feeling within the group that money invested in American land and agriculture would bring a better return than was possible in Britain, where so much was taken by rents, tithes and taxes. The simple prospect of land ownership naturally suggested that more of the profit was bound to accrue to them as owners-producers. The same motivation was expressed by agricultural labourers and farm servants and also, although the point was less clearly made, by general labourers and various urban and industrial workers. Where farming in the United States was concerned, all too few of the immigrants recognized the folly of projecting British norms of accounting on to a situation in which labour was expensive or non-existent, the physical environment was strange and far more demanding, and adequate transport and markets were lacking.

Where the hardships of pioneer settlement were apparently more or less known or suspected, the motivation expressed by emigrants exhibited one common characteristic which outweighed their worries. Their private 'future images' of Britain were thoroughly pessimistic, especially regarding the maintenance or improvement of their social status; emigration in these cases was described by Erickson as 'a defensive measure, a means of not slipping backwards as the nation did'.[22] There was an expectation of revolution in Britain shortly after the Napoleonic Wars, it is true, yet those predicting the event were not always confident that it would bring about lasting improvements. But the most frequently mentioned goal was independence, which was usually associated with farming one's own piece of land, the employee and tenant of no man. This motivation was peculiarly related to a faith in self-sufficiency and a desire for leisure — partly based on the assumption that there was little incentive to hard work in areas devoid of markets and partly reflecting a confused rejection of the commercial life, a need for a return to the kind of life they believed their British forefathers had enjoyed.

These ideas were less commonly expressed after 1850, but it is important to note Erickson's observation that they typify attitudes which conflicted directly with what we might presume to have been optimal requirements for an industrializing society. So the filter of emigration did not always select the most ambitious or profit-conscious types—'Many of the British who went to American farms in this period of social unrest in Britain were social conservatives who clung to a partly idealized view of the past which was their agrarian myth.'[23]

Approximately ten million people left Britain permanently for the New World during the nineteenth century, and this total was roughly equal to the enumerated population of Great Britain in 1801. The 15–34 years age group predominated and the departure of these younger folk influenced British society in numerous ways — affecting, for example, the Gross Domestic Product, birth and marriage rates and the distribution of national income. And there is probably some justification for the belief that the unusual victory of consensus politics over the politics of conflict in nineteenth-century Britain, shown in the relatively peaceful and evolutionary character of that country's reforms, may have depended upon the 'safety valve' of emigration. This view is a little exaggerated. Certainly Erickson's most interesting subjects showed very little passion for politics or reform movements, and emigration itself was probably their chosen form of protest. On the other hand an unknown but significant number of British Chartists also emigrated, and the notions of this creative minority — concerning land reform in particular — were very influential in the United States and Australia.[24]

Chartism in Britain in the early nineteenth century was undoubtedly nourished by a hazy and emotive version of America's agrarian and revolutionary experience; it was a highly simplified interpretation which came to emphasize the general material prosperity of the United States under democratic institutions, with which Britain was compared very unfavourably. The well-publicized liberal constitutions of such states as Indiana, Illinois, Michigan and, above all, Wisconsin, had special appeal for the Chartists. But many of the radical immigrants of this persuasion swiftly became disillusioned with America, or were 'converted' to less extreme beliefs. One important exception, however, was the Chartist émigré Thomas Ainge Devyr. This uncompromising Irishman achieved great prominence in the American labour movement and devoted more than forty years of passionate agitation to the cause of free farms for the landless, the workers' best alternative to wage labour. Devyr's activities contributed directly to the passage of the Homestead Act in 1862, although he continued to demand much more than that famous piece of legislation offered.[25]

'Back to the Land' was also the solution favoured by many of Devyr's contemporaries in Britain. It offered a tangible and comprehensible goal, and an excellent rallying point at the lively Chartist meetings. 'The land belongs to the people. It is the people's heritage. Kings, princes, lords and citizens have stolen it from the people.' The remarkable Feargus O'Connor promoted a plan for 'land colonies' based on small holdings of less than five acres. As presented to the proletariat, these diminutive patches were the epitome of comfort and the 'just reward for honest toil', and a form of secure, unassuming and 'cosy' self-sufficiency appeared to be an aim in itself. There were a few bold experiments which lasted sufficiently long to make their marks locally, but (apart from organizational and other handicaps) private ownership dominated Britain to the extent that there was only limited scope for such innovative settlement projects.[26]

There was of course a close relationship between these revolutionary expressions and the earlier European debates concerning the relationship between land and life. Leading British scholars participated in those debates, and the Chartists and other nineteenth-century reform groups were therefore able to build upon a rich inheritance of social and philosophical thought. From the viewpoint of subsequent New World developments, and especially the example of settlement evolution in the United States, the most prominent of these influential British scholars was John Locke (1632–1704). His religious, political, educational and metaphysical philosophy proved immensely attractive in the New World, not least because it had work to do there: it was very well applied, that is, as a set of practical arguments suitable for pioneering societies. In particular, Locke had argued that land was the common stock of society to which every person possessed a fundamental right.

> God, who hath given the world to men in common, hath also given them reason to make use of it to the best advantage of life and convenience. The earth and all that is therein is given to men for the support and comfort of their being . . . all the fruits it naturally produces, and beasts it feeds, belong

to mankind in common, as they are produced by the spontaneous hand of Nature, and nobody has originally a private dominion exclusive of the rest of mankind in any of them . . .[27]

Similarly, a little less than one hundred years later, Professor William Ogilvie of King's College, Aberdeen, presented an impressive case for 'The Right of Property in Land' based upon general public utility as well as upon the natural law. Borrowing heavily from Locke and the European philosophers, Ogilvie included a number of propositions which were then beginning to be forcefully presented in the United States and were shortly to become very influential in the early settlement of Britain's colonies — including Australia, where the first penal camp was established only six years after the publication of Ogilvie's *Essay*. A small selection of these propositions will serve our present purpose.[28]

Cultivation, held Ogilvie, was good for the soul, and made valuable citizens; absentee use and/or ownership should be discouraged.

> The happiness of individuals, or of any great body of men, is nearly in proportion to their virtue and their worth. That manner of life, therefore, which is most favourable to the virtue of the citizens, ought, for the sake of their happiness, to be encouraged and promoted by the legislature. Men employed in cultivating the soil, if suffered to enjoy a reasonable independence, and a just share of the produce of their toil, are of simpler manners, and more virtuous, honest dispositions, than any other class of men. The testimony of all observers, in every age and country, concurs in this, and the reason of it may be found in the nature of their industry, and its reward. Their industry is not like that of the labouring manufacturer, insipidly uniform, but varied, — it excludes idleness without imposing excessive drudgery, and its reward consists in abundance of necessary accommodations, without luxury and refinement.[29]
> That every field should be cultivated by its proprietor, is most favourable to agriculture, and cultivation. That every individual who would choose it should be the proprietor of a field, and employed in its cultivation, is most favourable to happiness, and to virtue. In the combination of both circumstances will be found the most consummate prosperity of a people and of their country, — and the best plan for accommodating the original right of universal occupancy with the acquired rights of labour.[30]

Emigration should be positively encouraged by Old World governments; in the great new territories conditions were obviously optimal for the establishment of more enlightened concepts of the rights and responsibilities in land than could ever be found in Europe. Ogilvie continued:

> Princes, instead of imprisoning their subjects, may come to perceive that well regulated exportation of men, as of any other commodity, tends to secure and to increase the domestic produce. Even Britain will no doubt find inviting

occasions (and just now perhaps has them) of sending forth new colonies, on better digested plans . . . In every such settlement there is opportunity of establishing the just and natural system of property in land, in the most advantageous form. The fundamental laws of such a colony ought to ascertain, in precise and explicit terms, the joint property of the whole community in the whole soil — a right which in that situation of their affairs will be easily comprehended by all. They ought, further, to ascertain the permanent and indefensible nature of this right, which no possession of individuals, nor any industry by them applied to any portion of the soil, can ever cancel or impair.[31]

The principle of perpetual community ownership seldom received strong support in the New World itself until the latter part of the nineteenth century. This is not to say, however, that it was a totally ineffectual argument. The types of pronouncements made in Ogilvie's spirited account were, in fact, frequently resuscitated in many guises.

However extensive the tract of country may then be in proportion to the number of the first settlers, general rules should even then be established, having respect to the future period when the whole territory may be found too scanty for its multiplied inhabitants. By such precautions, occasionally enforced by practical examples, it seems not impossible to prevent the formation of those erroneous opinions of private right, and those habits of possession, which in countries long settled prevent the greater number of citizens from knowing or desiring to claim their natural rights in this most important point . . .[32]

The fundamental bond between land and society; the special opportunities in the New World for rediscovering and repairing that bond, for constructing a new society by regulating not only the distribution but also the use of landed resources: these were crucial arguments influencing the images held by Europeans of their own countries and of the new territories. There is no doubt that the diffusion of these ideas from the Old World frequently accompanied, but did not necessarily require, the emigration of European people. It is equally important to emphasize that the citizens of the New World were perfectly capable of reaching similar conclusions with some degree of independence. Certainly, the symbol of the 'yeoman farmer' became central to the rhetoric of a form of popular and politically useful agrarian idealism in the new territories. As the next chapter will show, this was strongly reflected in the production and operation of certain legislative frameworks which were designed to initiate and direct settlement expansion. Another vitally important characteristic of Old World–New World interaction which now demands attention is the 'filtering' or 'intermediary' role of promotion activity in environmental appraisal and in the communication process.

3

The 'Yeoman Farmer' and the Quest for Arcady

The log at the wood-pile, the axe supported by it,
The sylvan hut, the vine over the doorway, the space clear'd for a garden.[1]

The successful evocation of the theme of the New World's 'abundance' took various forms, very few of which depended upon the precise recording and reporting of factual information. One of the most influential types of communication offered a usefully blurred picture of the physical and social environments of the new territories, an image of attractive and bountiful rural landscapes inhabited already or in some future time by an independent, virtuous, patriotic and industrious population, which pursued small-scale farming as a way of life, rather than as a commercial enterprise. The powerful romanticization of the New World as a veritable Arcady was variously promoted in art and literature at all levels, but in addition — and in these cases the effort was more often deliberate and the results far more tangible, though not necessarily more pervasive — there were the commissioned accounts of individual agents and companies, and the interpretations of the officials, the politicians and of course the immigrant settlers themselves. A full analysis of this topic would indeed demand the identification of each type of actor as well as each category in the communication process, and the entire complex would have to be placed in its correct social setting. This enormous task is naturally beyond our present scope. It is possible, however, to explore and illustrate some of the important aspects of promotional activity and to discuss their relationship with the Arcadia imagery and with the types of agrarian idealism already introduced. This latter theme is particularly well displayed in the frequent employment of the 'yeomanry' motif.

The Promotion of the New World before 1870

Clearly, accepting the great breadth implied in the usual division of promotion activity into advertizing, publicity and personal selling,[2] it is not yet possible to attempt a complete and valid geographical analysis of this central process in the settlement experience. The following discussion therefore rests merely upon some representative works which may illustrate the scope and significance of the general topic of promotion. The first, following the studies of H. R. Merrens, considers the variable impact of major types of promoters and promotion activity, both American and European, upon the images of South Carolina's physical environment which were held during the colonial period — a time when the information components of most New World images were extremely blurred, to say the least. The second example further elaborates the theme of the distortion of environmental appraisals by the processes of promotion. It is based on J. M. R. Cameron's investigations of the early boosting of Western Australia for prospective immigrants from Britain. The third selection focusses primarily upon some American-based efforts which were directed towards specific groups in Europe: it is concerned with Scandinavian settlement in the Middle West in the latter half of the nineteenth century.

The Image-Makers and South Carolina[3]

Between 1680 and 1740 South Carolina was enthusiastically presented in several languages and by a wide range of private and officially-sponsored authors. Unlike the highly successful propaganda for Pennsylvania during this period which emphasized favourable economic prospects and religious attitudes, the literature which marketed the idea of South Carolina portrayed its physical environment as a definite terrestrial paradise. This first group of writings, noted in Merrens's five-fold classification as the type of literature most unequivocally *promotional* in intention, naturally became increasingly cautious in tone with the arrival of more sober accounts and the accumulation of first-hand experience in the colony. Accordingly, many contributions in this category were eventually based upon the selection of proven resources and the celebration of their singular potentials. Others chose to substitute some high praise of the mild winters and springs for the previous adulation of the summer months, which had been shown to be distinctly unhealthy. Similarly they attempted to challenge, and frequently succeeded in blurring, the emerging picture of coastal insalubrity, by suggesting that this problem might largely be due to the importation of European ailments and life-styles.

In this context it is also relevant to point out that South Carolina figured prominently in the famous climatic theory of Jean Pierre Purry, and particularly in his designation of 'optimal' environments for European settlement, which he argued to be situated between latitudes 30 degrees and 36 degrees in both hemispheres.[4] Drawn inevitably to South Carolina by the wonderful naivete of his pseudo-scientific reasoning, Purry became engaged in a most enterprising programme to bring out Swiss colonists. In fact the publicity given to his theory coincided very usefully with the inauguration by the South Carolina government of a campaign to settle large numbers of white immigrants in order to offset the rapidly increasing slave population. Purry achieved only limited success, but in general there is an indication of the comparative efficiency of the works in this first category, as Merrens relates, in the careful development of a form of 'counterpromotion' by certain European governments.

Where the information component of the image of South Carolina was derived essentially from the reports of government representatives, missionaries and other *officials*, the available evidence emphasizes two features: first, the least favourable events and conditions were commonly ignored or underplayed during the early years of settlement, possibly to retain British interest in the area and to justify their appointments to their superiors and themselves; secondly, with increasing colonization and the British Crown's assumption of more comprehensive responsibility, the official sources simply took the form of more objective and realistic responses to fairly orthodox queries from London, occasionally employing sweeping but useful regionalizations in their appraisals of the environment. In comparison with this the next two categories presumably gained wider circulation, although they differed widely from one another in terms of their readership. The most interesting published accounts of *travellers* in South Carolina — Merrens's third category — were predominantly concerned with social and economic conditions, and in their detailed coverage even the most reliable of them were highly subjective and regionally selective. The *natural history writers* relied rather on the careful observation, mapping and analysis of climate and terrain and, although they must have communicated at first with a much smaller public, their influence later became more pervasive. Merrens's final information category is that of the written accounts of actual *settlers*. It was shown to comprise an insubstantial, fragmented and haphazard record which was seldom available to other contemporary interpreters — though the corresponding verbal accounts presumably were — and it may indeed be of greater utility as a guide to the modern researcher, indicating some of the settlers' own perceptions of seasonality and terrain, together with their choice of environmental indicators, botanical and otherwise, in the selection of sites and situations for settlement and cultivation. For other areas of the New World and for later periods, it is probably true to say that this last element in the classification of written evidence may be identified as a less discrete entity in the image-making process.

The utility of such a common-sense typology based on a recognition of the interests or motivations of the writers concerned has already been implied in the first chapter of this book. Contrasting images were thereby projected of the physical environment of South Carolina, at different times and to various audiences. These images were favourable, distinctly negative, strongly or hesitantly defined; but a most important theme which emerged from the survey of all these classes of literature involved the boosting of a vaguely defined region west of the settled districts. Merrens argues that this was one of several early expressions of the evocation of a mysterious 'West' in American literature: it was later to become a very dominant motif in the great saga of Western expansion.

Eden in the Great South Land[5]

The belief in the existence of a southern continent probably developed from the Pythagorean view that, since the sphere was the most perfect shape in nature, then the earth itself must be spherical. The concomitant conditions of equilibrium and symmetry suggested to scholars of the ancient world the existence of a landmass which was similar in shape and size to that north of the equator; and, as this Southern Hemisphere 'reflected' the other half of the globe, it was therefore expected to have similar physical environments and equally civilized peoples. These notions persisted despite bitter opposition from the Church throughout the Middle Ages. Scientific analogy or latitudinal comparisons were employed to compensate for gaps in the geographical record: the concept of twelve distinct climatic zones in each hemisphere, for example, was a by-product of these approaches and it was very well established by the eighteenth century. Purry's 'climate five', already encountered in our discussion of South Carolina, therefore encompassed most of southern Australia.

Dutch navigators had returned with most unfavourable reports of the new region during the sixteenth century, but cartographers' inventions, travellers' tales and an increasing number of fictional works continued to add to the mystery and romance surrounding the Great South Land. In 1718 Purry himself tried in vain to persuade the Dutch East India Company to colonize the south-western part of the continent, and it was then practically dismissed for another century until the British seriously considered the establishment of settlement in the area.

A resourceful naval officer, James Stirling, pointed out the potentials of the location for Indian Ocean trade, demonstrating that it marked a transition between the trade winds and the westerlies; the same locational argument was said to hold out a guarantee of a healthy and productive climate. Stirling's official survey of the 'Swan River' district, in which he was supported by Charles Fraser, a botanist, was completed in a mere sixteen days in March 1827, under highly favourable environmental conditions. It was also narrowly confined to the immediate coastal plain and river flats, omitting by accident rather than by design the sandy soils, interdunal swamps and scrub vegetation screened by the high banks of the river. Sir John Barrow, an acknowledged 'expert' on the Southern Hemisphere, gave Stirling's report his blessing in 1829, and strongly supported the idea of the establishment of an agricultural colony at Swan River. The new district could be compared with Goshen, the Biblical 'land of plenty', and with Hesperia, the Greek 'Isles of the Blest'. Stirling's detailed survey had actually covered a mere 260 sq. km., yet Barrow gave the impression that there were 'from five to six millions of acres, the greatest part of which . . . may be considered as land fit for the plough and fully capable of giving support to a million of souls'.[6]

Cameron points to the existence of an important sequence of transformations in the communication process. Stirling's initial assessment, though intemperate, was at least based on some personal observation; Barrow's dissemination of the information was distinguished by its extravagances and was enthusiastically received by an intellectual élite for whom the topic of emigration had become a matter of engrossing debate. Barrow's article stimulated widespread publicity and there soon emerged a group of secondary disseminators, frequently with political, commercial or philanthropic interests in the encouragement of emigration. During the ensuing 'Swan River mania' the British public was assailed with the most glamorous descriptions of the new territory. Their primary message sources were the press, commercial agents and shipping companies, most of whom strove to provide information which was compatible with the frames of reference of the receivers. Those frames of reference included several inaccurate preconceptions. For example, the Australian environment was naively viewed as a British variant, a notion which made possible a number of wild inferences which the original reporter never intended to be drawn: so Stirling's relatively conservative account of the generous water supply and the luxuriant vegetation eventually gave rise to descriptions of a twelve-months' growing season supporting an extensive range of valuable crops, including maize, flax, cotton, vines, sugar and all the British grains. The system was therefore multi-channelled, with abundant 'noise' to block or distort the original messages. The receptors' reactions were best shown in the rapid movement of people

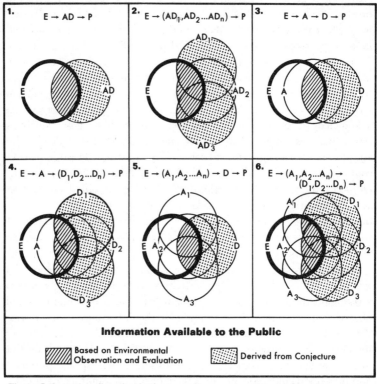

Fig 4   Information distortion in the promotion process. Adapted from Cameron, 'Information distortion in colonial promotion' (1974). In the first case, the appraisal of the environment (E) and the dissemination of that appraisal are conducted by the same person or persons, who may be labelled assessors-disseminators (AD). In example 2 there are several individuals carrying out this dual function, but the public (P) therefore receives a range of varying and overlapping interpretations. In case 3 the disseminator (D) has very little direct contact with the environment, yet the public gains most of its information from this source and not from the original assessor (A). The lower three cases illustrate instances of a single assessor and a multiplicity of disseminating agents; several assessors linked by a single disseminating agent; and a complex overlapping of assessment and disseminating functions.

and money to the Swan River settlement. And of course the immigrants' expectations were ridiculously optimistic. One of them chose to invest wholly in pointers, greyhounds, rabbits and pheasants; his wife arrived with a lap-dog. Their idea was to bring in servants from India and live out a life of ease. Within weeks of their arrival most of the colonists saw all of their dreams fade. The fertile soils were in very short supply, the winter storms abundant and dangerous, the coastline greatly overrated for shipping. The bewildered Stirling complained that 'people come out here expecting to find a Garden of Eden', only to be thrown into complete despondency when they failed to discover it. Immigration virtually ceased in 1830.

The importance of the general behavioural setting of the communication process, as outlined in our first chapter, is well illustrated here. The assessor-disseminator Stirling, communicating at first only to a small public (his immediate peer group and administrative superiors), together with the subsequent writers on the subject who selectively plagiarized, invented and borrowed, 'tried to elicit a behavioural response by presenting their information in a form that was in accord with their own objectives and was compatible with receptors' frames of references'. Similarly, the receptors only accepted information consistent with their own objectives, experiences and attitudes. Figure 4 presents various types of information fields as a series of permutations resulting from the above processes.[7] Although the diagram is derived essentially from the Western Australian example, the suggestion of its wider utility should be fairly clear.

The Middle West for Scandinavians[8]

The greater 'visibility', as it were, of the United States in the New World–Old World interaction, together with the early establishment in that country of a number of religious and other communities of Scandinavian origin, strengthened the 'push' factors of social, economic or political derivation and focussed the hopes of prospective emigrants in Norway and Sweden. It has already been suggested, however, that there were also many 'pulling' forces within the United States. And certainly there were innumerable 'salesmen' operating at federal, state and local levels, who were engaged in marketing three major tangible 'goods' — land, work and transportation.

It is difficult to discern the specific international and regional impacts of the organized propaganda campaigns. Further research may show, for example, that promotion in the first half of the nineteenth century mainly contributed towards a reinforcement of the natural environmental advantages and abundant land enjoyed by certain states, and that for the century as a whole most success was actually achieved amongst the native-born Americans, assisting them in their decision to move west. Also, there is some evidence to suggest that the earliest waves of European immigration showed very little correlation with the type and amount of promotional effort emanating from the various American regions; and again, it seems clearly proven that immigration to the industrializing eastern states required no great advertizing programme from either government or private enterprise, while the particularly strenuous endeavours of some southern states were largely unrewarded. It is possible, nonetheless, to offer confidently two simple observations. First, the net effect of all this promotion was obviously to saturate Europe with news of America and to emphasize the apparent advantages of the United States over those of her New World rivals. Second, where the organized propaganda was distrusted, there was usually another more subtle and penetrating form of publicity, the emigrants' letters home — 'let no one listen to anybody but only his relatives whom he has here, in this golden America.'

The interrelationships of these information sources are particularly well represented in the following vignettes from the history of Scandinavian settlement in the Middle West, in which settlers' correspondence was crucially significant.

> The nineteenth century witnessed a new discovery of America. It came about, not through the daring of a new Columbus, but as a consequence of letters written by immigrants to the people of the Old World. It was a progressive and widening discovery that played an important role in the migration of millions of Europeans from their home countries to the United States . . . the realities of the New World meant little, and indeed were almost unknown, to the everyday people of Europe until they began to read, in their own homes, the firsthand narratives of friends and relatives who had braved the Atlantic and had seen for themselves what America really was like.[9]

The 'America fever' which swept through the towns and villages of Sweden and Norway was indeed largely due to the widespread diffusion of what were called the 'America Letters'. They provided 'a composite diary of everyday people at the grass roots of American life' and, most of all, they became the means by which individual settlers were able to transmit most directly and efficiently some of the detail of their own experiences — from the very inception of the story, with the initial decision to emigrate, to the continuing consequences of that decision. This mode of communication was naturally particularly powerful where the receivers were relatives and friends. But in other cases the letters were addressed to newspapers in the home country, or were forwarded thence by relatives, and the 'filtering' action of skilled editors served to introduce a much wider audience to parts, at least, of the material.

A few of the more persistent and literate correspondents achieved great notoriety in this way. One of the best known of these was the Swede Gustav Unonius, a government official from Uppsala who settled in Wisconsin in the 1840s. Attracted like other educated immigrants by the promise of political, social and religious freedom in America, Unonius underplayed the fundamental problems of isolation and soil sterility in his own selected area, and challenged his countrymen to improve dramatically upon their miserable condition by moving to the New World.

> Its rich soil and its industrial possibilities invite just at present thousands of Europeans, who in their homelands have in one way or another been hampered in their hopes by the economic circumstances of their homes, or by a precarious livelihood. Work, in any industry only that it is honorable, in America is no shame. Every workman has there the same right of citizenship as the nobles. Conventional judgements, class interest and narrow-mindedness do not hang to your coat tail nor trample on your heels.[10]

Letters home were inherently more credible and generally provided, in addition, a more continuous flow of information than any of the organized promotion literature. The filtering function of the press probably resulted in a bias towards rather more commentary on the political and other 'freedoms' offering in the United States. But in the last analysis the decision to move was an individual act, and the millions of personal letters from the vanguard, of which only the smallest fraction remains for modern scrutiny, were collectively far more influential than the pieces from Unonius and others in the newspapers. Perhaps it could be said that the latter selections contributed mainly towards the formation of a favourable public or national image of the United States which included some emphasis on regional variation, while the private correspondence assisted in focussing the vitally significant private images of individual Scandinavians. The important content of these messages might be entirely personal, even trivial to other readers outside the circle of intimacy — some crucial reassurance concerning the establishment of a few familiar and favoured customs, the location of old friends and relatives, the apparent consequences on the health of immigrants, the price of a plough, a blanket or a day's labour, the suitability of imported seeds and farming methods, adjustments to weather and climate, and so on. A letter might simply wax eloquent on the extraordinary abundance of good breakfast fare, rapturously indulged by the writer and his family, and a common boast was the growing list of prized possessions — cattle, corn, hogs and, that most desired of all assets, land itself. Lest the comparison with the immigrant's previous condition be forgotten, it received frequent mention in the letters, and the implications for those who had stayed behind were not always very generously or subtly put. So the Wisconsin pioneer Ole Knudsen Trovatten castigated his former neighbours for their continued timidity.

> You, my true friend, together with many others of my acquaintance, probably censure me for my emigration considerably, and perhaps even yet believe that I regret having left Ødefjeld. NO! not so. In no circumstances would I return to live in Ødefjeld, not even if I could be the owner of half of the Annex. Ødefjeld is such a wretched place that one ought by no means to live there. Every inhabitant would do better by selling his farm to people from Lower Telemark. It seems rather foolish to me to abide by one's ancestors' ignorance of better regions and their fear of emigration and live in so poor a place and upon such barren ground as Ødefjeld. Fertile fields lay uncultivated in America partly for ignorance of the fertility of this land and partly for fear of emigration. Here in America a much better mode of living is open to every honorable citizen, as I hope most inhabitants of Ødefjeld are.[11]

The intimacy assumed in the private correspondence was of course its greatest strength in the communication process, yet it is unfortunate that, in addition to the fragmented nature of the surviving records, there is so little which documents the opposite flow — that is, of news, replies and especially of requests for information, from Europe.[12] The newspaper link may have fulfilled part of this function after the New World–Old World dialogue became sufficiently well established to define certain issues or points of interest. There is a little evidence for this speculative observation in the discussion of the therapeutic effects of emigration which appeared in Scandinavian newspapers in the 1860s. A letter from one Paul Hjelm-Hansen, from Minnesota, is a good example of this, though it is also a reminder that the immigrants had their own reasons for carefully selecting the information to be transmitted.

> In twelve days spent under the open sky on Minnesota's high plains, about halfway between the Atlantic and Pacific oceans, I have become free of my rheumatism, and in place of it I have gained physical strength and a cheerful disposition. In that respect alone I benefited greatly from this trip. In truth, the air here is just as wonderfully invigorating as the land is beautiful and fruitful. As I have drawn deep breaths of this clean air, I have often thought of the pittiable creatures who resort to Ayer's Pills or Sweet's Blood Renewer, and occasionally I have caught myself in sorrowful consideration of that lovely half of humanity, whom young men love so much, and who, in order to please us, get their rosy cheeks at the apothecary's. Oh, if only these fine, lovable human beings could come up here and move about in this clean air! Then the prettiest natural roses and lilies would come of themselves, and to doctors and druggists one could justifiably say, 'Goodby.'[13]

Since the promotion campaigns differed in style, intensity and ethnic orientation from state to state, it should be useful to narrow the focus in order to consider an example from one of these young political units. In the later 1860s the state of Minnesota hardened its resolve to compete with other states in the Middle West in order to attract immigrants from Europe and from other parts of the United States. Milwaukee and Chicago were the principal points of entry for the region as a whole, and it was discovered that agents from the other states were meeting the newcomers at these places and directing their subsequent journeys at the expense of Minnesota. It was therefore decided to appoint Special Immigration Agents in each of the gateway cities for the 'protection' of new arrivals.

One of those appointed was the Swede Hans Mattson, who soon displayed a skilled and dedicated interest in Scandinavian immigration. Mattson was a prime mover in subsequent legislation which extended the principles learned from his highly successful experience as Minnesota's Chicago agent. In 1867 a Board of Immigration was established, with Mattson as one of its three members, and its chief responsibility was immigrant 'protection', the publication of promotional literature in Europe and the United States, and the appointment and supervision of the official agents for protection and propaganda. These agents were to be representative of Minnesota's major ethnic groups, and indeed the various community leaders were closely consulted on all aspects of the Board's work. This was particularly clearly reflected in the engagement of a number of prominent individuals who contributed newspaper articles for release in America and Europe, and advised on the production and circulation of authoritative private correspondence in response to important queries or simply to publicize the state's advantages. It was similarly shown in the choice of content in the promotional literature. Whereas, for example, the material designed for English speakers attempted to reassure readers about the supposed severity of Minnesota's bleak winters, the fare offered to Scandinavians was intended to dispel their nightmares about the summer heat-waves.[14]

Hans Mattson was then well known and respected amongst his own people and in his new position he assiduously exploited his contacts with the Swedish and Norwegian press in America. At about this time, however, Mattson also became closely connected with the St. Paul and Pacific Railroad company. A decision had been made to allow the railroad companies of the Middle West enormous land grants which they could sell or offer as security for the bond loans they took out to finance their construction work. When the granted lands were sold to new settlers the railroads thereby gained construction hands as well as additional freight and passenger traffic, and so each company became deeply involved in the promotion of inter-regional and international immigration to its own territory.[15] Mattson's various writings on Minnesota diligently promoted the central area of the state which was to be served by the S.P.P.R., a district in which he was also personally involved as a farmer and land speculator. Shortly after a remarkably skilful public relations visit to Sweden in 1868-9 — where he represented his state, individual Scandinavian settlers or settlers' associations, the S.P.P.R. and a steamship company — the celebrated Mattson was elected Secretary of State for the Minnesota legislature. This new honour proved to be a useful asset in his continuing role as the major land agent for the planned 'New Scandinavia' which rapidly emerged along the main line of the S.P.P.R.

There is insufficient space here to discuss the rest of Mattson's important work, but some qualifications are essential to set his efforts in right perspective. His individualistic role as an agent in the transformation of the social geography and cultural landscape of Minnesota was made possible by the strongly supportive activity of local Scandinavian-Americans for whom he provided the spearhead. They were intensely interested, for social, personal, commercial and political reasons, in the attraction of more of their countrymen to their chosen part of the New World. Certainly, Mattson's most persistent and successful argument was that fellow Scandinavians had already tested the product and liked it. The statement was confirmed by immigrants' letters and by more than a few triumphant homecomings in which a great display was made of their wealth and general well-being. Without the direct and indirect support of an existing communication network and established nuclei of Scandinavian settlement, Mattson's work would have been rendered impotent, as his later endeavours for the Canadian government testify. In this respect it should be noted that Mattson never found it necessary to beat the drum during his visit to Sweden, though it is true that he did manage to win very favourable personal publicity for some outspoken political comments which were scarcely related to his primary objectives. Usually, apart from fulfilling his numerous commissions to contact the friends and relatives of Minnesota settlers, he was approached independently by prospective Swedish emigrants. And Mattson was somewhat less popular with the Norwegians, yet they moved to Minnesota in even greater numbers than did the Swedes.

Again, where his contribution towards the 'Scandinavianization' of central Minnesota was concerned, it is a fact that by law, general land sales in any area could not proceed until all government land of good quality in the locality had been purchased, so that Mattson was obliged to focus his promotional efforts on areas already partly colonized by Scandinavians. His best ploy had presumably been made during his tenure on the Board of Immigration, where he was more or less personally responsible for directing Scandinavians to the government land in the central district: at the same stroke, therefore, he eliminated the competing element which would have handicapped his later plans for the railroad grants, while ensuring the establishment of the crucial settlement nuclei.

In 1860 Scandinavians formed seven percent of Minnesota's population and they were outnumbered by immigrants of both German and Irish origins. By 1870 the first effects of the promotion activity which has been briefly outlined here were reflected in a marked increase in the Scandinavian sector to over thirteen percent, a proportion which exceeded that of any other foreign group, and this leadership was amply confirmed in the censuses of 1880 and 1890. At the latter date there were over 250,000 Scandinavians in Minnesota, constituting more than half of the foreign-born residents and over nineteen percent of the state's total inhabitants.

Vedder and Galloway have demonstrated that the geographical preferences of Scandinavian emigrants to the United States between 1850 and 1960 exhibited fairly good responses to actual interstate differences in labour demand and income, that distance itself was not an important consideration and that the factor of land availability declined in significance over time; and above all, that there was an avoidance of the southern states and a marked and persistent affinity for climatic regions similar to those in Scandinavia.[16] Their interesting statistical survey appears to indicate therefore that the archetypical Scandinavian immigrant was a fair example of the economist's 'maximizing individual', since a fairly accurate perception of the sources of economic abundance in the United States was displayed. The brief discussion offered above is surely a useful reminder, however, that in the formative period of emigration locational choices were made within a complex but accommodating matrix which was based in no small measure upon the pooling of information, and especially on the availability of some sophisticated guidance through formal and informal channels.

The Yeoman Symbol in America and Australia

The European inheritance of ideas and ideals was generously

distributed between the various centres of the New World, and the significant contrasts between these new nations should not be allowed to mask the essential similarities which reflected their common inheritance and what they made of it. The relatively homogeneous population of Australia maintained its close economic, political and social connection with Britain throughout the period under review. In comparison, the United States was politically independent from an early date, was geographically far less isolated, and her population was rapidly enriched by a more varied input of Old World immigrants. Yet the evolution of rural settlement in each of these two countries was profoundly influenced by a similar type of agrarian idealism derived essentially from Europe and considerably modified by promotion, by political initiatives and aspirations, and by a growing appreciation of the natural resource base.

The American 'Fee-Simple Empire'

The restatement and revision of European political and economic philosophies in eighteenth-century America — particularly those French and British arguments which emphasized universal land rights and the high status of the cultivator — imbued them with a very strong nationalistic flavour. It was indeed frequently asserted that American society was already the embodiment of what many Europeans appeared to regard as a utopian dream. During the revolutionary era the vast majority of Americans lived in rural areas, and there were large numbers of small family farms. Franklin, Crèvecoeur and Thomas Jefferson were the leading expositors of the agrarian ideal in America, and Jefferson was particularly influential in communicating what he perceived to be its primary political implications. The independent cultivators were the very foundation of the new republic — 'the most precious part of a state' — and the successful promotion of the westward expansion of this simple agricultural society would be the best guarantee of the survival of republican institutions. Jefferson's more extravagant rhetoric clearly exhibited a close familiarity with the European literature of the day.

> Those who labor in the earth are the chosen people of God, if ever He had a chosen people, whose breasts He has made His peculiar deposit for substantial and genuine virtue . . . Corruption of morals in the mass of cultivators is a phenomenon of which no age nor nation has furnished an example. It is the mark set upon those, who, not looking up to heaven, to their own soil and industry, as does the husbandman, for their subsistence, depend for it on casualties and caprice of customers. Dependence begets subservience

and venality, suffocates the germ of virtue, and prepares fit tools for the designs of ambition ... the proportion which the aggregate of the other classes of citizens bears in any state to that of its husbandmen, is the proportion of its unsound to its healthy parts, and is a good enough barometer whereby to measure the degree of corruption.[17]

In the statements of Jefferson and Crèvecoeur and in the descriptive and romantic works of the new republic, the visions evoked were those of a completely new and happy society that was being brought into existence under the influence of an abundance of good land ready for settlement. The communication of the associated future images was bold and simple, and it had wide appeal. Most significantly, it underlined the promise of a massive transformation of the geography of the West based upon a host of small-scale holdings, each to be controlled by an owner-occupier. The grand scale of this transformation naturally provided a major share of its attraction, but the most useful of the complementary literary metaphors emphasized instead a much smaller spatial unit, suggesting the potentials for more intimate and mutually beneficial man–land relationships. So the Mississippi Valley itself was the 'Garden of the World', and the rich symbolism traditionally attached to images of the garden was exploited with skill and dedication.

Henry Nash Smith has already explored this theme with great aplomb, and it will suffice here merely to point briefly to some of his interesting observations concerning the evocation of Arcady in America.[18] Travellers in Kentucky's frontier districts in the late eighteenth century, for example, were apparently moved to describe the new country in scriptural terms. It was 'like the land of promise, flowing with milk and honey', where 'you shall eat bread without scarceness, and not lack any thing in it'; it offered a climate without any threat of disease, a beautiful wilderness where 'nature makes reparation for having created man', and a promise of a return to the age of rural bliss which Britain and Europe were rapidly losing. Smith has also drawn special attention to the example of J. K. Paulding's early work, *The Backwoodsman* (1818), which announced the great opportunities of the western frontier in recounting the progress of Paulding's hero from grinding poverty to comfort and independence, both of which are attained through land ownership. Thus 'our meanest farmer's boy' strides out in the great West to seek his 'competence', finally to achieve the singular dignity 'That springs from holding in his own dear right/The land he plows, the home he seeks at night.' And similarly, Timothy Flint's fictional and non-fictional writings contrasted the peace and prosperity of an agrarian West with the new urban and

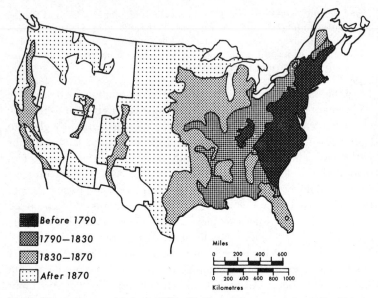

Fig 5   Westward expansion in the USA. Blank areas denote regions which still had a population density of under two per square mile in 1910.

industrial order which was threatening in the north-eastern states. So he depicted the emergence of a bucolic Ohio as a welcome reproduction of the best features of New England's landscape and society before the vile depredations of the textile mills began to rob that region of its charms. Those hordes of 'independent and happy yeomen' who had made their homes in the garden of the West were scarcely likely to regret their decision. Consider their improved position:

> With the ample abundance that fills their granaries, with their young orchards, whose branches must be propped to sustain the weight of their fruit, beside their beautiful rivers, and beech woods, in which the squirrels skip, the wild deer browse, and the sweet red-bird sings, and with the prospect of settling their dozen children on as many farms about them . . . and the ability to employ the leisure of half of their time as they choose . . .[19]

In their 'peace, plenty and privacy' they were fortunate indeed compared with those who were confined within factory walls, condemned to 'contemplate the whirl of innumerable wheels for fourteen hours of six days of every week in the year'.[20]

In conformity with this type of agrarian idealism the 'yeoman' expressed an attitude of spiritual attachment to his own small piece of land by fulfilling three major non-commercial conditions, duties, or responsibilities. He diligently cultivated the soil, resided on the land throughout his working life, and in due course ensured that it was passed on to one or more of his progeny as a revered heritage. During the eighteenth century this ideal had certainly approximated to actual conditions in some districts—although land speculation was not unknown, and where self-sufficiency did occur it would seldom have been described as the attainment of a cherished goal. By the late 1820s and into the 1830s surpluses of grain and livestock were appearing. The American farmers demanded access to markets and all kinds of internal improvements, and as these were provided there was an increasing divergence between the cherished ideal and the new economic organization. Steamships and railroads subordinated the yeoman farmer to the merchants and bankers of the growing urban centres; increasingly, the farmer himself became more of a businessman. Yet, as Hofstadter has indicated very well, the agrarian ideal displayed astonishing longevity, for it remained the accepted view of western society in the United States.[21] It became indeed an agrarian myth, which profoundly influenced political development and the subsequent legislation for the disposal of the public estate. Whereas the notion began as the preserve of the educated classes, by the early nineteenth century the agrarian ideal, with the yeoman as its central component, had become part of the national ideology.

Political and economic conditions, and especially bitter opposition from the southern states, kept land reform in the background for a number of years, but vigorous demands were repeatedly made for the granting of free or cheap homesteads for all the people. These inspired crusades were based on the contention that it was plainly sinful to continue to sell land as 'mere merchandise, like molasses or mackerel':[22] furthermore, it was morally unjustifiable to deny men their 'natural right' to use any portion of the earth's surface. As one prominent champion of the proposed homesteading legislation argued,

> if a man has a right on earth, he has a right to land enough to rear a habitation on. If he has a right to live, he has a right to the free use of whatever nature has provided for his sustenance — air to breathe, water to drink, and land enough to cultivate for his subsistence. For these are the necessary and indisputable means for the enjoyment of his inalienable rights of life, liberty and the pursuit of happiness.[23]

The Homestead Act was finally signed by President Lincoln on 20 May 1862. Full title to a maximum area of 160 acres — one quarter of a surveyed 'section' — could be acquired by continuous residence and improvements over a period of five years; after six months' proven residence and suitable improvements the claimant might commute his original tenure to full title by paying the usual price of $1.25 per acre.

His title was declared inalienable: that is, the land could not be transferred to satisfy any form of debt. Other major regulations demanded citizenship of the United States, the payment of survey fees and an affidavit stating that the land was not taken up for the benefit of another person.[24]

The Homestead Act continued with a few modifications during the remainder of the century, but it was largely irrelevant east of the Mississippi and in the more established areas of the Middle West — in a line running from Michigan and Wisconsin through Iowa, Missouri and Mississippi into Alabama. The bulk of the remaining federal land in these states had been purchased during the boom of the previous decade; further west, Arkansas, Minnesota and Louisiana still offered good opportunities for the small man, but most of the available land was located in the drier plains and the mountain states (Fig. 5). Special

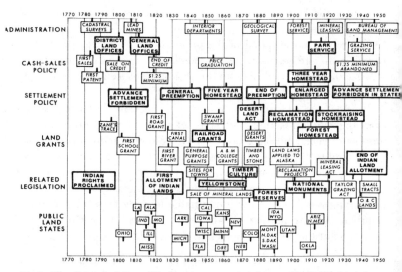

Fig 6   The disposal of the public domain: a crowded time profile. Public lands legislation was a major slice of the life of those lively times, consuming a good deal of political and popular attention throughout the nineteenth century and the early decades of the present century. Some of the major decisions discussed in this book, together with a few related events, have been emphasized for reference purposes.

amending legislation was soon required to cope with the new conditions. From 1873, for example, the Timber Culture Act was introduced to facilitate the settlement of the semi-arid High Plains by providing for a free grant of 160 acres to any person who planted ten acres of wood. The second official effort to transform these marginal areas was expressed in the Desert Land Act of 1877. Its purpose was to encourage intensive irrigation in the western and south-western states, principally by means of similar land grants.[25]

But neither the Homestead Act nor its subsequent modifications and appendages (see Fig. 6) created the type of fee-simple empire envisaged by Jefferson and his successors. Reduced to its essentials, the cultural landscape of the agrarian ideal, which was perhaps the most tangible component of the 'future image' shared by most of the reformers, was one of regularly distributed holdings which were closely spaced and intensively used. The deep commitment to the 'domestication' of the wild garden was very well shown in the rapid progress of national surveying under the rectangular grid system, so uncompromising in its emphasis upon a type of civilized or civilizing 'order'. Unsurveyed land was deemed 'unprepared' for the planting of yeomen settlers and inevitably, the framework of the grid dominated the general pattern of westward expansion — the landscape was structured accordingly to a utilitarian value system, to approximate profit maximization and/or cost minimization.[26] But processes of rationalization or accommodation emerged in each locality, as natural responses to real or perceived environmental conditions, and to individual and family needs and aspirations. In terms of the evolving forms of spatial organization, one obvious result was that early amalgamations commonly destroyed much of the homogeneity which had been built into the initial design: in fact, the minutest forms of subdivision were frequently more or less ignored from the outset as each pioneer set about the task of achieving what he considered to be a satisfactory working unit. Associated with these processes, the chronic lack of capital meant that short- and long-term tenancy became increasingly common and in some areas there was also a rapid turnover in ownership, linked with formal and informal partnership arrangements and a complex pattern of local mobility. In these respects the Australian experience exhibited many similarities, as will be shown. One eminent authority has estimated that for every 'free' American farm taken up and retained by a *bona fide* settler between 1800 and 1890, there were nine which were bought directly from railroad companies, speculators, or from the government itself.[27]

Although the local achievements of the legislation should not be too easily dismissed, it seems clear that the values and attitudes underpinning the belief in the yeoman myth were already anachronistic by 1862. Whatever the rhetoric, the character of the American farmer was essentially career-directed, not tradition-oriented; or, rather, he was at best an *ambivalent* agrarian, for the perpetuation of the imagery and a particularly vigorous revival of it from time to time could be socially, economically and politically useful. Even allowing for this, agricultural society in the United States during the nineteenth century was obviously distinguished by an inversion of the old European ratio of expensive land and cheap labour, and attitudes to farm management became markedly 'businesslike', as compared with the idealized 'craftsman's' approach and emotional attachment to the soil. Furthermore, a penchant for speculation and the continued lure of new and different country meant that the promise of cheap and permanent homesteads was virtually self-defeating; the sale of one homestead could mean security in the next. In short, the assumptions on which the Homestead Act appear to have been based were clearly incongruous with most of the new demands and opportunities which the industrial revolution made available. Again, the residential requirements seem to have assumed that settlement would be gradual and stable after the fashion of the mythical yeoman, and in general the provisions of the Act implied some confidence in the beneficence of nature, trusting to permanent and 'yeomanlike', non-speculative farming, which was particularly incongruous with the environment of the western plains. In those areas, climatic hazards and insect plagues were normal ingredients in the ecological system, and successful adaptation necessitated a certain amount of empirical testing which was bound to include considerable mobility at the local and regional levels. The Acts of 1873 and 1877 fared little better: many small farmers manipulated the loose provisions of the Timber Culture Act of 1873 and increased the size and flexibility of their original units by taking up adjacent or nearby blocks, but the more substantial landholders also benefited by employing this ruse; regulations under the later Desert Land Act were on the whole too demanding for the small-scale settler and the big ranchers were able to acquire an increased share of the diminishing public estate.[28]

The gap between rhetoric and reality was wide indeed, and the grand frauds and innumerable 'innocent deceits' employed to obtain land in the United States still constitute the greater part of the written record of the disposal of the public domain. But a vast number of homesteaders realized the dream without defying either the spirit or the letter of the legislation, and immigrants from every European country were drawn to America by the good news of generous land laws. This part of the story, which illuminates such profound geographical transformations, deserves further scholarly attention. So too does one peculiarly neglected feature of the impact of the agrarian ideology on the development of public policies for enlightened resource management. Contemporary discussion at the highest levels of decision making was almost always centred upon the 'disposal' of the public domain

Fig 7   Arcady in California. (Source: *Chicago Daily Tribune*, 21 November 1911)

rather than upon its management: the issue of continued public ownership, for example, was seldom explored in any depth. Similarly, the consuming pre-occupation with tillage as the *sine qua non* of a landscape of sturdy yeomen oriented the policy-makers away from grassland, timber and minerals which actually constituted the major resource endowment of several large regions. This often resulted in the early consignment of these vital resources to the ignorant, careless and wanton exploitation of private enterprise.

But to all appearances Nature's generosity towards the splendid new country was unparalleled. The alarm was only infrequently sounded, and then with little effect. Certainly, unusual restraint and extraordinary vision would have been required for the design and imposition of rigid control measures in an age of expansion, and in any case this would have stretched the capabilities of America's fledgling bureaucratic systems far beyond their limits. And finally, returning to the positive aspects, it should be pointed out that the disposal of the public domain was itself a very prolonged management exercise of enormous magnitude and complexity; despite its shortcomings, its multifaceted contribution towards the modernization of the whole spectrum of public administration in the United States must be stressed.

Urban and suburban expressions of a rather more transparent Arcadianism may be seen in the increasing vogue for public parks, private gardens and 'garden suburbs' throughout the nineteenth century, supported by a phenomenal growth of related community organizations whose avowed purpose was to make their own towns and cities as 'rural' as possible. The fabric of the American townscape was rapidly transformed by these efforts. It is more central to our present argument, however, to point to the development of modern irrigation technology during the last quarter of the nineteenth century and the early decades of the present century. Irrigation opened up new possibilities for those urbanites with rural aspirations for whom the back-breaking toil of the impecunious homesteader held no real attraction. The vision of compact civilized communities in the fragrant and ordered landscapes of California's valleys was romance enough. Like a prophecy, the seemingly self-renewing orange and vine were to replace the gamble of wheat, corn and hogs. So the railroad men and the land agents took up their pens once more (Fig. 7). And the city folk rushed in.

Arcady in the Antipodes

From the dumping of the first convicts in 1788 to the beginning of the gold rushes in the 1850s, a large proportion of the white population of Australia was brutalized and illiterate, and for most of that time the colonists were fully occupied in taking possession of an immense continent and in attempting to grasp some of its unique ecological relationships. Whether they studied their immediate surroundings or speculated on the future they were primarily concerned with improving their own living conditions. A number of blurred images of the continent were evoked by and for a small educated élite which was inevitably very British in taste and outlook, and in fact it was not until the 1880s that creative workers began to capture and communicate recognizably Australian flavours.[29] In the interim, while the mass of the

Australian population continued to pursue a very simple utilitarian dream, British images of Australia's present and future became inextricably linked to reactions to changing conditions in the mother country. This applied especially to the frustrations and insecurities associated with the industrial revolution, and a strong connection was established thereby with British interpretations of the agrarian idealism. In the late eighteenth century the British thought of Australia as a small and incredibly distant cesspool of depravity; during the middle of the nineteenth century it was successfully evoked for them as a veritable Arcady, in which the Golden Age of rural prosperity and individual dignity might be recaptured.

The beginnings of this transformation may be traced back to the conditions which gave rise to the ill-fated Swan River project. More directly relevant, however, was Edward Gibbon Wakefield's promotion of a simple new scheme of spatial organization to unite Europe and the New World.[30] From the second decade of the nineteenth century Jefferson's American vision of a compact continental empire of small-scale farmers was matched by a grandiose British dream — of a global empire which would be made an economic, social and political whole through colonization from the mother country. Wakefield was largely responsible for the popularization of an attractive and coherent scheme of 'systematic colonization' based upon a 'self-regulating' mechanism of colonial land values — that is, relatively high prices were to be established and, although these could be altered from time to time, they were at all times to be made sufficient to finance emigration from Britain, and to maintain a rural proletariat in Australia by restricting the upward movement of landless labourers. Settlement in the colony of South Australia, and also in New Zealand, was to a large extent founded upon these principles, which in simple geographical for-mulation meant the slow extension of the agricultural frontier into the interior, set within a matrix of tight government management of the direction and pace of the expansion. Official control deeply influenced the detailed character of the emerging cultural landscape in terms of its major structural elements — small farm sizes, intricate road patterns and, to some extent, the familiar South Australian and New Zealand features of an orderly style of settlement morphology and fairly intensive land use. These organizational tactics were less rigidly applied in the other Australasian colonies, but high land prices and the principle of government supervision became accepted props of their settlement policies, and for the remainder of the century important land debates in the colonial parliaments were seldom free of useful 'Wakefieldian' phrases dredged from the memory of these years.

A movement which expanded these views emerged later under the leadership of Samuel Sidney. Coral Lansbury has shown how Sidney, who never saw Australia, produced a spate of evocative writings on the country and encouraged others to do likewise, extolling its Arcadian virtues as a ready-made paradise for the abused British workers.[31] His attitude to Australia was in essence rather patronizing and, if we are to consider the 'intention' field within which his offerings were set (*cf.* Chapter 1), then it should be noted that the most significant ingredients were the benefits he saw for Britain in the new emigration field. His first salvo was fired in *A Voice from the Far Interior of Australia* (1847), which was incorporated into *Sidney's Australian Handbook* in 1848. Seven editions of the latter work, each of 1,000 copies, were sold within five months. He also opened the columns of *Sidney's Emigrant's Journal and Traveller's Magazine* to accommodate essays by the philanthropist Caroline Chisholm and other champions of small-scale farming for Australia; and all of these efforts attracted the admiration of noted writers, including Dickens and Lytton, who borrowed extensively for their information on Australia. Dickens's earlier works had already helped to change the mythic consciousness of Englishmen, who now looked back with nostalgia to a Pickwickian era without factories and spoil-heaps: 'it was becoming increasingly true that Pickwick's England was the historical past for most Englishmen, and it was this idealised past which Sidney and Caroline Chisholm hoped to establish in Australia.'[32] *Pickwick Papers* was immensely popular in Australia, where over 30,000 copies of the first edition were sold, and the most immediate point of reference for travellers visiting Australia in mid-century was said to be the world of Mr. Pickwick. The tranquillity of a vine-covered cottage in a new land provided a useful concluding image for the popular novels of the day, and Dickens's characters had no monopoly over this comfortable scene. In another place, Coral Lansbury has shown that Dickens's influence can be traced through a variety of Australian newspapers and periodicals, providing a host of readers with reassuring images and not a few colonial politicians with a good catch phrase. In Dickens's phenomenally successful magazine *Household Words* a series of articles on the qualifications of Australia as a migration field was offered to an international public, and Sidney contributed six major essays. Sidney's major work, *The Three Colonies of Australia: New South Wales, Victoria and South Australia* (1852), sold 5,000 copies in its first year of publication, and was full of lyrical descriptions of the Australian landscape. Most of it was hopelessly inaccurate, but highly attractive, and this is the point.

Australia-New South Wales-Botany Bay — these are the names under which, within the memory of men of middle age, a great island-continent at the antipodes has been explored, settled and advanced from the condition of a mere gaol, or sink, on which our surplus felonry was poured — a sheepwalk tended by nomadic burglars — to be the wealthiest offset of the British crown — a land of promise for the adventurous — a home of peace and independence for the industrious — an El Dorado and an Arcadia combined, where the hardest and easiest, best paid employments are to be found, where every striving man who rears a race of industrious children, may sit under the shadow of his own vine and his own fig tree — not without work, but with little care — living on his own land, looking down to the valleys to his herds — towards the hills to his flocks, amid the humming of bees, which know no winters.[33]

It is not difficult to accept the argument that English popular fiction saw Arcady as established in Australia, and that Samuel Sidney's contribution towards the promulgation of this 'myth' was paramount. For Cassirer, myth implied a real belief in the image, whereas David Bidney claims that to merit the title myths must be disbelieved. Other scholars have emphasized instead the 'play-quality' of the mythic response.[34] The application of the term to the image then being established for Australia adds very little to this debate, since evidence can be found to support each of these statements on the nature of myth: as will be shown, it was a most versatile product. Sidney's hitherto neglected contribution towards the promotion of the Arcadian myth deserves, therefore, the prominent place in Australian history which Lansbury has accorded it. The very boldness and apparent conviction expressed in Sidney's repeated assertions must have contributed to the success of his campaign to market the idea of Australia.

The discovery of gold in the 1850s brought scores of British travel writers to Australia, but the literary delineation of the continent was by that time so well established that no amount of personal experience could greatly modify it. Lansbury cites the case of Henry Kingsley's novel *The Recollections of Geoffry Hamlyn*—which, though set in Australia, could well have been written in London, despite the author's colonial experiences. Kingsley was writing commercially, for an established market, and his book was crammed from cover to cover with the accepted clichés and the familiar underplaying of natural hazards, particularly drought. He knew better, but the stereotyped formula proved to be a financial success.

Australia was the Arcadian settlement of verdant plains and wooded heights, seamed with gold, where small farmers dwelt in rustic content supplying food to the diggers. The young pastoralists galloped freely through the bush, no whit different in appearance from the humblest shedhand or shearer. It was

an expression of English social aspiration that men had no desire to see
fulfilled in England itself, and an elegy to the way of life that had passed away
before an age of industry and machines.[35]

These and a host of similar examples demonstrate that Australia was
subjected to the concentrated attention of some of Britain's most
influential writers at a most crucial period in its history. It would have
required a writer with the contemporary prestige of Dickens himself to
change the image of Australia in English literature, but Dickens had no
equal in his field. He refused an offer to tour Australia in 1862 and
maintained his rustic vision until the end; a personal visit would surely
have changed his whole concept of the country. In the last quarter of the
century, Britain's farmers were struggling against the competition of
imported produce from the New World. Despite some persuasion most
of her workers felt that they could no longer 'look back to the land'
which offered such insecurity, but forward to co-operative strength in
trade unionism, in which they might force society to change according
to their needs. Socialist doctrines proclaimed the imminent liberation of
the worker and the elementary palliative of emigration was rejected.
But Lansbury maintains that as this British version of the Arcadian
myth became unacceptable to the rapidly industrialized urban societies
of the home country, it was transferred to Australia where it maintained
a vigorous literary existence.

Ward and others have offered evidence which qualifies Lansbury's
thesis, arguing that the myth was really a virile hybrid of British and
Australian stock.[36] Its British characteristics are best seen in the root
structure, certainly, but we should therefore be wary of over-exposure;
the largest and most attractive part of the plant became thoroughly
Australian since it was adapted to, and for, the political and social
environment of the new nation. There is no doubt that a major factor in
its healthy growth was the continued learning process of identifying,
interpreting and communicating the qualities of the Australian
landscape. The romanticization of the Australian 'bush' (the whole of
the area beyond the urban centres) was obviously an important part of
this process, and it assisted Australians to accommodate and ultimately
to accept their strange environment, yet this was essentially the
contribution of locally-based interpreters. The so-called 'bush ethos',
for example, involved the investigation and celebration of distinctive
characteristics of life and landscape in rural Australia, and included a
rejection of city life. Originating in the earliest days of the penal camps,
it gained momentum after the middle of the century and was quite
deeply ingrained by 1914, our terminating point. The development of
the bush ethos is possibly best observed in the contemporary songs and

ballads, and also in the contributions of Australia's poets, writers and painters whose works exuded an increasing sense of national identity. For our present purposes, however, a most important feature associated with the evocation of Arcady during this period was the formulation of a type of ritual to accompany the myth: it involved the introduction of new legislation for the disposal of the public domain, fresh guidelines for the transformation of the rural landscape and the making of a new society. As in the United States, the conjurers were for the most part practising politicians and the yeoman farmer provided them with a very powerful symbol. And once again, in Australia as in North America, the attempt to bring about a social and geographical transformation by simplistic legislation met with very mixed success.

The land reform issue throughout Australia was always tightly intertwined with the demand for political and social reform, and European immigrants were at the forefront of every campaign. Immigration was strongest during the middle of the century in the gold mining colony of Victoria, which received the major input of British Chartists, Irish rebels and other radical elements, including a small but influential number of American miners. It was these newcomers, together with the city bourgeoisie, who initiated the land reform movement. A good deal of this argument concerning 'land for the people' was borrowed from the Chartists and after responsible government was granted to the colony in 1855 and goldmining commenced its decline, the reformers declared that the stage was set for a massive programme of small-scale settlement. By throwing open the big sheep and cattle stations then held under short-term tenure they would create 'a little England in Australia', a naive promise which ignored completely the contrasting potentials of the mother country and its colony.

> Cottage farming, if pursued only with spade, fork, pick axe and long iron punch power, would make any country great. It requires not such herds of cattle and horses to labour at the soil to make its inhabitants comfortable; where such are employed, and often over worked, men are placed in the same predicament, while the farming lord is often found with a spur on his heel, hunting, horse racing, or gambling. A few acres of land, well drained and well cultivated, may be made to produce enormously; and if the owner cannot have his cow, goat, poultry or horse, he may still produce wine, oil, vegetables and bread, and from his surplus supplies all other accessories may be produced.[37]

Between 1860 and the mid 1880s a series of Land Acts was passed in Victoria and in each of the other Australian colonies, with the urgently expressed intention of placing small-scale farmers on the public domain. Imbued with very British tastes in landscape, colonial politicians appear to have cherished an image of an ordered landscape with small fields, intensively cultivated, 'softening the horizon' or yielding 'a pleasantly settled aspect'; and they were held fast by an inherited political and philosophical ideal for which the small freeholder had become the symbol. The functioning of this motivating image was exhibited in the efforts of each of the colonial governments to mould the cultural geography of its territory. Survey systems, for example, varied regionally and from colony to colony and they were repeatedly modified, but permanent settlement was usually expected to advance according to the blueprints laid down by the official survey plans: land could not be sold without prior survey, and so the State had an opportunity to control the pace, direction and detailed pattern of settlement expansion. In Victoria and South Australia especially, efforts were frequently made to organize the land in such a way that it conformed to a rudimentary appraisal of quality, so that the farm blocks varied in size and sometimes in shape. In the same colonies, township plans were carefully drawn up to provide well-designed local centres for the densely packed rural population which was anticipated.[38] Even when the stipulation of pre-sale survey was removed, the maximum size of new holdings permitted under the law remained very low over most of the continent, usually ranging between 320 and 640 acres, and this was particularly stringent considering the difficulties of Australian conditions. Furthermore, it was not expected that the legislation alone would bring into existence the 'yeoman' class envisaged by the politicians: it had to create itself, by dint of sacrifice and manly endeavour, on a foundation of opportunities presented by the State in the form of small holdings. Contemporary parliamentary debates, newspaper campaigns, official emigrants' guides and the like all suggest that the idealism which assisted in spawning the land legislation assumed that the independent Australian farm, like the homestead in the United States, would be a home for the pioneer's lifetime, to be carefully tended and eventually passed on to his children. Consequently, the official regulations included severe penalties for non-residence and neglect.

The intricate details of the land legislation took up a major slice of the time available for discussion in the young parliaments, but (with notable exceptions examined elsewhere) very little energy was directed towards evaluating the real potential of the land for intensive settlement and the incumbent pastoralists justifiably complained of the incompetence of their political opponents, 'whose knowledge of laws and ideal of a country has been founded in the culture of a cabbage garden or flower pot of a city suburb'.[39] Certainly, they appeared to know very little about the practical business of agriculture in general, and even less about farming conditions in Australia; on the other hand, they were well aware of the vital importance of the income to be derived for their infant treasuries from the prudent disposal of their greatest asset, and accordingly, whatever the idealism, they were not inclined to allow the public lands to be sold for a song.

To some degree Queensland and Western Australia devised their own versions of controlled expansion, but these were overshadowed by developments in the older and more populous southern districts. As successive Land Acts gained only local successes in their stated objectives and vast areas of these colonies were freeholded by speculators and the sitting pastoral tenants, it was frequently pointed out that the small grazing property, or at least the practice of mixed farming on a moderate-sized holding, was the only realistic land-use. The price of land was quite as unreasonable, especially when the meagre resources of the potential settler are considered: for a standard 320-acre farm in Victoria in the mid 1860s, for instance, a total investment of £1,000 was required in short time and a third of this outlay was directed merely to the purchase. Credit facilities were gradually introduced to improve this situation, but the conservatives continued to hold strongly to other principles which they believed to be the basis of the yeoman ideal. The hallowed tenet of intensive cultivation was for them the ultimate test of the *bona fides* of the settler. Perhaps a furrowed acre or two and a bristling field of stooked corn made the most pleasant or tangible change which the traditionalists were capable of acknowledging, and anything resembling a continuation of the despised and 'wasteful' pastoral economy was usually rejected out of hand — 'Let a man take his 320 acres, at a shilling a year if you like; but let him remain on the land; make him cultivate it, because, if he does not cultivate it, it may be very reasonably assumed that he does not want it.'[40]

With the exception of premium locations near the towns, however, cultivation was not a paying proposition, and until the development of refrigerated shipping in the 1880s dairy farming suffered the same handicaps. In addition, it was normally essential for the pioneer to raise sheep, but this was hardly possible on the small acreage permitted under the law. Yet in the general process of adaptation, each new Land Act contributed towards the learning sequence; and since this was in large measure a 'controlled' situation, a recognition of the characteristic official/popular dichotomy is of fundamental significance to any analysis of settlement evolution. Whereas the official viewpoint was obscured throughout the learning sequence by a recurring mirage or blinkered by an abiding ignorance of Australian conditions, the 'man on the land' had to work within an environment conditioned by the legislation, as well as by physical and economic processes, and he sought his own solutions to achieve a viable working unit in spite of the deficiencies of the law, and frequently in plain defiance of it. Until the last quarter of the nineteenth century neither markets, railways, nor port development were properly studied by any of the colonial governments, and the agricultural research and education so vitally needed was largely ignored. A good case could obviously have been made, or it could have been put more often, to show that American soils were normally richer, cheaper and more readily available for farming than those of Australia. And obviously, Australians desperately required the positive support of their governments.

Without this assistance, various settlement techniques developed as spontaneous 'folk contributions' to the emerging cultural geography of the frontier regions. One of the best examples occurred in South Australia, where farmers and prospective farmers insisted on the opening of the dry northern plains for pioneer settlement. The subsequent rapid invasion of the northern country, supported by frequent extravagant descriptions in the local press and by a run of unusually good seasons, was inevitably checked when the droughts returned with a vengeance. Yet this very process of advance and retreat clearly established the existence of an extensive 'marginal' zone for which a wide array of novel management techniques was required.[41] The public image of the region was challenged, then radically changed. Mixed agricultural practices and an encouragement of medium-sized grazing farms were now urged at every level. Other examples which became well-known throughout Australia and New Zealand were the common-sense adaptations devised to combat the problems raised by the lack of capital and the restrictions on farm-sizes and land-uses which the settlement legislation imposed. These included the emergence of intra-family supports, partnerships, formal and informal types of co-operative activity and inter-family linkages, all of which were expressed spatially in the landholding and land-use arrangements of each locality. These processes became particularly common following the 'bursting-up' of great freehold estates by the colonial governments before the First World War.[42] Similar adaptations must have been made, however, in frontier regions throughout the New World.

The hypothesized sequence in Figure 8 is broadly illustrative of the structural transformations which marked the gap between rhetoric and reality in Australian land legislation. The first map displays the 'ideal'

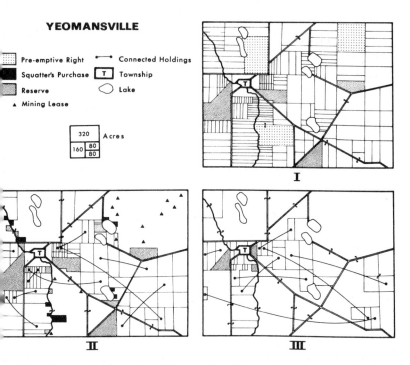

Fig 8   The changing geography of Yeomansville. This reconstruction of some changing landholding patterns in an imaginary parish in nineteenth-century
Australia is broadly illustrative of the structural transformations which marked the gap between rhetoric and reality in the era of land legislation.
I: *the geography of the ideal*, in which the image of a 'Little England in Australia' inspired carefully prepared blueprints of 'parkland towns' and intricate survey patterns, incorporating a rudimentary environmental appraisal which emphasized the scarcity of water frontages.
II: *the geography of evasion*, created by big and small men alike. Pastoralists 'picked the eyes' out of their hard-won acres. Some smaller men gained a genuine foothold, especially in and around the township; others simply earned a good fee by 'dummying'—selecting land in their own names and making it over to the incumbent pastoralist.
III: *the geography of adaptation*, in which a metamorphosis has taken place, 'rationalizing' the earlier pattern by amalgamation and the interlinkage of previously separate holdings. Small relict holdings, usually uneconomic, are lost in a landscape dominated by the large freehold estates of the pastoralists and some mixed farms of intermediate size: the development of the fledgling township scarcely progressed beyond the main shopping street and much of its original parkland has been subdivided.
Sources: based primarily on discussions in J. M. Powell, *The Public Lands of Australia Felix* (Melbourne, 1970) and S. H. Roberts, *History of Australian Land Settlement 1788–1920* (Melbourne, 1924 and 1968).

landholding pattern in which the image of a 'Little England' inspired carefully prepared blueprints of compact villages and 'parkland towns', together with intricate survey patterns incorporating a rudimentary environmental appraisal which emphasized the scarcity of water frontages. It also shows a major difference between the Australian and North American experiences, the early establishment of pastoral lessees and licensees who were determined to repel the threatened invasion of small 'selectors'. In the second map, the pastoralists are shown to have 'picked the eyes' out of their hard-won acres — by judicious early purchases, the filing of claims for 'mineral leases' in key locations which could never justify the raising of a single spade or pick, and the successful reservation of other small but vital areas, ostensibly for travelling stock, construction timber, firewood, and other public purposes. In this latter ploy they usually enjoyed the collusion of local officials. Some smaller men managed to gain a genuine foothold, especially in and around the township and the bigger 'commons' reserves. In these areas they could graze some additional stock and supplement their income by working on the new roads or for their more prosperous neighbours; others simply earned a good fee by 'dummying'—selecting land in their own names and making it over to one of the bigger men. The third map illustrates an advanced stage of adaptation or accommodation after a relatively short period (say ten years) of intense activity. A metamorphosis has clearly taken place, 'rationalizing' the earlier pattern by amalgamation and the in-terlinkage of previously separate holdings; the fledgling village has scarcely progressed beyond the main shopping street and much of its surrounding parkland has been quietly subdivided amongst the handful of citizens. And overall, the final management complex is dominated by the large freehold estates and some mixed farms of intermediate size, together with a very small number of relict smallholdings which seem locked in a state of chronic pioneering.

Later in the nineteenth century, as pioneering advanced into Australia's more difficult farming country and indeed, as a wealth of practical settlement experience accumulated and disseminated, another element in the yeoman symbolism, the freehold principle, was subjected to closer scrutiny. This was the result of a new reforming impulse, nurtured in Australia's growing cities but borrowing articulation and direction from British and American developments. Its challenge was resolutely opposed by the traditionalists.

> This love of a freehold, of having a home of his own to live in, and to leave to his children, was intricately and deeply connected with the qualities which

went to make good citizenship . . . Any one who had been among the farmers and the peasantry of the mother country must know that the very idol of their hearts was to get somewhere where they could have a freehold.[43]

With the useful public domain swiftly diminishing, however, there was an increasing demand for the repurchase and subdivision of the great pastoral estates and — especially in the urban centres — for the substitution of a closely policed system of leases which would bring in a continuous revenue. The movement was home-grown and based upon the economic arguments and bookish research of local scholars and politicians, yet it was also deeply influenced by ideas of land nationalization and the philosophy of a 'single-tax' (on land alone), which were then being promoted in Britain and the United States.[44] Leasing successfully challenged the yeoman myth and was widely introduced in Australia in the 1880s. The severe depression of the 1890s led to further experimentation in settlement planning, following a wave of enthusiasm for some forms of State-aided group settlement which swept through the country. Although the detailed implementation of the collectivist schemes for 'labour colonies', 'village settlements', 'homestead associations' and the like appeared to contrast sharply with the yeoman ideal of independence and hardy individualism, in essence the two remained closely related. With the prior example of a number of New Zealand attempts to encourage them, Australians were greatly assisted by the political and philanthropic associations which focussed on the plight of the unemployed population of the urban centres. They were also attracted and instructed by at least one minor utopian novel which sketched out a new landscape created by and for the working man — 'a return to the dreams of the cultivation of the land as the good life, and universal land ownership as the solution to all problems'. Most of the host of new settlements survived for only a very short period, but the present rural landscape still bears the imprint of the efforts of the 'reluctant Arcadians' of the last decade of the nineteenth century.[45]

The young societies of Australia and New Zealand experienced urban and suburban expressions of a kind of Arcadianism similar to those shown in North America, although in the antipodes they usually arrived somewhat later and were more directly influenced by British precedents. 'Back to the land' movements have continued to ebb and flow throughout the twentieth century, and farmers' political organizations still exert extraordinary influence in the government of each nation. The most significant geographical expressions of a sustained political attachment to the agrarian myth, however, were the efforts to settle scores of thousands of discharged servicemen on the land after each World War.[46] Similar massive undertakings were attempted in Canada, and a comprehensive analysis of these experiments is overdue. It is nevertheless clear that the yeoman symbolism still appealed and that traditional beliefs in land as the most bountiful resource, the great panacea, were far from dead: were not the original 'yeomanry' considered to be the backbone of any nation, the defenders of their native soil? Yet the early legislation in particular was too often rapidly enacted in an atmosphere charged with emotion, and its administration was frequently confounded by the pressures of various interest groups and well-meaning local associations who wished to play their part in repaying the 'Debt of Honour'. The more organized and commercially-orientated farmers in the United States, fearing the increased competition, successfully opposed the introduction of similar schemes for soldier settlement.[47]

*   *   *   *

In the 1870s an agent of the Santa Fe railroad told prospective Kansas settlers that the only thing he could imagine which might give them some bother in cultivating was the humble pumpkin: 'The seeds come up quickly. The plants blossom full. Pumpkins set and grow about the size of a sugar bowl. Then the vines begin to grow and run so fast that they wear the pumpkins out dragging them over the ground until they die from exhaustion.' And one of Oklahoma's country newspaper editors, commenting on the opening of an Indian reservation for settlement, assured his readers not only that there were silver dollars in every mud puddle, but also that they would be able to raise 'corn bigger than sawlogs and watermelons bigger than whales'.[48] The expectations of thousands of pioneers, perhaps those of most pioneers, were never realized; a very large number made decent homes for themselves and their families, however, and achieved something like the kind of independence and security which the possession of land in the New World appeared to offer.

The spacious territories of the New World offered European man a unique chance for experiment, for exploration, which the Old World could never match. That great opportunity was based essentially on their possession of abundant public lands. It was an unparalleled offer which was open to interpretation by all sectors of society, by ordinary individuals as well as by the most visionary leaders and decision-makers. It has not been possible to determine the levels of agreement in interpretation, or to distinguish between public and private images; we must therefore proceed to investigate this important theme in some different contexts. Accordingly, this forms one of the principal objectives of the next chapter, for which it also provides the controlling basis for the selection of three different types of image. But our exploration of the Arcadian ideal may have succeeded thus far in establishing one major premise. The complex geographical transformation which occurred in the countries of the New World during the nineteenth century and in the early part of the present century cannot be understood without examining the gap between rhetoric and reality; and the measure of that gap is nothing less than the measure of human strengths and weaknesses. Each of the succeeding chapters in this book attempts to retain a central explanatory focus which researches basic human qualities for the light they can throw on geographical change.

4

Refractions: Identity, Wilderness, Illusion

The geography of the world is unified only by human logic and optics, by the light and colour of artifice, by decorative arrangement, and by ideas of the good, the true, and the beautiful. As agreement on such subjects is never perfect nor permanent, geographers too can expect only partial and evanescent concordance.[1]

Geographical analysis at any time and at any level — for all men, women and children are by nature geographers — depends equally on the degree of candour or opaqueness in the subject matter and the aims, skills and background of the interpreter. In other words, human geography is, was and always will be differently fashioned and differently interpreted according to the vantage point employed. This chapter presents three themes which appear to be representative of some special ways in which the changing geography of the New World reflected man's own self-images, his views of his fellow-man, and his evaluations of local physical environments. It illustrates some of the spatial expressions of certain major types of societal conflict, and of plain disagreement and confusion over societal goals and the means of achieving them.

Identity: the 'Native Lands' Question

The relationship of a tribe to its land defines that tribe: its identity, its culture, its way of life, its fundamental rights, its methods of adaptation, its pattern of survival. Land also defines the Indian's enemies — those who covet the land and desire to expropriate it for their own use. Because Indian land is, or may be, of value, it has been, and remains, the source of almost every major conflict and every ongoing controversy between the Indian and the white man. Indian land is synonymous with Indian existence. A tribe's title to land often proves to be its death warrant.[2]

The 'native lands' issue is long-established as a focus of teaching, but the recent rapid increase in the attention it has received reflects in part a growing conviction that it should weigh more heavily on the conscience of the whites as yet another flaw in the story of their great inheritance. In some large measure, we can identify ourselves in our actions towards others; so the past informs the present and can change the future. But from another viewpoint, the issue is also intimately connected with the primary motivations underlying the settlement process in the New World: motivations which the native peoples seldom shared and found difficult to comprehend, for their image of the world and their place within it contrasted profoundly with that of the white. On logical grounds alone, therefore, this confrontation of cultures must be seen as a major component in the geographical transformation of each of the New World territories with which this volume is concerned. The inevitable tyrannies of space confine our enquiries to two brief examples, from the United States and New Zealand.

The Dispossession of the American Indian[3]

The Europeans clearly entered the New World with a vital sense of mission. Part of that mission entailed a conversion of the native peoples to 'civilized' ways, and it incorporated a strongly ethnocentric application of the increasing emphasis in post-Reformation Europe on the 'perfectability of man'. So, for example, the Indians could only be 'improved' if they were settled upon their own cultivated farms. Despite all the evidence to the contrary in the eastern woodlands, the dominating concept of contemporary Indian life in the minds of America's policy-makers became based on the idea of a complex of primitive hunting cultures. And, since the hunter required a vast area to support his savage traits, whereas the white farmer was maintained at a far superior level by the intensive cultivation of a fraction of that area, it was scarcely difficult to decide which group had heeded the command of Genesis to 'Be fruitful, and multiply, and replenish the earth, and subdue it.'

Puritan–Indian relationships were usually far from violent, but the white culture was 'unified, visionary, disciplined, and dynamic' and the native culture was in comparison 'self-satisfied, undisciplined, and static'.[4] Of course, these latter characteristics could have been readily noted at the time by the whites, yet may not have been recognized at all by the Indians themselves; some recent efforts at reconstructing the cultural interplay do, however, suggest that they proved to be real and significant differences between the two peoples. Puritan society successfully expanded as the Indian culture disintegrated. Towards the end of the colonial era, ideas of the 'noble savage' continued to modify white attitudes to the extent that they supported a relatively neutral stance based on the expectation of gradual assimilation, but the rapid westward expansion of white settlement produced a complete change of mood in the 1820s and 1830s.

The Indian was then increasingly seen as an inferior being who was blocking the 'progress' of the divinely sanctioned white race in the civilization of the New World. He would have to change, or give way — 'be moralized or exterminated'. In 1830 President Jackson signed an Indian Removal Act aimed at moving all eastern Indians to the west of the Mississippi. The Act authorized the President to negotiate the relevant treaties guaranteeing full payment for the relinquished lands, legal titles for the new territories and a degree of self-government. Contemporary rhetoric invoked the idea of progress and stressed the benefits to the white race which would accrue from the displacement of the noble savage. Some tribes were moved a number of times, and despite the white government's declared intention of reaching mutual agreements in every case, forced removal was by no means unknown.

Between 1778 and 1869, 370 treaties were made between the United States and various Indian 'nations'.[5] The major early concentration of this activity occurred in the periods 1815–19 (48 treaties) and 1825–9 (35), but 221 treaties were drawn up in the period 1830–69, largely focussed on the Midwest and Western frontiers of white settlement. By 1869 the pattern of modern Indian reservations was already firmly established, and in 1871 Congress decided that 'Hereafter no Indian nation or tribe within the territory of the United States shall be acknowledged or recognized as an independent tribe or power with whom the United States may contract by trading.'[6] The American Indians were merely Indian Americans; their friendship and support as independent peoples were no longer required. Even the best intentioned philanthropy functioned as an aggressive declaration of white identity insofar as it was an extension of the civilizing' effort.

The effective destruction of Indian culture then seemed inevitable, and the passing of the General Allotment Act (or the Dawes Act) in 1887 was really an affirmation of the superiority of American goals and values. This Act authorized the President to divide Indian reservations into individual holdings and assign a parcel of land to each inhabitant, leaving a 'surplus' available for orthodox homesteading by all-comers. The ultimate result of the allotment programme was to create a host of white-owned and -operated farms on the former Indian territory.[7] Government agricultural advisers despatched to the former reserves usually found the administrative burden of the new system so great that they scarcely had time to offer instruction. The state of Indian agriculture declined still further on the greatly reduced areas then available, until the very survival of many groups was threatened. After 1900 white neighbours and land agents indulged in an unseemly scramble to relieve many of the Indians of a burden of 'ownership' they had never asked for and could barely understand. By this ploy and related enactments, the Indians were relieved of almost two-thirds of their greatly diminished land base — approximately 90 million acres — between 1887 and 1930. Naturally, the legislators saw wisdom and kindness in their bland preoccupation: 'We must stimulate within them to the very largest degree, the idea of home, of family, and of property. These are the very anchorages of civilization; the commencement of the dawning of these ideas in the mind is the commencement of the civilization of any race, and these Indians are no exception.'[8]

Opposing concepts of property rights had been a common cause of friction between Indians and whites from the outset. A type of private or exclusive ownership had always been understood and accepted in some Indian tribes, but the greatest emphasis was usually placed on user's rights rather than on the rights and powers of nominal owners, whether they were individuals, groups or tribes. The nominal owner was in most cases bound by long traditions of customary use held by members of a kinship group, and he could not prevent that use or arbitrarily dispose of any property without reference to pre-existing rights. And those traditions were built upon a sense of territoriality which was frequently place-specific and rich in definitions of sacred grounds; it was also abundantly expressive of a reverent I-Thou relationship with nature which was, in practice, a far better guarantor of ecological integrities than anything in the contemporary repertoire of the white settler.[9] The Indian–white confrontation was an unequal contest in which modern concepts of space and time, and of man's dominance in nature, quickly displaced those of the indigenous peoples: for the white man, the image of the Indian was always distorted by the most powerful of cultural lenses; the native groups were on the whole rather less myopic, but they must have found it equally difficult to understand the invaders. One likely reason for this latter problem was, however, the whites' ceaseless projection of their own self-image in their dealings with the new environment and its inhabitants.

The geography of dispossession took different forms and may be graphically represented at a variety of scales. At the lowest level there were and are the individuals and families, frequently disoriented fringe dwellers in urban and rural white communities; at the next level of

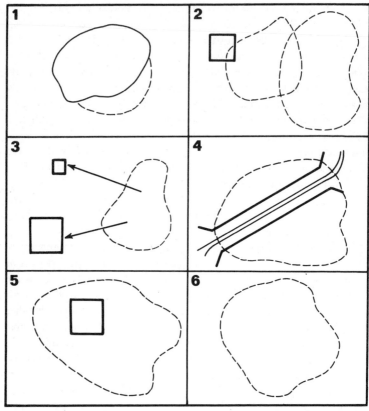

Fig 9   Indian territorial adjustments (Source; freely adapted from the examination of treaties in McDonald, 1976) 1 *No adjustment:* pre-European boundaries maintained virtually intact; 2 *Drift:* movement away from European settlements or towards them; 3 *Relocation:* Indians moved to an area beyond their own existing territory; 4 *Withdrawal:* prohibition of camping within or otherwise approaching an area within a specified distance of certain settlements or facilities; 5 *Concentration:* Indians were contained within a small part of their tribal territory; 6 *Extinction:* specific groups disintegrate or disappear, via annihilation or assimilation. Solid lines indicate reserved Indian lands; broken lines indicate the area of Indian lands at the time of first contact with the whites.

analysis, the fates of particular tribes and regional groupings of tribes, and the peculiarities of the social, economic and political metamorphosis on certain reservations, would require investigation. Unfortunately, we must be restricted here to two more general categories of analysis which may usefully amplify the spatial perspective adopted in this book. The first (Fig. 9) reproduces McDonald's interpretation of the range of territorial adjustments introduced by the many treaties and

Indian Land Cessions

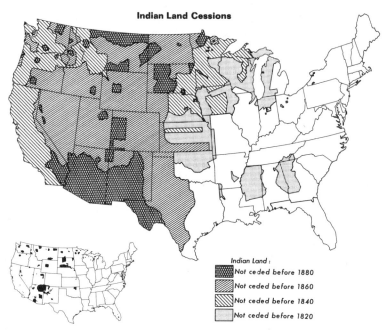

Indian Land :
- Not ceded before 1880
- Not ceded before 1860
- Not ceded before 1840
- Not ceded before 1820

Fig 10 A geography of dispossession: the cession of Indian lands. (Source: adapted from Hilliard, 1972 and McDonald, 1976. *Inset:* present Indian reservations)

gives a somewhat simplified impression of a kind of 'planned acculturation'.[10] In reality, of course, these patterns were not always the product of conscious design, but they clearly display some tangible spatial aspects of the passing of a culture. The second (Fig. 10)[11] illustrates the dispossession on the widest scale and emphasizes the unrelenting thrust of white expansionism, a process which one author has condemned as a strangely neglected feature of the belief in 'Manifest Destiny', an early version of American imperialism.[12] A detailed interpretation of this map would require a discussion of many variables — the degrees of Indian resistance; the direction of the expansion of pioneer farming, the local intensities of change, and the associated modifications in the evaluation of 'Indian Lands'; the process of urbanization and industrialization; regional and national trends in racial attitudes, economics and politics; the emergence of articulate champions of the Indian cause, and so on.

The emphasis on the era of farming expansion in the later nineteenth century is plain enough on this map, however, and this simple observation also suggests that it can never be sufficient to direct the entire analysis at the highest level of decision-making. The pioneer farmer must be seen as the leading agent of white expansionism, often defying official policy to move independently into Indian territory. The State and Federal governments had neither the will, nor the popular support, nor indeed the military and administrative resources, to prevent the ensuing confrontation. Thus the American pioneer and his family provided 'the practical surrogate of the white man's brash and aggressive society as it met and proceeded to accomplish the demolition of the native culture'.[13]

Whether it is regarded as the major vehicle for Indian assimilation or the primary weapon in the destruction of native identity, the agrarian ideal is again a primary explanatory focus in the interpretation of geographical change. Note, for example, the agricultural symbolism in the 'Ritual on Admission of Indians to Full American Citizenship', which was employed until 1924:

> To complete the initiation, the Indian subject first shot an arrow into the air, intoning an oath to end his wandering days. Then placing his hand upon a plow he swore to abandon the hunt, take up agriculture and live the life of a white man.[14]

How soon forgotten was the dependence of the first New England settlers on the abundant maize, squashes, beans and pumpkins of the Indian gardens. This ironic citizenship ritual was presumably to mark the final 'transformation' — as Wessell ruefully comments, 'the Indians had beaten arrows into plowshares'.[15] How complete the cultural distortion had become over the years.

The Land Wars in New Zealand[16]

Our New Zealand example begins with yet another treaty. But in this case we are concerned with a most singular document which has taken on considerable symbolic significance in a small modern democracy now characterized by a relatively compatible mixture of whites, Maoris and Pacific Islanders. In 1840 scores of Maori leaders gathered at Waitangi on the Bay of Islands north of Auckland. Until that time, missionaries had purchased a small amount of Maori land and the New Zealand Company was beginning to develop its new possessions for the white colonists or 'Pakehas'. Under the terms of the Treaty of Waitangi the Maori chiefs yielded sovereignty to the British Crown and in return were guaranteed continued possession of their lands, forests and fisheries. The Maori signatories also yielded to the Crown the exclusive rights of pre-emption to purchase such lands 'as the proprietors thereof may be disposed to alienate'. Land for European settlement could only be obtained by a Crown (government) purchase, via Maori consent.

The stage was then set for a complex confrontation over the disposal and settlement of land. The main actors were the Maoris, the Pakeha settlers, the Provincial Councils and Central Parliament constituting white government in New Zealand, and the imperial authorities, interested institutions and influential individuals in Britain. And the situation was further complicated by divisions within each group founded on prejudices, misconceptions and honestly-held attitudinal differences over various racial, economic, social, political and even religious issues. The locational focus of the conflict was the fertile and heavily wooded North Island, where for some years the Maori population far exceeded that of the Pakehas.

Maori tradition did not recognize the rights of individual tribal members to sell land; even on the basis of general tribal consent land was only rarely transferred, and then as a type of gift. But land-selling and land-holding factions gradually developed in the 1850s and these divisions were fostered by the under-cover activities of white settlers and government purchasing agents. Eventually the local authorities openly supported individual vendors who defied tribal opinion, and in 1858 a Territorial Rights Bill was passed in New Zealand to abolish Crown pre-emption and to legalize direct private purchase. Although the latter measure was rejected in London, further rapid incursions were made into the Maori lands with the full connivance of the local officials. The reaction of Maori traditionalists was to organize pan-tribal land leagues pledged to resist the purchasing process, and they were also determined on violence, if necessary, to preserve their heritage. The main force behind this reaction was the desire to preserve and strengthen what was left of the Maoris' distinct cultural identity within New Zealand: to keep European settlement at a distance, and thereby limit the demoralization which excessive drinking, materialism, prostitution and the inevitable ethnocentrism of missionary activity had brought to Maori society.

The whites regarded the land as 'the property of the colony, merely encumbered with a certain native right of occupancy' and considered the proclamation of that right to have been a matter of expedience rather than one of justice. Like their contemporaries in North America they based their claims on the conception of a superior moral right which had been demonstrated by their ability to use natural resources more intensively. In fact many of the Maoris, like the eastern woodland Indians, were quite accomplished agriculturalists. It is also true, however, that the introduction of the European pig and the potato appeared to render large areas of native land 'redundant' in strictly economic terms, though this was not acceptable from any social and spiritual viewpoint. For the traditional Maori, the connection between authority over land and political and social status was absolutely central — and ultimately it included, therefore, the entire question of law and order.

In 1858 the Waikato tribes formed a land league and selected Potatau Te Whero Whero as king.[17] In 1860 the opposition of Wiremu Kingi and his Ngatiawa tribe held up the purchase of the Waitara country in Taranaki and the resulting skirmishes precipitated that frenzied period of land spoliation which is still known as the 'Maori Wars'. The entry of some 10,000 imperial troops eventually assisted the colonial forces to defeat most of the tribes in a series of pitched battles before the end of 1864. Subsequently London gradually withdrew the imperial support, expressing rather more praise for the valour and integrity of the native adversaries than for the land-hungry settlers, and the war took the form of periodic guerilla campaigns against a number of militant religious or quasi-religious sects. This 'fire in the fern' lasted until 1872. Already, however, the new Maori King Tawhiao and his followers had fled (in 1864) to the vast Ngatimaniopoto stronghold in the centre of the island. Tawhiao refused to surrender until 1883 and the 'King Country', which retains the title to this day, was not opened to settlement until 1885.

Government land policy during these years displayed two main features. Assimilation was the stated aim of the Native Land Acts and their amendments passed in 1862, 1865, 1867 and 1873. The legislation was expected to 'destroy, if it were possible, the principle of communism which ran through the whole of their institutions' and the resulting individualization of titles would ensure that 'their social status would be assimilated to our own'.[18] A Native Lands Court was established with the nightmarish task of determining the 'ownership' details. Its early operations were restricted by the fighting to the districts of 'friendly' or neutral tribes, where the Maoris seldom showed a great deal of genuine interest in gaining land titles, and sham proceedings were usually initiated and controlled by the whites. When a few individuals were persuaded in various ways to attend the court all those who opposed their claims had to attend, often to find that they became so embroiled in transportation, accommodation and legal costs that they were obliged to accept a title themselves and almost immediately had to dispose of it to satisfy their creditors. It became a normal and elementary practice for the settlers, speculators and government agents to manipulate this scandalous situation to their own advantage. The tribes were further demoralized — and the process occurred more rapidly, in fact, in those very areas which had shown little or no resistance to the settlers.

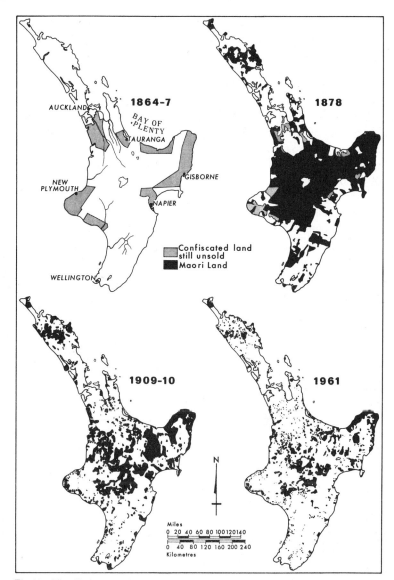

Fig 11 The diminution of Maori lands, North Island, New Zealand. (Source: Turnbull Library, Wellington)

Confiscation was the more overtly punitive aspect of the policy. As enunciated in the New Zealand Settlements Act of 1863, the intention of confiscation was to punish the rebellious Maoris and to provide land for strategically-located 'military settlements', while at the same time selling the surplus to offset a £3 million loan which was to be raised to defray some of the costs of these projects and of the fighting itself. The military settlements were to be based on a distribution of 5,000 men to form a strategic screen south of Auckland, with the township of Hamilton centrally placed along the line.[19] The men and their families were enticed from the goldfields of Australia and from Otago, in the South Island, with the promise of a freehold allotment after three years' satisfactory service. They were to qualify for different amounts of virgin land according to their rank: the scale ranged from 50 acres for a private to 400 acres for a senior field officer, and the planned contiguity of each of the blocks of allotments would have made for reasonably efficient mustering. It was a nice Victorian touch, but for the most part the scheme became lost in a confusion of hesitancy and careless mismanagement. Many of the military settlers were left stranded and idle, a drain on public funds; others who moved on to their bush allotments found that they had neither the capital nor the experience, nor indeed the markets, to convert them in reasonable time into viable enterprises.

With some exceptions, the military settlements were small and evanescent features in the North Island landscape. The other related processes, of confiscation and individualization of tenure, produced more powerful transformations in the landholding pattern and thereby exhibit far more clearly the spatial expression of this tragic confrontation. The progressive diminution of Maori lands is naturally the most obvious feature of Fig. 11, but the intricate mosaic comprised in this broad picture represents the outcome of a number of important related themes: the sharp and direct effects of confiscation; the early duping of the neutral and friendly tribes; the significance of the successful resistance of the King movement in the centre of the island, now the Maori heartland.[20]

From time to time the Maori people have shown an enviable capacity to find inspirational leaders who have assisted them in the re-assertion of their self-confidence and collective identity.[21] The early series of religious cults, despised and feared by the whites, were really intensely secular in their functions, sustaining the oppressed people, aiding them in their organization, and articulating their needs and aspirations. The Maoris were also assisted, of course, by the continuing political influence of Britain, where religious bodies and general humanitarian movements often intervened in the interests of beleaguered native peoples in the Empire. So, towards the end of the nineteenth century and in the early decades of the present era, the Maoris found that they had ridden the storm into a comparatively more enlightened age, in which they achieved a genuinely separate political representation. Although they continued to suffer injustices, this political strength gave them rather better hopes for the survival of their traditional land base than the unfortunate American Indians ever enjoyed.[22]

The preceding discussion is naturally intended as a brief and highly selective account of a complex theme, but the selection of two case studies exhibiting at least as many contrasts as comparisons may suggest pertinent approaches for further reading. Canada and Australia, the other New World territories touched upon in this book, obviously demand separate treatment, but the following paragraphs may serve to add useful perspective to this section.

Canada's varied Indian populations have had the advantage of a special and long-lasting relationship with the first white settlers.[23] The fur-trading interests of the French in the east and the Hudson's Bay Company in the north and west required the co-operation of the natives. In fact, private ownership of land, that great and pernicious concept, was neither necessary nor desirable in the very profitable fur trade. Also, the rigorous climate and terrain of the vast interior provided ample refuge for at least some of the native peoples living beyond the small hospitable strips in the south and west. Together with the vague but on the whole usefully moderating influence of the British and French connections, these factors sustained Canada's Indians and Eskimos, as similar influences and opportunities sustained some of the Maori people, until the modern era. Technology now seems as powerful an enemy, and as tempting a seducer, as those ideals and institutions of the pioneer farmer which the native peoples were able to avoid or resist. The description of this new crisis of identity is, however, beyond our scope.

The Australian Aborigines had a great deal to offer the invading Europeans, for their ecologically sophisticated culture was in many respects highly adapted to the environment of that huge continent which the white man found so difficult to appreciate.[24] But they were thinly distributed, few in number and usually organized in small family groups; they were certainly no match for the self-confident, aggressively materialistic and comparatively well-equipped European culture. When they were not ignored or exploited, the Aborigines were frequently hunted and poisoned like verminous creatures. Their highly localized and sporadic resistance was mercilessly answered and only hastened their rapid decline. Apart from a small number of urban fringe dwellers, barely a trace of them remains in the regions most favoured by the whites; most of the survivors now occupy Australia's most arduous and remote sections, usually on missions and reservations. For many years the best treatment they received was that odd brand of patronizing care, tinged with a kind of high-minded fatalism, which characterized the experience of each indigenous group in the New World in varying degrees: it was born of a white belief that either the natives themselves, or their culture, or both, were irrevocably doomed. Therefore the geography of dispossession in the case of the Australian Aborigines was really agonizingly simple, for the removal was usually swift and virtually complete. The reformation in white Australian attitudes commenced in earnest only recently, primarily in the 1960s, and it is probably best expressed in the continuing debates over the mining of immensely valuable minerals in some of the Aborigines' most sacred grounds.

Changing Images of Wilderness

The term 'wilderness' does not lend itself to succinct definition. As Nash has indicated, it is almost entirely subjective, denoting merely a type of quality which may evoke a wide range of interpretations and feelings in any given set of people. If we accept that its root is probably 'will', then the descriptive meaning must imply something like 'self-willed' or 'uncontrollable', and the associated ideas therefore include confusion, disorder, unruliness. Italian usage stresses these latter associations, whereas the Spanish and French equivalents favour respectively lack of cultivation and desertion or avoidance. An Old English derivation, closely related to the German usage, is *wild-deor-ness*, a place of wild beasts. And frequently, for the modern era as well as for the past, a far stronger anthropocentric focus may be discerned — 'The image is that of a man in an *alien* environment where the civilization that normally orders and controls his life is absent.'[25] For our present purposes, however, it is sufficient to point to the basic dualism inherent in the term: 'On the one hand it is inhospitable, alien, mysterious, and threatening; on the other, beautiful, friendly, and capable of elevating and delighting the beholder.'[26]

This dualism became well established in the Old World between the seventeenth and nineteenth centuries. In the New World, the dominant public images of the wilderness were founded in part upon the older traditions and upon close observation and analysis of contemporary developments in Europe, but they were also substantially influenced by indigenous forces; by cumulative local experience in and with the new environments, dissatisfaction with some current trends and, above all, the promotional activities of prominent groups and individuals.

Wilderness and the European Mind

The fundamental needs of food, shelter and clothing must have governed the attitudes of primitive man towards his environment. Those areas which could be made to provide man's requirements most abundantly and conveniently were naturally favoured, while feelings of abject fear and hostility were generated towards incomprehensible and unyielding wild territory. These deep-seated attitudes, so inextricably tied to restrictive definitions of man's survival capacity, were essentially unchanged until recent times. Classical mythology, for example, populated the unknown and untamed areas with minor gods and demons, and treasured the primary landscape artefacts of civilized man — his towns, villages and fields. Pan and the satyrs controlled the woods and forests, the profane spaces, and the settled areas were sacred, Edenic.[27] Similarly, Europe's early peasant societies invested their wild areas with nightmarish legends and a bewildering assortment of supernatural creatures — werewolves, wood sprites, ogres, trolls and other fantastic beings — and so the wilderness was the very antithesis of 'civilization', for that, of course, was man's dominion. Christianity was no more generous to the wild places. They were the symbols of original sin, constant reminders of man's enforced sojourn in a chaotic material realm. The good Christian aimed at heavenly bliss; not for him the adoration of mere 'natural' scenic assemblages of mountains, valleys and other earthly constructions. As for his relationship with his fellow animals, the 'stewardship' of man appeared to be unequivocally proclaimed in that bold Genesian message: man was made in the image of God, to 'fill the earth and conquer it', to be the master of all the earth's creatures.

But these propositions, now all too familiar, should not be allowed to disguise the important fact that a degree of ambivalence, even some ambiguity, was always present in the Western image of wilderness. The free or 'abandoned' spirit of Pan himself is not so readily categorized as might be supposed; certainly, it was by no means universally feared, for he also represented the energetic celebration of nature's mysteries and called out a unique challenge to unliberated, civilized mortals. More generally, the influence of animism led men to interpret nature in terms of intimate individual and social experience. Conceptions of gender offer one example of this. Consider the 'Earth Mother' concept, obviously a primary metaphor. Some societies have spurned tillage

because it injures her body, torments the plants, soil and rocks which
are her skin, flesh and bones. We still have this metaphor, of course:
witness the growing list of Dame Nature's champions, or protectors,
pledged to halt the repeated 'rape' of the environment, to bring the
chauvinistic miners, lumbermen, land developers and all those
seemingly insatiable types before that great court of public opinion
which has been so long neglected. Representations of desert environments offer another example. Judaic tradition commonly portrayed
the desert as an evil place, manifestly carrying the curse of God. It was
Eden's clear opposite, yet it was also described as a type of earthly
Purgatory — a region of sanctuary, of purifying retreat, providing an
essential preparation for the good life in the promised land. And it was,
after all, in a very wild district, on Mount Sinai, that Moses received the
ten commandments; and Elijah and Jesus Christ both chose the desert
to seek communion with God. Again, in Europe's Dark Ages, the
missionary spirit certainly led to the destruction of a good deal of the
natural or semi-natural forest which had accommodated the sacred
groves of the pre-Christian tribes and had even encouraged their pagan
rituals. Subsequently, however, the flourishing monastic movement
deliberately sought out the wilderness: like the hermits of antiquity the
leaders of the monastic orders perceived the sense of privacy, of isolation
from the mass of humanity, as a major environmental resource. On the
other hand, the vigorous agricultural activities of the monks were eventually responsible for massive transformations of their lonely territories.
Indeed, most of Europe's settlement frontiers expanded rapidly between the eleventh and fourteenth centuries, when man appeared to
be fiercely asserting his God-given dominance in the earthly realm.[28]

It would be ridiculously impertinent to attempt any unravelling of
the extraordinary complexity of medieval scholarship at this point.
Perhaps it is sufficient for our purposes to note Glacken's authoritative
commentary upon the preoccupation of the great medieval thinkers
with the story of the creation.[29] The most compelling reason for the
investigation of the natural environment in the medieval world was
simply that it assisted towards a better understanding of God: Nature
contained a proof of God's existence, a demonstration of His design for
the world and therefore of the very truth of the Christian religion. With
some significant exceptions, Nature was seldom studied or enjoyed for
its own sake during the Middle Ages. In the fourteenth century,
however, the focus began to change. Revelation gradually became a
matter of faith alone and reason, or 'scientific' argument, henceforth
supplied the philosophy and the methodology for the observation and
analysis of natural phenomena.

Over the next four centuries there was a growing awareness of man's power over nature; an increasing conviction in European thinking about the purposive human control of nature, following the dramatic declarations of Bacon, Descartes and others. The religious theme of man's dominion on earth was also strengthened, especially after the discovery and exploration of the New World and the observation of its rapid transformation by human ingenuity, but the alternative perspective provided by Europe's leading philosophers led to 'an emphasis on human society and its accomplishments, to the possibility of improving society by the purposive application of scientific law to the needs of food, housing, transportation and the like'.[30] This was the essentially secular viewpoint of an increasingly self-conscious, anthropocentric culture. Industrialization, urbanization and the rise of commercial agriculture, particularly during the eighteenth century, added an air of considerable optimism as the secular forces of science and technology reached across the globe. And yet in some quarters, following the emergence of the challenging new field of 'natural history', that same growth of self-consciousness also nurtured the idea that man was capable of any number of undesirable changes in the natural environment: that he was, indeed, already responsible for ecological disruption on an alarming scale.

Although the consuming drive for material 'progress' tended to underline the overriding emphasis on man's dominance over nature, contemporary attitudes to the European environment continued to incorporate the full range of practical and spiritual perspectives. In Western Europe especially the growth imperative was certainly paramount and the remaining wildernesses rapidly diminished in every reasonably accessible area, but there was a rather stronger antiphonal in the eighteenth and nineteenth centuries, led by a small number of influential philosophers, scientists, poets and creative writers. They were largely motivated by increasing apprehensions over what they perceived to be the declining dignity of the human condition, as well as by some closely related fears concerning the reverberating,ecological destruction wrought by advancing 'civilization'.

Associated with these developments was a 'revolution in taste' effecting fundamental reorientations towards landscape painting, architecture and landscape gardening. There was a fresh evaluation of the 'diversity' and 'interest' of those pristine mountain environments which had previously been feared or scorned,[31] and the new trends became linked to the idea of extensive travel as a type of compulsory 'finishing' pilgrimage, or a form of therapy for battered aesthetic sensibilities. For some Europeans, this incorporated a sharpened focus on landscape which may be interpreted as an effort to fill the spiritual vacuum created after the break between philosophy and revealed religion. But this 'break' can be exaggerated. Other Europeans, who might be called the Deists, developed an interest in landscape as an extension of their own interpretation of the recent scientific discovery of the immensity and complexity of the universe: they accepted this revelation as further evidence of the might and mystery of God and eventually projected the argument to the earth's grandest physical features. So the mountains, seas and deserts were the works of God, made in His image, for man to behold.

The transformation of aesthetic standards was directly and indirectly associated with these developments. The concept of the sublime, for example, became widely used to emphasize the crucial aesthetic qualities of apparent chaos and grandness of scale in nature appreciation, and in this context awe and terror were to be accepted as vital sensuous pleasures of the wilderness experience. Accordingly, the Romantics enthusiastically proclaimed the value of the wilderness areas and rejected the comfortable order of the built environment of the towns and countryside, filled as it was with society and its small works. The most extreme expression of this approach was indeed a form of Primitivism which argued that there was an inverse relationship between civilization and the very well-being of man: following the works of Jean-Jacques Rousseau and Daniel Defoe, the literary convention of the 'noble savage' became as useful as the general romantic enthusiasm for wild nature in all its aspects.[32] The discovery of the New World was of special interest to this group, as we have already seen (above, Chapter 2).

The investigation of the changing images of wilderness in Europe must be seen against the background of philosophical and scientific re-orientations and profound social, economic and geographical transformations. Clearly, although the long record of human occupation of the continent shows that there was always a variety of public images for every aspect of the man–environment relationship, there was undoubtedly distinct and sustained support for a more positive or favourable interpretation during the eighteenth century. And in this respect the key role of the educated and leisured classes requires further emphasis and clarification. Allowing for a very generous interval, it might be said that it was they who 'led the way' towards a more conservative approach to the natural environment, but this also suggests a degree of 'other-directed', purposive activity which is very difficult to discern. Succeeding generations were (and are) mightily influenced by the inheritance of creative work from this period, but in the eighteenth and nineteenth centuries there were very few marked or tangible achievements in terms of wilderness use and preservation which can be directly related to these developments in aesthetics and philosophy. The New World story proved to be a little different.

Two final qualifications must be made quickly here. The first concerns the romantic evocation of a relationship between nationalism and certain 'unspoilt' regions. European Romanticism in the late eighteenth and early nineteenth centuries was dominated by Germany: by Goethe, scientist and poet; Schinkel, the great architect; and the composer Richard Wagner. The mountains, forests and valleys of southern, central and western Germany were represented as the true cultural hearth of the nation and were celebrated as such in music, aesthetic literature and philosophical argument. The second type of qualification regarding the romanticization of the natural environment also involved an interesting spatial focus, but the scale was more intimate: there was an effort to 'improve' on nature, involving a degree of selectivity in nature preservation and imitation which was expressive of varying degrees of intricate and conscious design, deeply influenced by the 'discovery', interpretation and diffusion of Chinese attitudes towards the environment. Unhappily, Europeans never came to terms with the complicated symbolic expressions of the man–land relationship which had been built into the meticulously contrived 'harmonies' and ordered 'irregularities' of the Chinese scene. From Russia and Scandinavia to the southern tip of Italy, however, the design of great private and municipal parks and formal gardens showed enthusiastic responses to the fashion for *chinoiserie*. The English landscape school shared in these developments, but it also established a distinctively blended national style based upon three primary elements — the 'Ornamental Farm', in which that simple utilitarian object was rendered artistic; the 'Garden Connecting a Park', developed around a large number of great houses by William Kent, Lancelot ('Capability') Brown and Humphry Repton; and the idea of the 'Forest Garden' or 'Savage Garden', the so-called Picturesque, which was essentially confined to the scholars, painters and the Lake District poets.[33]

The images of wilderness which were held in the Old World were from the outset multi-faceted. Although the Judaeo-Christian tradition gave most support to the unfavourable or negative public images, the opposite view was frequently well represented and there was always some ambivalence or ambiguity which drew upon a more ancient heritage. The increasing secularization of society and the economic and social upheavals accompanying industrialization, urbanization and the rapid commercialization of agriculture brought about widespread cultural confusion. This must have been due in part to the disruption of imperfect but comparatively stable ecological relationships: and in this respect, it might be argued that Western man himself also appeared to be facing a crisis of identity, from the eighteenth century onwards. In the midst of the general chaos a very small number of private individuals and groups made their own admirably creative responses to the changing situation, and some of the most significant of these responses were spatially expressed—in the selection, celebration, preservation and reproduction of distinctive landscape elements and regional landscape types.

Keeping the New World New

Nash, Hays, Huth and others have amply demonstrated that the changing public images of wilderness in the United States were heavily

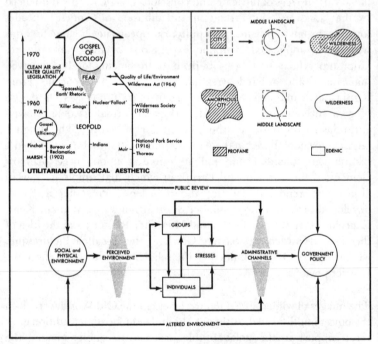

Fig 12 Wilderness and conservation: some approaches. *Top left:* major motivational streams in the conservation movement, after Nash, 1972; *right:* sacred and profane landscapes in the nineteenth and twentieth centuries, after Tuan, 1971. *Lower:* political involvement and decision-making in resource management.

influenced by the intellectual legacy of the Old World to the New, and furthermore, that the wilderness theme is a vital ingredient in the analysis of the deep-seated motivational shifts on which conservationism was based.[34] It is important to emphasize here that this statement is not intended to diminish the role of social, geographical and political change within the United States, which clearly activated and reflected these motivational shifts, giving additional strength and positive, practical and innovative expression to the concepts inherited from Europe.

Nash has argued that the motivation for conservation in the United States can be conveniently separated into three divisions. He writes of the aesthetic and utilitarian streams, which are both anthropocentric in so far as 'either man's stomach or man's spirit is the paramount concern', and the ecological stream, which 'puts man back into the biotic community, and its welfare, not that of *homo sapiens*, is given top priority' (Fig. 12).[35] Individuals, groups, institutions and key events and periods are variously located according to their most important contributions to one or other of the major streams of thought. The model is naturally highly simplified in this respect, since many of the leading contributions were made 'across the board', as it were; it is, however, a convenient heuristic device and the reader is referred to Nash's original diagram, which is rather more detailed.

The culminating events leading in recent years to a more public 'gospel of ecology' were largely based on that most powerful emotion, fear, and derived from growing popular awareness of environmental degradation and various pollution hazards at the local, national and global scales. But we are now concerned with the earlier part of the story preceding the development of massively increasing public participation, when very small numbers of people defined alternative wilderness images which challenged those held by the majority — new and positive images which insisted on the highest of valuations for the surviving wilderness places, at the same time emphasizing new attitudes ranging from rejection to reverence, and associated new behaviours which highlighted the enjoyment of the 'wilderness experience'. This was but one facet of the process in which a minority of committed people defined certain stresses in the American society as its relationships with the environment evolved (Fig. 12, lower). They provided an essential articulation of those stresses for the community at large and/or pressed the cases directly to the bureaucrats and elected representatives, so influencing public policy in the field of environmental management. As major resource conflicts received increasing national attention in the contemporary press, the process outlined in Fig. 12 quickly became more sophisticated and far more politicized.

Four main themes appear to offer good potential for a comparative historical–geographical approach. The first of these, the romanticization of the wilderness, must be omitted here. In this case, the American examples have become very familiar, from the early ambivalent, genteel, and anti-urban sentiments borrowed from the European inheritance to the development of an increasingly nationalistic focus on the 'uniquely American' wilderness favoured by nineteenth-century writers, poets and landscape painters. The subtle comparisons and contrasts in time and space in the Australian, Canadian and New Zealand stories have also provoked considerable interest in recent years.[36] Accordingly the following examples are merely intended to give some useful impression of the three remaining and equally important themes: the national park concept, the role of key groups and individuals, and attitudinal and structural changes in the broader social setting. None of these can be treated in sufficient detail in the available space, no effort has been made to distinguish them as artificially separated entities, and for economy, the discussion has been restricted to the American scene.

The development of the park movement in the nineteenth century was intricately associated with certain responses to the urban condition. American architects and landscape gardeners gave a fresh and more extensive application to the philosophy of British and European reformers in their efforts to design an urban fabric more conducive to the production of a socio-spatial environment which might 'improve' the urban residents. Public gardens were becoming common in the 1820s; 'naturalistic' suburbs and cul-de-sacs in the 1830s; garden suburbs, boulevards, decorative leisure resorts and planned industrial communities had arrived by the 1870s; metropolitan parks and playground systems for active recreation were introduced in the 1890s. But this was strongly associated with another response to the urban condition: some city-dwellers chose instead to turn 'back to Nature'.[37] In some ways this was simply an urban version of the search for Arcady, exhibited in the wider taste for house gardens and in the growth of the popular literature of nature essays and adventure stories. It was also displayed in the new principles for urban education based on G. Stanley Hall's 'genetic psychology', which demanded that children be assisted to recapitulate the basic stages of human development, from the primitive rural condition to the sophistications of city life: so the Outdoor Camps, Boy Scouts, Campfire Girls and similar institutions mushroomed from the 1880s onwards. With increasing leisure and a comparative improvement in the distribution of income, citizens' groups of all kinds developed to provide for the new interests in outdoor recreation and the aesthetic appreciation of nature. In 1904 the American Park and Outdoor Art Society (formed in 1897) combined with the American League for Civic Improvement (formed in 1901) to establish the American Civic Association. Under J. Horace McFarland, its energetic president between 1904 and 1923, the Association became a very powerful national influence in urban planning, conservation and outdoor recreation.

The reaction to crowded urban conditions and the increasing interest in all forms of recreation as mental and physical therapy were major factors leading to a gradual revision of the American concepts of 'sacred' and 'profane' territory. As Tuan indicates, the classical concept of a dichotomy between sacred urban spaces and hostile or despised wildernesses gradually made way for the entry of the Edenic middle ground of the yeoman farmer and, in time, a rejection of the city and a corresponding elevation of the status of the wilderness.[38] Although this extreme example of the transference of spatial imagery scarcely has universal application, there seems to be no reason to doubt its broad utility — and indeed its increasing validity over time (Fig. 12, top right). The mounting threat to the wilderness from the expansion of the middle ground in modern times, for example, has led to some impressive battles in defence of the ever-more hallowed territory against a triple encroachment — from equally profane farmland, industry and urban-based tourists. The national park movement, so closely related to the changing images of wilderness within an increasingly urbanized society, obviously displays this 'social construction' of the national space.

Urban parks were familiar expressions of change throughout the nineteenth-century world, but the national park concept was arguably an American innovation. It was probably first announced by the painter George Catlin, in the early 1830s and subsequently in his book *North American Indians* (1841). In 1864 Congress established Yosemite Valley as a grant to the state of California 'for public use, resort and recreation'. On 1 March 1872, Yellowstone National Park, a federally-administered area of over two million acres, was created in Wyoming; it was the first of its kind in the world. Yet its creation owed very little to the efforts of any true wilderness movement. The region was then a high, remote and newly explored federal territory full of geysers, hot springs and other spectacular natural scenery, but seemingly of no orthodox utilitarian value. The Act defining the park was the result of the opportunism and salesmanship of a handful of scientific explorers, landscape artists and photographers, assisted in part by some railroad men who saw the possibilities of tourist traffic.[39] Yellowstone was then largely regarded as a great 'museum' full of Nature's 'freaks'; its value as a true wilderness reserve and even, as the Act itself declared, 'a public park or pleasuring ground for the benefit and enjoyment of the people', was only slowly realized.

But the realization came during the pioneer administration of that new type of space in the public domain. The first great park was not only a massive geographical fact: as an institutional reality it also required the development of entirely new forms of bureaucratic management. The park administration made its way by cautious experimentation through innumerable trials of strength with miners, hunters, tourists, prospective farmers, railroad companies and other parties who had their own forceful ideas for its development. At the same time it proclaimed its mandate and the unique quality of the territory in its care to an ever-wider public, so extending the very support base of the park ideal and the promise of similar reservations in the future. The National Park Service Act of 1916 built on the pilot experiences of Yellowstone and other early ventures to ensure a more sophisticated and integrated management body throughout the country. In that year there were thirty-seven national parks and monuments under federal control. By 1973 the National Park Service controlled 298 areas, including 14.7 million acres in thirty-eight national parks and 9.9 million acres in eighty-three national monuments, attracting a total of 15,348,000 individual overnight stays.[40] The park system obviously constitutes an impressive spatial structure within the national economy and life-style. It has directly influenced the rapid evolution of new movement patterns and a wide range of decision-making situations concerning local economic planning and regional residential preferences.

The activities of certain key figures lent special force and direction to the image-making processes in the wilderness movement. Foremost amongst these gifted individuals were Henry David Thoreau (1817–62) and John Muir (1838–1914).[41]

Thoreau's Transcendentalism was revolted by the confusion of materialism and insecurity in the growing cities and in *Walden* (1854) and other works he looked to the wilderness as an environment in which spiritual truths could be more easily discovered. Neither his writing nor his public speaking were wholly concerned with the natural world, *per se*: he preached instead the intellectual value of the wilderness, which he identified in the spiritual sustenance it provided for man himself. And, following on from this, Thoreau called for the preservation of wilderness areas for the frequent use of the truly civilized man. In 1859 he urged the setting aside of a sacrosanct park 'or rather primitive forest' in each of the townships in his own Massachusetts region: 'let us keep the New World new, preserve all the advantages of living in the country'.[42] His repeated arguments obviously provided a firmer philosophical base for the influential urban-based opposition to dominant environmental attitudes which had been stirred by the Romanticist and Naturalist movements. Thoreau's emphasis on the preservation of continuing access to opportunities for contemplative outdoor recreation was greatly expanded by educated urban élitists over the next few decades.

The extraordinary John Muir — author, scientist, poet and philosopher — was the leading publicist for the wilderness from the 1870s until his death in 1914. Muir was deeply influenced by Emerson, Thoreau and other American Transcendentalists, but he became far more committed to a new wilderness ethic which recognized the 'rights' of all animate and inanimate things and man's kinship to them; man had both a need and a responsibility to rediscover and express that kinship, instead of continuing to act out the dangerous and discredited mission of 'dominion' over nature. Conservation was becoming a national issue as Muir moved towards the peak of his powers. But the young conservation movement was divided on utilitarian and aesthetic grounds—between 'wise use' and 'preservation'. The forests administrator Gifford Pinchot became the leading light of utilitarianism and Muir took up the cause of the preservationists. In collaboration with the journalist Robert Underwood Johnson, Muir focussed on the Californian Sierras, making good use of Marsh's treatise on man's destructive potential and of Henry George's attack on the principle of private ownership in land. They succeeded in achieving the proclamation of the Yosemite National Park in 1890. In 1892 the Sierra Club was founded in San Francisco; Muir was elected President and he held the office until his death.[43]

Muir eventually clashed with the Pinchot school over the use of the millions of acres of new forest reserves. With the passing of the Forest Management Act of 1897 the utilitarians had really won the day, but the bitter conflict heightened the awareness of a wider public to the issues involved in crucial decisions over land-use planning in virgin areas. During the early part of this century 'wise use' was the more accepted meaning given to conservation in powerful official circles and in the public mind generally. Muir and his supporters (including J. H. McFarland) failed in their aggressive campaign to defeat the application of the San Franciscan authorities for a permit to construct a reservoir in the Hetch Hetchy Valley in the heart of the Yosemite wilderness. But the conflict raged from 1908 until 1913 and drew national and international publicity.[44] Despite its contemporary defeats the minority preservationist view became the inspiration of a veritable 'wilderness cult' whose passionate adherents could not be ignored.

From the outset the Sierra Club was a central organizing focus for protestation. After the mid twentieth century it began to throw off its élitist origins and swiftly became one of America's most influential vehicles for the expression of a more radical voice for conservation in general and wilderness in particular. In the process, Muir — like Thoreau before him and the forester Aldo Leopold who preached the 'ecological conscience' and the 'land ethic' in the inter-war period— acquired the status of a secular saint. The present commitment to activism in the international wilderness movement is John Muir's best memorial.

The Role of Illusion in Pioneer Settlement

If hope, fear, challenge and uncertainty are central to the human condition, then they have to be accorded due weight in the study of human geography. This is sufficient reason for including the following guide to some more specific aspects of the role of illusion in the settlement process. At various times we are all, of course, 'deceived by appearances'. We may be the victims of an imperfect interchange of communication, or of what is really the reverse of this — that is, we may be manipulated by highly skilled communicators. On the other hand we frequently deceive ourselves and we also make ourselves specially receptive, individually and collectively, to incoming messages which conjure for us a view of the world in which we would like to believe.

One of the strongest traditions of research and teaching in the historical–geographical field argues that certain major regions and certain kinds of environmental relationships were entirely 'misperceived' by the pioneer settler. These are the 'illusions' which provide the material for our present section. Their separation from some of the other images discussed in this book is somewhat artificial. But this is nevertheless a very convenient and valuable pedagogic device, and its simple epistemological significance should become clear as we proceed.

Of Trees, Rain and Soil

The use of 'botanical indicators', particularly trees, was a part of normal procedure in the earliest days of white settlement in the New

World. Extensive grassland areas were regarded with some suspicion by small-scale cultivators and mixed farmers partly because they seemed incapable of supporting such an obviously impressive natural 'crop'. In time, empirical testing also succeeded in matching individual woodland species to certain types of agricultural potential, but the luxuriant profusion of some natural woodlands, notably in Australia, continued to encourage massive clearing efforts for modes of occupation which proved to be very questionable from most economic, social and ecological viewpoints. Applied science gradually supplanted tradition and folk mythology, but it also incorporated something of the old-established empiricist approach. Williams and others, for example, have illustrated the significance of the recognition of certain livestock diseases as a central diagnostic procedure in the identification of trace element deficiencies in Australian soils.[45]

New World notions of the reciprocal relationships between vegetation, soils, weather and climate certainly reflected quite conventional deductive processes; where they became more sophisticated, they borrowed directly from Europe's Enlightenment and from the scholars of antiquity, but there was always a distinctive New World flavour. Characteristic optimisms, a fundamental naivete concerning environmental processes, and the complete absence of reliable meteorological data encouraged travellers on the first American frontiers to accept and promote the idea that the physical environment might somehow be 'ameliorated' merely by white occupation. These writers were particularly susceptible to local reports of increased streamflow, higher lake levels and unusually wet seasons. Yet even the most gifted of contemporary observers must have found it impossible to evaluate these reports in the spatial and temporal setting we now accept as essential: so, in the 1850s, F. L. Olmsted noted the Mexican claim that the west Texas region had experienced a significant increase in precipitation since the arrival of the Anglo-Americans, and a British visitor found no reason to doubt that the Indian maxim 'the pale-face brings with him his rain' was equally applicable to pioneering areas in Utah, Kansas and New Mexico.[46] In these contexts the introduction of irrigated tree crops, amongst other 'improvements', was believed to have reduced evaporation, conserved soil moisture, retarded surface runoff, and thereby supplemented the water vapour available for precipitation.

Now in some measure, this latter argument was simply an elaboration and extension of the debate on environmental degradation in the more established districts of Europe and eastern North America. There was indeed mounting apprehension in educated circles over the continuing rapid removal of the tree cover, its clear association with accelerated runoff and soil erosion, and the apparent consequent reduction in surface springs and local rainfall. In 1864 George Perkins Marsh brought these views together in his remarkable survey, *Man and Nature*, which Kollmorgen has described as 'the bible of the rainmakers of the West'.[47] Individual champions for the forest emerged in every state, but in the west the enthusiasts went far beyond Marsh in advocating extensive afforestation as a remedy for the recurring droughts. At the Federal level, Egleston, Fernow and Hough pressed the case for scientific forest management on climatic as well as economic grounds, and the debate on the Timber Culture Act of 1873 articulated similar convictions. The intimacy of the forest-climate linkage continued to provide a favoured scientific theme until the 1930s and it still attracts considerable interest, albeit of a more sophisticated variety.

The idea that 'rain follows the plough' was another example of folk mythology or popular science. Kollmorgen and Kollmorgen claim that this was essentially an American climatic theory which came into vogue with the breaking of the prairie sod in the west.[48] They quote an enthusiastic description of the resources of Kansas in which the transformed prairie soil is portrayed as a kind of cistern or reservoir — slowly releasing the rainfall it has received into an increasing number of springs, at the same time 'recharging' the water vapour of the atmosphere — and note that Nebraska's Professor Samuel Aughey was convinced that prairie cultivation had been more important than afforestation in increasing the precipitation.

Perhaps the claim for another American 'first' is in this case rather loosely made. The dubious correlation between the expansion of pioneer settlement and coincident increases in local rainfall was certainly common enough in the scientific and promotional tracts of the later nineteenth century, but the idea itself is surely so central to the engrossing anthropocentrism of Western man in the Judaeo-Christian era that one must expect to find it in different guises at much earlier periods, possibly even in medieval Europe. A nascent concept of this type was, in any case, apparent in the early stages of small-scale farming in Australia during the first decades of the nineteenth century.[49] And, since it provided such useful psychological support and strengthened the moral sanction which immigrants believed they had inherited in their possession of new territory, it can be safely assumed that in America too the idea that 'rain follows the plough' was essentially a firmer restatement or adaptation of the traditional self-image, at a propitious time, with particularly useful local application.

The popular acceptance of both types of rainfall theory was

consolidated and skilfully exploited by the New World's promoters, particularly when they were faced with the task of 'marketing' a doubtful product — notably, the opportunity of settling in a condemned or hitherto neglected territory. The best-known example of this situation is provided in Meinig's account of the northward movement of settlement in South Australia in the 1870s, already briefly mentioned in Chapter 3. Urged on by newspaper editors and interested politicians, an army of pioneer farmers moved beyond 'Goyder's Line' of reliable rainfall.[50] Exhilarated by the success of a few good years and encouraged by the enthusiastic revival of the anthropocentric climatic theories in the local press and parliament, the settlers seemed content to put their faith in further cultivation mixed with a little afforestation, and moved on into the difficult Northern District. In the 1880s the droughts returned and the pioneers retreated in bewildered disarray.

For Australia generally, however, the advocates of the afforestation panacea continued to press their case. They had taken an early cue from Victoria's internationally respected Baron Ferdinand von Mueller, who had expressed the opinion (in 1866) that 'in the Australian vegetation we probably possess the means of obliterating the rainless regions of the globe, to spread at last woods over the deserts, and thereby to mitigate the distressing droughts, and to annihilate even the occasionally dry heat evolved by the sun's rays from the naked ground throughout extensive regions of the interior.'[51] Mueller soon modified this view, but others did not. John Ednie Brown, for example, an energetic Scottish forester and South Australia's first Conservator of Forests, campaigned for 'climatic afforestation' in several colonies during his varied career in Australia.[52] Yet the record — admittedly sparse — shows thus far only two tangible contemporary effects of the advocacy of this peculiarly resilient rainfall theory: most importantly, it lent invaluable support to the Australian governments' fledgling forest departments and to the nascent conservation movement in general; secondly, in the 1880s it influenced the design of some innovative laws for land classification which included the proclamation of forest reserves, for climatic as well as for utilitarian purposes.

Conjurers and Exorcists: the Great American Desert[53]

For roughly three centuries, Spanish, French and British contact with the North American region now known as the Great Plains was restricted to a generally insubstantial and occasionally precarious settlement of its periphery, accompanied by an occasional penetration of the region proper by small numbers of explorers. The environmental appraisals made by these initial European groups reflected their respective preoccupations with the search for gold and other valuable minerals, and with the possibilities for an extension of the fur trade; another important constraint was the quest for relatively advanced native tribes amenable to religious conversion and other forms of 'assimilation'. The Great Plains scored badly on each of these points, but the area was at least vaguely proclaimed as an extensive region with its own unique character. For these reasons, modern scholars have judged the initial European image to have been dominantly 'negative'. It is equally valid, however, to point to the very indistinct information component of the image and its neglected dynamic characteristics, in terms of the related values and attitudes. The picture was never, so far as we know, precisely articulated, and over that lengthy period between the sixteenth and eighteenth centuries there was a subtle alteration in the Spanish appraisal, as the 'empty' interior took on the character of a useful buffer zone between the rival European powers, and the Spaniards themselves expanded into California and Texas.

Apart from the distorting veil of their consuming preoccupations, the Spanish explorers displayed a propensity for arduously lengthy south–north drives which emphasized the apparent homogeneity of the area and, as bad fortune dictated, they frequently encountered delicately-balanced local ecosystems in conditions of physiological drought. Had they made more lateral drives and had better luck with the seasons, their evaluation might have been a trifle more generous. Similarly, their meagre bequest of printed information with which the Anglo-Americans had to deal was almost inevitably characterized by descriptions of personal reactions to some 'unusual occurrences' which punctuated the monotonous treks: thus, the dessicated appearance of some small areas took on an inflated importance and accentuated the air of frustration in the official journals. And the repeated use of Southern European terminology introduced some semantic confusion, particularly in subsequent translation. The very term 'desert' was itself ambiguous, since it might only have implied an 'empty' area — devoid of people (or even of relatively advanced people), of domestic and wild animals, trees, or a rich cover of productive native vegetation. Similar crucial processes of image-making may be identified in the early Anglo-American period, beginning with a series of official explorations in the first decades of the nineteenth century. These explorations had specific and dominating commissions which controlled their choices of route, the kinds of information they sought, and the mode of reporting their findings to their superiors and the American public.

The relevance of a re-examination of this old case study should now begin to emerge. As our earlier chapters have attempted to show, it is never sufficient to portray any major public image as simply 'positive' or 'negative': such images are essentially multi-dimensional and multi-functional. The traditional approach to the controversy is therefore misleading. Again, it has already been established in the previous sections of this book that direct 'perception' is by no means the only method of image-construction. It will be shown that the 'Great American Desert' theme illustrates quite efficiently two of our basic common-sense principles: first, images are often born of the fears and longings of a society; secondly, this is a dynamic process in which gifted communicators at the local and regional levels and the inspired, articulate and gifted leaders of society at large, can and do play central roles. This argument would not have to be put in most other social science disciplines, but human geography has become increasingly mechanistic and inflexible. Traditional structuralist propositions which have guided so much of our teaching and research in this area must now be made to accommodate the necessary balancing perspective which the existentialist philosophy guarantees.

The powerful figure of Thomas Jefferson may be discerned once again throughout the early development of the Anglo-American appraisal. This is not only evident in the context of his persuasive commitment to the formation of an agrarian republic, but also in the contemporary pre-eminence of his geographical knowledge of the trans-Missouri/Mississippi region. Jefferson accumulated an impressive collection of maps and books which were broadly representative of the earlier British, French and Spanish appraisals, but the approach he adopted in sieving through this immense quantity of fragmentary evidence was unquestionably influenced by a very American brand of imperialism. He concluded that the territory lying to the north-west of the settled districts was a veritable garden awaiting yeoman settlement, while at the same time offering the best of all prospects for the discovery of the long-awaited 'Passage to India'.[54]

Jefferson's visionary proposals instigated the Lewis and Clark transcontinental expedition of 1804–6 and were carried over into the explorations made by Pike (1806–7) and Long (1819–20). Zebulon M. Pike's account of 1810 argued that the higher plains would become 'as celebrated as the sandy deserts of Africa'; Stephen Long found the area between the Rocky Mountains and 96 degrees west 'tiresome to the eye, and fatiguing to the spirit . . . a sea of sand . . . wholly unfit for cultivation, and of course, uninhabitable by a people depending upon agriculture for their subsistence'.[55] Long was also the author of a manuscript map on which the title 'Great Desert' was given to a large slice of western Oklahoma and northern Texas. G. M. Lewis has noted that a very widely publicized version of this map first appeared in 1822, using the same description for southern Kansas and eastern Colorado. The publication of the official account of Long's expedition during the following year applied the title 'Great American Desert' to the same area, and the 'desert myth' is said to have been widely held until about the mid 1870s.

The controversial works of Walter Prescott Webb more or less dominated the teaching of this story of regionalization between the early 1930s and the mid 1960s. According to Webb, the desert image had its origins in the earliest days of European contact and was strengthened during the first encounters of Anglo-Americans who moved in from the humid and well-timbered east. It was, furthermore, a substantially accurate image of aridity or semi-aridity which acted as a deterrent to pioneer settlement, but major American innovations in transportation, weaponry, ranching management, fencing, water conservation, dry farming and so on gradually demonstrated that the future of the Great Plains lay in livestock farming. Webb wrote compellingly of the contemporary perception of a kind of 'institutional fault' running from central Texas to Illinois or Dakota along the 98th meridian; the eastern ways of American civilization were forced to change as the Americans responded to the environmental challenge west of that fault line: 'east of the Mississippi civilization stood on three legs — land, water, and timber; west of the Mississippi not one but two of these legs were withdrawn — water and timber — and civilization was left on one leg — land'.

More elaborate statements, while rejecting Webb's deterministic stance, clarified the sequence thus: the desert notion was born of disinterest, neglect and misperception in the earliest days of European contact; it was then fostered by the imperfect transmission of information to the Anglo-American inheritors, who in turn exaggerated the supposed characteristics of aridity, leaving it to their more enlightened successors to demonstrate by careful promotion and scientific research, as well as by technological innovation, that the region was predominantly a massive and complex subhumid grassland ecosystem. The best of these later works wisely placed more emphasis on the social setting rather than on the physical environment, and they succeeded thereby in demonstrating the operation of an involved and continuous learning system. Thus, G. M. Lewis has shown that the widespread acceptance of the desert concept never fully excluded other notions, particularly those proclaiming the existence of the 'Great Western Prairies' in the same region. Lewis has also drawn attention to

the vigorous promotional activities of William Gilpin, which commenced in the 1850s and offered an elementary kind of 'synthetic
regionalization' which proved more useful in the communication
process than the contemporary 'analytical regionalizations' of a
number of scientists who were then similarly engaged in breaking down
the sweeping statements of earlier days. Gilpin's wide experience in the
west and his commitment to its more intensive settlement was allied to
his varied background in administration, law, politics, business and
journalism to fit him admirably for his role as a promoter. He predicted
that his 'Great Plains' would become 'the great pastoral belt of the
continent' and, according to Lewis, he eventually succeeded in evoking
'a new and timely motivating image', a positive 'regional image,
calculated to induce widespread and permanent settlement'.[56] The task
of regional promotion was later taken up in earnest, with the
application of all the customary, consummate skills, by the land agents
and railroad companies. And so the last vestiges of the forbidding image
of the Great American Desert would be patched over by the power of
the mighty dollar, dispersed to the quiet store-rooms of the mind by
windy rhetoric.

The significance of the wider social environment has been noted by
several authors over the past ten years or so. Some have pointed to the
influence of the prevailing agrarian ideology on the negative appraisals
made by the first Anglo-American explorers; others have indicated that
the development of the concept of a desert barrier would have helped to
quell the fears of many easterners who found the westward expansion of
settlement extremely threatening, for political as well as for economic
reasons. But the contribution of similar factors in bringing about the
rejection of the desert myth has received rather less attention.

Goetzmann, particularly, and also Bredeson and Emmons, have
gone some distance towards correcting this omission.[57] In brief
summary of their arguments it could be said that motives other than
those related to the pursuit of scientific accuracy must have influenced
the principal image-makers of both the 'garden' and the 'desert'
schools. These 'external' motives must have reflected the political,
social, economic and environmental theories which were prevalent in
the observers' own communities. This leads to the obvious question:
were there any deep-seated reasons which persuaded Americans to
challenge the image of a sterile western interior? As the nineteenth
century 'advanced', surely the possession of a barren desert in the young
nation's geographical heartland was increasingly seen as a giant heresy,
an affront to that secular faith in 'Manifest Destiny'? Moreover, the
existence of an interior desert in North America did not conform with

the widely-held tradition of environmental unity; it was unacceptably *odd*. Above all, however, the conflict between North and South redefined regional ambitions and priorities in which the 'desert' began to loom very large indeed. A simple desire for territory lay behind much of this changing orientation, but at a purely ideological level there were several good arguments which appealed to one political faction or another. The strengthening of the Republican belief in the virtues of an increasing population of independent yeomen was one notable expression of the unfolding conflict, but in its extreme form this belief could suffer a desert as much as it could endure the idea of slavery, which was not at all. Again, the moderate Republicans sought a more homogeneous union of the entire nation — hence their opposition to the South's aberrant ways and also their reluctance to accept the 'desert' as an immutably barren area, given over to mere natives, for this doomed it as yet another unconformity: 'American nationalism demanded a homogeneity at once institutional, geographical, and racial.'[58] And the real and supposed designs of the South to check the expansion of the North into the western plains were sufficient transgressions for some Northerners, slavery notwithstanding: proponents of the 'desert' theory would therefore get short shrift and might even be seen as outright enemies.

So, in a sense, we have merely flipped the record to uncover a rather different expression of that search for identity discussed in the first section of this chapter: after the middle of the century, American Republicanism identified with a denial of the desert. The ideological legacy of the Northern victory therefore required the extension of the institutional features of Northern society into the western interior as well as into the defeated South. The west would be 'civilized' by the North — 'cleansed of deserts, Indians, and any other barbaric remnants'.[59] In the late 1860s and early 1870s, Northern officials chose to sponsor an impressive campaign to promote the settlement of the Great Plains, and a deluge of pamphlets, gazeteers and emigrants' guides flooded every part of the country.

Perhaps the true moral of the story so far is that there is no such thing as 'disinterested evaluation' of the environment. The observation itself is far from novel, but why have we been so reluctant to apply its underlying assumptions to the environments of scholarship and teaching? Like any other person, the teacher and research worker is, after all, a creature of his several environments, and the kind of healthy introspection and mild exorcisms and penances demanded by the present cautionary pause in academia will no doubt be productive as well as chastening. In the present context, there is one very interesting analysis which illustrates this development quite well. This is Martyn Bowden's interpretation of the historiography of the Great American Desert concept, which forms the basis of our final section.[60]

Bowden's earlier work was clearly pointed towards iconoclasm. But the clumsy pun is apposite: reluctant to accept the hallowed orthodoxies, Bowden diligently researched the regional texts, maps and newspapers of the day and offered two strong complaints. First, the image was far weaker and possibly more restricted in time than we had been led to suppose; secondly, its contemporary acceptance was geographically and socially selective, being primarily among the educated classes in the north-east. In a more recent essay, Bowden has claimed that the changing interpretations of the subject amongst professional historians have reflected the fluctuating environmental conditions actually experienced on the Great Plains during the twentieth century, together with the general official and popular concern for what was deemed to be a problem or 'marginal' region, and the emphases selected by a group of gifted scholars. In the first of these ebbs and flows, roughly between 1880 and 1905, the Romantic Plains historians — working from promotional and biassed sources, and assisted for some of the time by the prevalence of severe drought conditions — popularized the idea of an authentic desert region made over to settlement by the genius and sacrifice of the American pioneers. Subsequently, the preference for rather grandiose locational theory shown by the Turner school until the early 1930s minimized the strength of the physical environment as a factor in Plains history. Unusually favourable seasons at that time, and open neglect and misinterpretation of the basic ecological data, further persuaded most of the Turnerians against the possibility of a strong contemporary image which stressed aridity. The third change came with the droughts and depressions of the 1930s, when Walter Prescott Webb revolutionized the historical interpretations by insisting that there was, indeed, a distinctive area sufficiently arid to create an 'institutional break' which the settlers perceived and to which they adjusted. Webb and the other 'later Turnerians', and also the geographers, therefore paid far more attention to the physical environment.

Webb's academic *credo* and individualistic personality cannot be divorced from the analysis; Bowden might have indicated that Webb is known to have been very irritated by his fellow historians' indifference to the story of his own region, and that a main part of his effort was directed towards promoting the development of a *bona-fide* Western literature to counteract the influences of the pulp novelists and the screenwriters.[61] He found the theme of the physical environment much stronger than any other available material and it clearly served his purpose by helping immeasurably in the very definition of his region. Similarly, James C. Malin was then the only notable scholar who stressed the crucial complexities of the relationships within the grasslands ecosystem. But Malin was too often regarded as a mere maverick — owing allegiance to no particular school, communicating with very few senior students, and acting as his own editor and publisher.[62] He contended that the desert myth was largely restricted to those who opposed the expansion of settlement into the area, and that the pioneers themselves were usually fairly optimistic and resourceful empiricists. Malin struggled alone against the main academic and popular currents of his day. His grasp of basic ecological principles was partly intuitive and partly the result of some original and painstaking research in local history, on which he based his rejection of the frontier model. This forbade him to indulge in fads and fancies born of unrepresentative environmental conditions and real and perceived academic needs. The droughts of the 1930s therefore had relatively less effect on his thinking because he could not accept such short-term deteriorations as anything more or less than what they were.

Since the 1950s, Malin's approach has clearly made a marked impact on a new generation of scholars concerned with settlement processes on the subhumid margins. In Australia alone, for example, most research in this field has occurred since 1960, and the works of Heathcote, Jeans, Meinig, Powell and Williams have all described the introduction of European attitudes towards the Australian environment as the input of a partially destructive new agent in the ecological system and as the commencement of a difficult and continuing process of learning, or 'adjustment'.[63] Also, in each of the countries discussed in this book, the growth of 'environmental history' courses in the 1970s, together with comparable developments in the related sub-branches of geography, must incorporate some guarantee that Malin's contribution will at last receive its due recognition. The pertinent signs all indicate that approaches sympathetic to his holistic 'ecological' schema are destined to balance, and perhaps replace, Webb's classical statement on the settlement of the western interior of the United States. As that re-orientation occurs, the idea of a contemporary belief in the desert image may be accorded its proper weight — as one focus in the analysis of a wide range of appraisals, adjustments and maladjustments in the process of making a living on the western plains.

5

Elysium: the Search for Health

Complete and lasting freedom from disease is but a dream remembered from imaginings of a Garden of Eden designed for the welfare of man.[1]

In Greek mythology 'Elysium' was vaguely conceived as a realm to which heroes were taken before death. It was a place of perfect happiness in which every inhabitant was free to follow his favourite pursuit; a pre-Hellenic paradise, completely free of worldly cares and infirmities. Homer located it at the farthest end of the earth on the banks of the mythical river Oceanus. But it was also equated with the legendary Isles of the Blessed, with which the New World in general and North America in particular came to be identified in the later Middle Ages and during the great age of discovery. In its original sense the wide-embracing concept of Elysium could scarcely be separated from that of 'Arcadia'. During the eighteenth century and especially throughout the nineteenth century however, a narrower definition of the term was occasionally employed by New World promoters to evoke images of extraordinarily healthy localities and health-giving regional environments. It is this more restricted interpretation with which we must now be concerned.

This chapter deals with some aspects of the influence of 'medical promotion' and inadequate medical knowledge upon environmental appraisal and settlement in the New World during the nineteenth century. The first two parts of the chapter examine the general setting and provide an example of a contemporary debate over the function of 'medical climatology' in the interpretation and settlement of California, with particular reference to regional and national images of tuberculosis and malaria. The second study concerns the promotion of the Australian colony of Victoria as a haven for British and European tuberculosis sufferers. It stresses once more that the most vigorous communication of many of the important public images of Australia was closely linked to the real or perceived requirements of particular sections of the population of the Old World, and especially those of the British public.

A New World Approach to Medicine[2]

There were very few notable American contributions towards the physical and biological sciences during the early colonial era, but the accumulation of novel experience in varied, rapidly changing environments, together with the very simplicity of pioneering life and its comparative lack of social and professional distinctions, meant that the new territories were for a time unencumbered by the kinds of stubborn and perverse dogmatism which severely hampered scientific progress in the mother countries. In medicine, above all, the Americans developed a distinctive style which also yielded a number of valuable professional lessons for their European colleagues. Their emphasis was on the concrete and practical rather than on grand abstractions and prolonged argumentation: on careful observation, respect for common-sense interpretations, and a laudable concentration on the delivery of relevant treatment as the most urgent focus of their service to the community.

Ministers of religion, rather than trained physicians, were responsible for the first diffusion of medical knowledge to North America. This was a significant factor, insofar as the European clergy often successfully opposed major medical 'interventions', especially in surgery. Similarly, the empirical spirit was probably strengthened by the Puritans' belief in original sin and their consequent interpretation of the marked dualism of man's nature. So Cotton Mather, in his *Angel of Bethesda* (completed in 1724) was content to see sin as the prime cause of all sickness. Most of his text was directed instead at surveying the symptoms of a large number of distinct diseases and listing their known or supposed remedies. The emphasis throughout the colonial era was indeed upon learning by the most direct forms of experience, in the field rather than in the laboratory, and there was a heavy reliance on a crude apprenticeship system which made for a surprisingly satisfactory if limiting kind of provincialism which stressed regional environmental differences. There was also a marked respect for clinical procedures which proved highly successful in coping with those occasional epidemics which were wont to strike ferociously at such isolated communities.

In the late eighteenth century, Paris was the Western world's scientific capital. French medicine, encouraged by Napoleon himself, by an intellectual climate relatively free from moral objections to medical research (unlike contemporary Britain, for example) and by the general success of the physical sciences, made sound progress in statistical techniques, detailed clinical work, and surgery.[3] Wealthy Americans were then attracted to Paris as well as to London and Edinburgh to study medicine, yet their return made little impression upon their countrymen, who maintained their disrespect for academic theorizing. Thomas Jefferson was once more prominent.

> Having been so often a witness to the salutory efforts which nature makes to re-establish the disordered functions, he [the wise doctor] should rather trust to their action, than hazard the interruption of that, and a greater derangement of the system, by conjectural experiments on a machine so complicated and so unknown as the human body, and a subject so sacred as human life. Or, if the appearance of doing something be necessary to keep alive the hope and spirits of the patient, it should be of the most innocent character . . . But the adventurous physician goes on, and substitutes presumption for knowledge. From the scanty field of what is known, he launches into the boundless region of what is unknown. He establishes for his guide some fanciful theory of corpuscular attraction, of chemical agency, of mechanical powers, of stimuli, or irritability accumulated or exhausted, of depletion by the lancet and repletion by mercury, or some other ingenious dream, which let him into all nature's secrets at short hand. On the principle which he thus assumes, he forms his table of nosology, arrays his diseases into families, and extends his curative treatment, by analogy, to all the cases he has thus arbitrarily marshalled together.[4]

The widespread distrust of 'bookish' medicine assisted the Americans to escape some of the worst forms of European quackery, although the exaggerations of some of the early promotional literature and the very naivete and provincialism so characteristic of medical care in the United States did encourage some development of various 'nature cures', including seasonal movements to mineral springs and other areas seemingly well endowed with respect to relief and climate.[5] But this latter interest, harmless at least, rapidly intensified during the first half of the nineteenth century. In that period, public disdain for the medical profession was expressed far more bitterly throughout Western Europe and in the several regions of the New World; characteristically, however, the Americans were rather more extreme in their criticism and explored the alternative routes to good health with far more vigour and invention.

There were several reasons for this increasing loss of confidence in the medical profession. Rising standards of general education made people increasingly critical of their medical advisers and the rapid expansion of publishing facilities, especially the dramatic growth of the newspaper industry, gave the critics abundant opportunity to popularize their views. A very telling point which was repeatedly made contrasted the obvious practical successes of the physical sciences with the continued failure of the medical theoreticians to contribute to human welfare. After 1850 the traditional 'depletion procedures' (bleeding, purging, etc.) were gradually discredited by the new discoveries in medicine, but the educated layman demanded far more — and felt entitled to do so, for he already enjoyed the fruits of high technology in so many other areas which were far less vital. The naturally conservative responses from the painstaking medical researchers had left a massive vacuum.

Into that vacuum rushed the 'medical sectarians'. The *hydropaths* and *homeopaths* originated in Germany, and offered respectively mild and comfortable treatments based on 'water cures' (drinking, bathing) and on the administration of minute quantities of drugs to healthy patients with the expectation that they would be rendered immune to diseases with symptoms which were associated with those drugs. The Americans proved very receptive to these ideas and to variations on them. With the rapid increase in population and its extension to areas remote from the established centres of learning, an astonishing proliferation of private colleges generously provided a large output of second-rate doctors in short time, and further undermined the status of the profession. And the common acceptance of the importance of free competition and free expression actually supported medicine's expanding periphery, just as it supported business enterprise and the growth of new religious sects. Similarly, as the new medicine won a strong following, that very success became an assurance of further growth; when it also frequently proved to be a financial success, that added to its respectability.

> The truth is that Americans, as a result of the current exploitation of vast natural resources, had become a commercially-minded people, and were inclined to encourage only such science as was of obvious utility. The popular ideals were those of business success and of efficiency. This meant that in medicine there was respect for fashionable practitioners but little more than toleration for physicians who dabbled in apparently useless clinical or pathological studies.[6]

This judgement is a little harsh. It neglects the American preoccupation with novelty, with the prospect of change and the associated high status of youth; and it discounts the consuming passion for comfort and security in better and longer lives, which the bountiful New World seemed destined to provide. In addition, there was to some extent a continuity of style and emphasis between the medical sects of the nineteenth century and the environmentally-conscious, patient-oriented provincialism established in the colonial era. The monistic pathology and monistic therapeutics favoured by the sectarians were also based on familiar ground and greatly assisted their popular appeal.[7]

Hygiene became a secular religion as the popular health cults rapidly gained ground. One of the most influential figures was Sylvester Graham, whose *Science of Human Health* (Boston, 1839) proclaimed his opposition to harsh medication, offering in its place general temperance, careful dieting (including vegetarianism), personal hygiene, fresh air and exercise. Another was Dr. T. H. Trall, whose publicized 'cure' based on bathing, diet, exercise and electricity won a wide following in the eastern states and in the Mid-West. Graham, Trall and others undoubtedly succeeded in energizing and re-focussing the powerful core of suspicion and disappointment which characterized the public image of 'regular' medicine.[8] On the whole, the industrialized and urbanized American society gained considerably from the less extreme popular health movements, particularly from the increased emphasis on sport and physical education, and the growing demand for summer vacations and outdoor recreation greatly assisted the development of amenity resources in regions which were in most other respects poorly endowed. With increasing population density and improvements in transportation, the hitherto more remote mountain and beach locations took on new significance and some of the old spa resorts were resuscitated.

California was more deeply influenced than any other state by these developments, not least because of its relatively recent exploitation and the close connection between a most effective form of arcadian imagery, already discussed in Chapter 3, and what has been called here the search for elysium. These latter themes provided a most alluring promotional mix.

The Salubrity of California

The reputations of America's popular health cults and indeed those of the old mineral springs were largely built upon their contributions towards the cure or alleviation of such common complaints as lumbago, skin irritations, rheumatism, digestive disorders and the like. They had little to offer to those pioneers who suffered from malaria and rheumatic fever after the expansion into the wet lowlands of the Mississippi Valley. Nor did they reduce the alarming rise in the incidence of tuberculosis amongst the crowded populations of the growing industrial centres. For many medical practitioners, the most suitable response to the growing public distress over this deteriorating situation was an imaginative elaboration of 'climatotherapy' and its careful application to the American situation.

In 1850 Dr. Daniel Drake published his *Diseases of the Interior Valley of North America*.[9] This was primarily a medical geography of aboriginal America, but the widespread professional acceptance of some of its major explanatory themes and of the author's concurrent recommendations for therapeutic travel heralded the arrival of 'medical climatology' in the United States. Drake advocated lengthy journeys to California via the Great Plains, the Rockies and the desert country as a uniquely American version of the fashionable ocean voyages then favoured by wealthy Europeans. His advice proved popular, especially in the 1860s, but for a time there was no general agreement on the choice of destination. Throughout the country the bulk of public and professional awareness was being concentrated almost exclusively upon tuberculosis and rheumatic diseases. The fear of malaria was by no means dispelled, but its high degree of geographical concentration was recognized and for a time the discussion of its particular problems played only a secondary role in the controversy over the selection of resorts and resort regions.

Southern California, the low desert areas of Arizona, and the dry mountainous areas of Colorado and New Mexico were favoured more or less equally by the climatotherapists, but the first of these was furthest removed from the main centres of supply, the populous regions of the north east. The contest for invalids coincided, moreover, with an interval of great economic stress in California itself, in large measure the result of the decline in gold-mining and a series of crippling droughts and floods which brought the traditional grazing industry to its knees.[10] This precipitated massive programmes of land subdivision to accompany an energetic campaign aimed at attracting new settlers, yet recent events scarcely justified the promise of a secure and comfortable future and in addition, Californians had to contend with the huge fact that their fellow Americans still knew very little indeed about the distant Pacific state. As Vance has indicated, 'A straightforward economic pull could not suffice; what was needed was the *spatially independent* attraction of the geographical image.'[11] California was therefore promoted as an agricultural paradise and as the land of the restorative climate.

One-Lung Pioneers

One of the most interesting of American responses to California's climate and landscape was the evocation of their 'Mediterranean' aspects.[12] As a peculiarly rich metaphor for all that California had to offer as a regional civilization, 'Mediterreaneanism' proved to be extraordinarily attractive and useful. Quite apart from its literary and artistic utility, the metaphor supplied the state's promoters with a multitude of associations on which they could draw — Greek, Italian, Iberian, French, North African and Middle Eastern. The vine, the very touchstone and common denominator of the analogy, was of course regularly employed as the symbol of civilization, yet at the same time it was redolent with suggestions of historicity. California was new *and* old; past, present and future were blended enticingly for the American palate.

> Each refraction suggested an association which clung to the analogy as a whole. Italy called to the ordering of landscape and the enrichment of daily life. Greece connoted pageantry and art. The desert regions bespoke the mystic. Spain, the most compelling because it arose from history, asked for largeness of purpose, heroism — and romance.[13]

The first notable attempts to explore the Mediterranean metaphor were made in John Charles Frémont's two topographical models, the *Report of the Exploring Expedition to Oregon and North California* (1845) and his *Geographical Memoir Upon Upper California* (1848). Frémont was entirely captivated by the landscape and by the rich variety of produce in the old mission gardens, and he was drawn frequently to comparisons with Italy. Once this type of exploration was launched, however, the unlimited versatility of the metaphor soon became clear. Neglecting the comparatively youthful demographic structure of the state, some authors chose to portray California as one of those mythical lost paradises of antiquity in which fertility and longevity were guaranteed: it was claimed, for example, on dubious statistical grounds, that there was an unusually low incidence of disease, which suggested the presence of environmental conditions profoundly beneficial to mankind. Alternatively, they were at least performing wonders for the most important part of the white race, which was good enough: 'California will be found more conducive to the highest physical and intellectual development of the Anglo-Saxon race, than any other part of the globe'; and again, 'a multitude of instances have occurred of couples who, after having lived childless for ten, fifteen or twenty years in other countries, before coming to California, in a year after their arrival here have had children.'[14] California had everything:

When a northern American visits a tropical country, be it Cuba, Mexico, Brazil, or Central America, he is delighted with the bright skies, the mild climate, the wonderful productiveness of the soil, and the novel customs of the inhabitants; but he is repelled by an enervating atmosphere, by the dread of malarious diseases, by the semi-barbarous habits of the people, and often by a lawless state of society. Moreover, he must leave his own country, and is without the comfort and security he enjoys at home. California is our own; and it is the first tropical land which our race has thoroughly mastered and made itself at home in. There, and there only, on this planet, the traveler and resident may enjoy the delights of the tropics, without their penalties; a mild climate, not enervating, but 'healthful and health-restoring'; a wonderfully and variously productive soil, without tropical malaria; the grandest scenery, with perfect security and comfort in travelling arrangements; strange customs, but neither lawlessness nor semi-barbarism.[15]

The California Immigrant Union, founded by a group of prominent citizens in 1869, established promotional agencies in the eastern states and in Bremen, Copenhagen and Hamburg. The Southern Pacific Railroad Company, with over ten million acres of Californian land at its disposal, publicized the attractions of its region in a new company magazine, *Sunset*, and hired an energetic public relations man, Jerome Madden, to run its land office at Sacramento. Madden produced a steady stream of pamphlets and newspaper articles throughout the 1880s, culminating in 1890 in an interesting promotional tract, *California: its Attractions for the Invalid, Tourist, Capitalist and Homeseeker*. A rate war between the Southern Pacific and Santa Fe Railroad companies, possibly secretly contrived to boost their real estate sales, greatly assisted the development of Southern California. The $125 passenger fare from the Middle West to Los Angeles was successively reduced to a mere $17 and for a time was set at a nominal $1. In addition, voluntary 'state societies' of former Mid-Western residents were organized to write directly to their relatives and friends of the pleasures of California living, and to contribute regular pieces on the Californian climate for the editors of their hometown newspapers in such states as Illinois, Indiana and Ohio. In 1887 alone, over 100,000 immigrants and visitors entered California, supporting and supported by a real estate boom in which a large section of the local community shared indulgently.[16]

With the fear of tuberculosis — the 'Great White Plague' — increasing throughout the nation, it was inevitable that some of the Californian promotion should gradually become more specialized in the related areas of climatotherapy. It was eminently successful in attracting a host of invalids, especially sufferers from pulmonary tuberculosis, to Southern California. At the end of the main period of 'tubercular migration' between 1870 and 1900, contemporary estimates of the number of these invalid immigrants ranged from about eight to seventy-five percent of all the region's inhabitants.[17] The complex morphological expression of health-seeking was shown predominantly in the development of a strong middle-class element in the main 'sanitarium' belt, which stretched from Riverside and San Bernardino in the east along the edge of the San Gabriel range and as far west as Los Angeles and Pasadena, with San Diego and Santa Barbara as outliers.[18] Good railroad connections and well-appointed new hotels enabled the more wealthy invalids to winter in California, and encouraged many of their friends and relatives to visit them, thereby gaining for themselves the bonus of an extended winter holiday tour; poorer invalids crowded into the coastal cities in modest boarding houses and hotels. There were other consequences of what was called 'the health rush', and might have been more aptly entitled 'the health industry'. These included the differentiation, via intense inter-municipal rivalry and pseudo-scientific speculation, of supposed 'health regions'; an increased interest in dietary reform and outdoor living, especially that associated with the growth of Seventh Day Adventist settlements; and the appearance of important new spa centres.

Not unexpectedly there were also earnest efforts to challenge or to clarify the image of health which was originally projected with such unqualified enthusiasm. And, as we shall also see for Victoria, the strongest opposition to the established viewpoint stemmed from the consideration of observations made by local people directly involved in making a living in the boosted environments. This last aspect is best illustrated in the controversy surrounding irrigation and malaria, which provides the material for our next section.

The Appraisal of Health Hazards

Malaria and its associated diseases were extremely common in North America during the nineteenth century, reaching a peak of endemicity around 1870, when new waves of European settlement were reaching California.[19] Contemporary public images regarding the relationship between the natural environment and the incidence of malarial diseases derived from an established medical theory of the day which pointed to the pathogenic role of atmospheric gases or 'miasmata' created by decomposing organic matter. Although its particular correlations were later rejected, the theory was manifestly based on sound empirical observations dating at least from the time of Hippocrates, and there appeared to be no reason to doubt its validity.[20] Unfortunately, however, the fertile bottom lands of California's Central Valley presented a rich source of the dreaded type of 'pollution', and this was one of several important factors which frequently resulted in a negative appraisal of the region; it was therefore avoided by many pioneer settlers. And it was difficult indeed for some professional consultants to lend support to the promotion of arcadian images based on irrigated agriculture. No less a person than the Secretary of the Californian State Board of Health, Dr. Thomas M. Logan, expressed very great concern over the artificial extension of miasmatic conditions by the introduction of irrigation.[21]

Geographical responses to this disease hazard exhibited what we have recently come to accept as the full range of hazard behaviour-types.[22] These included a fatalistic acceptance of what was considered to be the normal or inevitable situation, which meant that immigrants stayed in the hazard zone; renewed mobility, in which cases they moved on to the coast, returned to their original home territory, or went elsewhere in North America or overseas; and positive efforts to neutralize what were perceived to be the dangerous elements in the environment. Allowing for the high degree of optimism which was common enough amongst such enterprising and future-oriented communities, the latter type of behaviour displayed almost as much logic as the original cognition of the disease. Arguments supporting this position stated that certain plants should be used as purifying agents — citrus groves, orchards, grain crops and eucalyptus plantations were all expected to reduce the hazard. In so far as they reduced or destroyed the breeding grounds of the mosquitoes this was perfectly true, of course, and the results of several experiments of this type naturally appeared to prove the point. The adventurous introduction of Australian eucalyptus trees is however a particularly interesting example in the special context of the present chapter: California and Victoria maintained close contact at private and official levels during the latter half of the nineteenth century, and there is no doubt that advice on the prophylactic properties of the eucalyptus was obtained directly from the Australian colony.[23]

The confusion over irrigation was not fully resolved until the turn of the century, but the balance usually favoured 'progressive' expansion. Engineers and agriculturalists who comprised the most influential proponents of irrigation either ignored the warnings of fellow experts, acknowledged them but adopted a neutral stance, or positively argued that well-regulated systems of irrigation necessarily involved improved drainage facilities, the clearing and replacement of the original offensive vegetation and the more efficient use of waste water. One very convinced engineer offered the happy observation that female figures had shown a marked improvement in California's irrigated districts.[24] Spurred on by the promise of such a splendid future, the developers ignored the nagging opposition and steadily extended their irrigated area.

Australia as Resort[25]

Environmental differences between Great Britain and Australia were always a source of speculation, but occasionally a mutually attractive interpretation was accepted and it functioned as a vital component in the processes of emigration and settlement. One example of this was a neoclassical interpretation of the connection between climate and health which led to an assertion that the Australian climate provided the most effective cure for 'consumption', pthisis or tuberculosis.

Until the contagious nature of tuberculosis was indicated by Jean Villemin in the late 1860s, and until the subsequent discovery of the tubercle bacillus by Robert Koch in 1882, the search for 'the cure' was often frantic, for tuberculosis was reputedly the major cause of death in Britain and in most of Western Europe throughout the nineteenth century. Frequently, medical authorities cited the favoured environmental theories of the classical writers to support propositions that were at worst fanciful and at best dubious — but they were, above all, articulations of hope. The popularity of open-air recreation in Great Britain, for example, was certainly the product of a changing economy, of concomitant alterations in social stratification and behaviour, and of improved transportation, but the special promotional role of a few notable doctors can also be identified. John Fothergill advised his patients to winter on the south coast and to sail to Lisbon; Richard Russell's research into the curative effects of seawater on the diseases of the glands boosted the growth of coastal 'health resorts'; and Ebenezer Gilchrist, drawing on Pliny, Celsus, and other familiar classical authors, distinguished the particular qualities of sea voyages in the treatment of consumption.[26] Later, one of Queen Victoria's physicians, Sir James Clark, whose influence was pervasive, international and durable, announced the benefits of lengthy visits to certain European resorts for tubercular patients.[27]

The promotional activities of Clark and his contemporaries were imitated by other professionals, and the industry thus spawned transformed the social and economic character of many regions. On the margins of Europe and far beyond, the concurrent promotion of overseas travel was just as successful, although the results were different.

The discovery and exploration of extensive areas with apparently favourable climates was welcomed by the British medical profession, and a small but important group of ailing voyagers and sojourners was added to the increasing flow of emigrants to the New World. For Australia, the cult of the ocean voyage contributed to a new appraisal: its remote location was said to offer the invalid a long and beneficial voyage, and the reports then being issued suggested in particular that the southern regions of the continent might prove to be genuine havens to accelerate the recovery of British consumptives.[28]

In the 1820s and 1830s several of the most prestigious British medical journals carried correspondence relating to the extraordinary absence of common ailments in the transplanted population of New South Wales and Van Diemen's Land (now Tasmania). *The Lancet*, a leading London medical journal, sometimes added to the attractiveness of these letters by its choice of headings. One issue boldly proclaimed 'The Healthiness of New South Wales', as an introduction to a letter reporting the absence of all epidemic diseases except catarrh, and of the principal children's diseases such as measles and whooping cough.[29] Ten years later (1837–8) the same journal announced a letter from a ship's surgeon thus: 'Uselessness of Medical Men in Australia'. The correspondent introduced in this rather flippant fashion insisted that the Australian colonists enjoyed the 'finest climate in the world' and, since they also had excellent working and living conditions, their health was 'of the highest order'. His major purpose, it seems, was to warn British doctors against going there: the adventurous medico should at least be sure to obtain a contract guaranteeing him a return passage, for he would scarcely be needed in the colonies — 'If he do not do this, he must become a clerk, or a cattle driver; or he must starve.'[30]

Some of *The Lancet*'s readers may have become better disposed towards Australia during the 1820s and 1830s, when major decisions were made for that continent by a handful of politicians and administrators in Britain. It is just possible that the transmission of highly favourable medical information may have helped to influence the emergence of British policy encouraging free emigation to the formerly convict-ridden antipodes. The same could be said for the more fanciful snippets which increased the appeal of Edward Gibbon Wakefield's persuasive writings on colonization: the conscious or unwitting assertions, based on unrepresentative data, which effectively disguised a want of firsthand experience.[31] So Wakefield drew upon a few contemporary works to dismiss Australia's minor health problems as an unfortunate but strictly temporary condition, requiring better 'adaptation'. And in *A Letter from Sydney* he chose to ascribe the unusual health and beauty of the first generation of Australians to the direct and indirect influence of soil and climate: they were surely reincarnated Greeks, who suffered only from prematurely decayed teeth, the result of a continuance of their low-bred English ways.[32]

High-ranking administrators and prominent members in the leading medical circles pointed to the dangers of easy and confident generalizations based on so little factual information. In 1829, the same year in which *A Letter from Sydney* appeared, a report to the Royal College of Physicians claimed that consumption in Australia was actually more common 'than from the mildness of the climate might be expected, and more in advanced life suffer from this disease than in England . . . In people who arrive in this colony labouring under this complaint it runs a much more rapid course than it is observed to do in colder climates.'[33] This claim proved to be merely an honest scholarly judgement removed from the wider web of communication, and it had no effect on the development of a regular cruising service of invalid ships along the Great Atlantic Circle Route to the antipodes. After Wakefield's arguments had helped to convert the politicians to the opportunities and necessities of colonization, increasing numbers of consumptive emigrants chose Australia as their new home. They had already heard about its advantages and could now command the blessing and the material support of the British government in establishing what they hoped would be — almost literally — a new life.

During the gradual implementation of some modified versions of Wakefield's systematic colonization, the professionals continued their practical medical education. Colonial doctors guided by field experience probably made greater strides than their British colleagues did, for an unusual degree of participant observation was afforded by the presence of a large number of medical men who had emigrated mainly to cure their own consumptive condition. But over this period the limited and varied experience of the individual doctors, the initial lack of formal institutions for communication between them, the absence of reliable local statistics and the general misconceptions about consumption, resulted in different attitudes toward the disease. Consumption was believed to be rare among the locally born population before the start of gold mining in 1851, and a myth arose that satisfied professionals and laymen alike: a 'native immunity' to tuberculosis was presumed to be established in the southern regions of the continent. After familiarity with colonial conditions increased, this heresy was successfully contested and was abandoned by most local practitioners during the 1850s, when it was proven that tuberculosis had emerged not only in native-born whites but also in full-blood

Aborigines.[34] Firsthand knowledge of consumptive immigrants suggested to many doctors that the environmental characteristics of hot summers and rapid diurnal temperature fluctuations in all seasons actually accelerated the deterioration of their patients' health.

As our third chapter related, Britain experienced a flood of popular literary works concerning Australia in the 1840s and early 1850s. This swept aside the cautionary statements supplied by those in Australia who were learning their lessons the hard way. In addition, the excitement generated by the gold rushes in the colony of Victoria in the 1850s appears to have distracted many of the most gifted locals from the pursuit of further scientific investigations into the link between climate and health. For the majority of Australians it also reduced the impact of some significant disclaimers then being forcefully presented. British novelists and travel writers 'discovered' the Australian frontier, often without leaving their own firesides, and the colonization business prospered in the new imagery. Prospective emigrants were thereby enlisted or encouraged, and even the toiling settlers were comforted and bemused. The romantic dream of novelty, comfort, and independence was presented as a plausible and accessible reality, and so it possessed a strong selling capacity. 'Elysium', 'Eldorado' and 'Arcadia' combined as a powerful triumvirate.

No major voice disturbed this euphoria, even though Lancelott's *Australia As It Is* demonstrated that the 'paradise' actually demanded extremely hard work, that the climate promised kidney, liver, and other gastric disorders, ophthalmia, and numerous skin afflictions, and that it could do nothing to cure the consumptive immigrant unless he arrived when the disease was in its earliest stages.[35] Although the message was lost to the public at large, major sections of this interesting book were deliberately directed at an involved, professional readership which may have been more impressed by the content than the style. For those in Great Britain whose investment in the colonies was intricately entwined with matters of health, rather than solely with economic conditions and prospects, works such as Lancelott's advised a cautious approach to the romantic literature, the lure of the goldfields and the confident predictions of the emigrants' guides. Significantly, British life insurance companies, for example, were unusually reluctant to commit themselves heavily in the Australian market. In the mid 1850s this mood of caution, shown also in the small volume of business, was associated with considerable intercompany and intracompany disagreements, and was reflected in the varied rates and conditions attached to insurance policies for Australian residents.[36] As the population soared during the mining boom it became even more imperative that efficient insurance operators should clarify the confused impression of Australia, but the only relevant correspondence in *The Lancet* merely emphasized the continuing dilemma and warned prospective emigrants not to underestimate the disadvantages of the Australian environment. In a forceful letter, John Webster, physician to the North British Insurance Company, reported the dangers and discomforts of long sea voyages and of conditions on the gold diggings, and he stressed the high mortality rate caused by heart attacks, influenza, scarlet fever, dysentery, ophthalmia, and liver complaints. Despite the much-vaunted clear skies of Australia, 'the climate is much less favourable to health and longevity than cool, wet England, with her pea-soup London fogs'. Consequently, Webster advised, 'wherever life insurance offices calculate New South Wales risks as ordinary business, they are most likely to be mistaken, and will ultimately find such policies become unusually hazardous'.[37] Clearly, the image of Australia as a resort had not been universally accepted.

Climate and Tuberculosis: Dr. Bird's Diagnosis

As the golden 1850s dimmed, each of the Australian colonies, then enjoying responsible government, embarked on its own vigorous campaigns to attract new immigrants and to establish the former miners and their service population on Crown lands. By that time, the emigrants' guides and settlers' handbooks could draw on a wide range of official statistics to paint the rosy picture even brighter and, for the majority of Britons, the ambiguity of the preceding years appeared to be more or less resolved. According to these publications, each colony was a veritable Eden, where unusually sturdy children could be raised by happy and healthy parents who were safely removed from European penury and stagnation.

The guidebooks took many forms. One that was directly aimed at the medical profession was entitled *On Australasian Climates and Their Influence in the Prevention and Arrest of Pulmonary Consumption*.[38] The author, Dr. Samuel Dougan Bird, credited his own recovery from tuberculosis to the Australian environment. Apart from its favourable promotion of Australia, the main distinction of the book was its lucid and informed summation of authoritative contemporary views on the pathology of tuberculosis. Bird's emphasis on the 'temperament' and 'constitutional predisposition' of the patient has in fact been regarded as one of the last great formal expressions of the 'humours' theory before its rejection by Pasteur and others late in the century. Whatever the shortcomings of his treatise, Bird's insistence that consumption was not simply a local condition, restricted to the lungs, is to his credit. He demonstrated that consumption was part of a general process of morbidity, so that the common therapeutic practices aimed at only one area of the body (bleeding, starving, the use of counterirritants, and so forth) merely treated the most obvious symptoms and did not attack the critical features of the disease itself. Certain types of climate, diet, and moderate exercise — the ancient trio — were prescribed again as the foundation of a new regimen for the invalid. And Bird's interpretation also provided a fresh, locational aspect: the unique advantages of an extensive and little-known territory.

Although he acknowledged Sir James Clark's early lead in medical-climatological research, Bird argued against the fashionable pre-occupation of British doctors with the relative ranking of European health resorts. Their attention to the nature of the disease itself, he said, had been insufficient. He offered the thesis that the following elements were necessary for any change in climate to have a curative effect:

> That it should have an alterative action so complete and powerful that it will open not only a new leaf, but a new volume in the patient's constitutional history; and so change and modify the course of his vital functions, and more particularly the operation of his glandular and secreting system, that the probability of his blood again assuming the conditions under which tubercle was first formed will be very remote.[39]

Bird then proceeded to reject the climates of various countries favoured by the Europeans; in fact, the only localities that could meet his standards were small sectors of the eastern coast of Spain and the Mediterranean coast of Africa. He could not resist pointing out that even in these areas the summer heat was probably far too oppressive.[40]

Australasia could offer much better climates and Victoria was the most suitable colony, according to Bird, for the rehabilitation of tuberculosis sufferers, since it was generally cooler than South Australia, Queensland, and New South Wales, and warmer and drier than Tasmania and most of New Zealand. Melbourne's mean annual temperature provided a good comparison with the plush resorts of Nice, Montpellier, Marseille, Genoa, and Florence, yet its annual range was much smaller and the occasional sudden changes in temperature so characteristic of southern Victoria were said to be particularly stimulating. To justify some comparisons with Great Britain, Bird demonstrated that the population of Victoria was similar to those of the fast-growing ports of London and Liverpool — certainly in terms of racial mixture, occupations, and the (supposed or suspected) hereditary predispositions to tuberculosis. With regard to sex and age structure, however, the Victorian population was actually more dangerously placed, since the disease was then known to be far more common in young adults between the ages of twenty and forty, chiefly among males. In 1863 Victoria probably did have a 'more susceptible' population, for it had only recently (in 1836) been officially opened for settlement, and had experienced a major influx of immigrants during the recent mining boom.[41] Bird could also have emphasized that some of the special occupational hazards faced by Victoria's large mining population might have increased the number of certain types of tuberculosis cases, but subsequent research indicated that other occupations were hit much harder.

On the basis of his superficial but generally accepted statistics Bird showed that whereas in England twenty percent of all deaths resulted from tuberculosis, Victoria's proportion was a mere seven percent. He also disposed of the argument that migration had been deliberately selective of certain stronger types of people, pointing out that for some time a broad cross section of British society had been represented.

The book enjoyed enthusiastic reviews in the British medical press. *The Lancet* was greatly impressed with the plethora of statistics and declared that Bird's effort would easily win the highest place in the medical literature of the colonies for its clear and practical exposition of the relationship between the local climate and consumption.

> As regards the climate of the great Australian continent . . . we have hitherto been without any precise information. Beyond a general idea that it was a country of sheep, kangaroos, gold-diggers, wild cattle, and still wilder bushrangers, our notions of the great colony have been rather vague . . . One can readily conceive this [Victoria's] to be a climate peculiarly adapted for the permanent residence of a phthisical patient, with a marked superiority over that of our most esteemed winter resorts of Southern Europe, which, graceful and salubrious though they may be in winter, are intolerable in summer.[42]

In 1865 Isaac Baker Brown's *Australia for the Consumptive Invalid* appeared.[43] Brown agreed with Bird's general hypothesis but modified the three ancient requirements. He emphasized change, a long sea voyage, and a desirable climate, ranked strictly in that order. He insisted that the climatic factor had been overrated, and he fumed at Bird's careless recommendations. The large number of immigrants suffering from advanced consumption who were visited by Brown in the Melbourne and Adelaide hospitals profoundly alarmed him, and he appealed to British doctors not to expect too much of the Australian climate.

Brown's slim volume was completely overshadowed by its predecessor at every level of readership, however, and most of the medical journals chose not to review it.[44] Nor did its direct rebuke of Bird's promotional efforts encourage more than a ripple in the correspondence columns in the late 1860s. In fact, the only other professional queries raised at this time against the idea of Australia as a resort for consumptives drew on the health records of the Imperial troops — an ever-ready set of data which was open to conflicting interpretations. The best example of this was a strong protest in *The Lancet* which illustrated that British soldiers appeared to suffer equally from the disease no matter where they were stationed. This point was not pursued, either in later issues of the same journal or in the remainder of the medical press, partly because *The Lancet* editor printed his own simple rejoinder that, where the Australian example was concerned, the troops' complaint did not after all *originate* in that country, and that overcrowded barracks and other unhealthy conditions normal to the military life scarcely made the analysis representative.[45]

Calling for Second Opinions: Victoria, 1870

Bird's book accelerated the trend towards the permanent settlement of consumptive invalids in Australia, particularly in Victoria, even though the transient trade continued. As the capital and most prosperous and rapidly growing centre of Victoria, Melbourne naturally received the largest proportion of consumptive immigrants. Repeated rejections of Bird's theory were clearly and urgently enunciated by a growing number of colonial practitioners, but these opinions were usually ignored by British journals. Large numbers of British doctors chose to live in Victoria in the 1850s and 1860s because they suffered from tuberculosis; later, the preponderance of middle-class consumptives appears to have been replaced by the immigration of working-class invalids and their families who were granted assisted passages by the confident Victorian government.

It is not yet clear how the diffusion of information influencing these decisions actually took place in British society, but the emergence of public and private benevolent institutions concerned with public health and poverty must have provided new channels of communication. Most of the Australian colonies were then campaigning in Great Britain for settlers, and it probably seemed likely that consumptive emigrants would find secure employment in the new territory.[46] So British workers swelled the ranks of consumptive emigrants in the 1860s and 1870s. In the same period innovative legislation for tariff protection, factory conditions, pioneer settlement and free public education gave Victoria an early lead in industrialization, massive growth in small-scale wheat and sheep farming, and an attractive and civilized social order for the working man. The result was a substantial increase in its population, which soon exceeded that of any of the other Australian colonies. The consumptive immigrant seeking a cure had no reason to look beyond Victoria.[47]

Now one of the most effective ways to undermine successful promotion is 'bad publicity'. Although a few doctors with experience in Melbourne openly questioned the wisdom of Bird's theory and its disturbing repercussions on a form of selective immigration, the fate of the consumptive immigrant did not become an issue until 1870, when a leading metropolitan newspaper, *The Age*, launched a bitter campaign against the unguarded practice of shipping out tuberculosis victims to Victoria. The catalyst for the campaign was provided in the death of a 29-year-old consumptive, Edward Denison, the Member of Parliament for Newark, son of the late Bishop of Salisbury and nephew of the Speaker of the House of Commons — only eleven days after he arrived to 'take the cure'. *The Age* saw it as a national tragedy, the last straw of a scandalous and drawn-out affair, which colonial practitioners with humanity and good sense should halt immediately. A stinging editorial announced that public interest would be reawakened

to the practice which has been long in existence of sending consumptive patients out to this country, under the expectation of their recovery by that means from the attacks of this most insidious disease. The profession, that is, at least, its more capable and impartial members, feel that a cruel imposition on the patient and a gross injustice to the climate of this country are perpetrated by those medical advisers in the United Kingdom who, when the consumptive cases in their hands become hopeless, have recourse to the charlatanism of sending the sufferers out here on a tedious voyage across the world, with the fallacious impression that the change will likely cause their cure. And the public, who are enlightened enough to sympathise with the profession in this matter, share their indignant feelings. It is seen that this portion of Australia, instead of getting the reputation for a healthy climate that is its due, will, by-and-by, become in the eyes of the British public the most unsalubrious country under the sun. The reason is plain. Almost every consumptive patient that comes out here from the United Kingdom, after a short residence in the country, dies . . . Repeated incidences of this kind occurring will, in the long run, produce the impression in Europe that Melbourne, and the region of Australia in which it is situated, are most unsalubrious, and the last place that a person suffering to the least extent in his health should go to, if he wishes to prolong his days.[48]

Whether *The Age* was more concerned with the good name of Victoria or with the fate of the invalids is not important here. The storm it raised in local medical circles reverberated widely, despite the support Bird received from powerful social and professional coteries, including the prestigious Medical Society of Victoria. *The Age* continued its crusade against 'the unfeeling barbarity that banishes from home and friends the dying victims of a yet unscientific medicine'[49] and opened its columns to Dr. William Thomson and other colonial researchers whose work had convinced them of the validity of the germ theory and the contagion principle.[50] And it provided an excellent forum for the views of gifted colonial statisticians, who now chose to enter the debate.

The Image and the Enumerator, 1870–1880

The large-scale entry of infected immigrants into the Australian population presented an excellent opportunity for empirical research to evaluate the contesting views on tuberculosis and its connection with climate. The available statistics confirmed William Thomson's suspicions: tuberculosis was the most frequent cause of death in Victoria in the 1860s and had risen markedly since the first registration of these data in 1853. In 1863, when Bird's book appeared, tuberculosis mortality in Greater Melbourne was 24 per 10,000 population, similar to the rate for England and Wales. The apparent improvement in 1871 was probably attributable to the inclusion of a wider variety of supposedly related diseases in the earlier statistics. Even though no actual improvement took place, it could be shown that whereas the rate for native-born Victorians was only 2.4 per 10,000, it was almost 19 per 10,000, calculated on the same basis, for the remainder of the population born outside the colony.[51] Encouraged by the potential significance of distinguishing these special characteristics, Thomson inaugurated his own intensive research project for the investigation of consumption in Victoria. But in the same period new government schemes were independently devised for the systematic collection of a formidable array of mortality data. The content and quality of this information far surpassed similar types of data collection in the rest of Australasia, and its particular contribution to the successful challenge of the specialized image of the Victorian environment merits brief consideration.

Each Australian colony devised, manipulated, and often drastically changed its own systems of statistical collection. Indeed, it is exceedingly difficult to discover any reasonable uniformity between the statistical records of Australia's different political units, except at the crudest level of analysis, before the Census and Statistics Act of 1905, four years after Federation. Some colonies chose to record causes of death simply by broad groups of diseases; some published the data only

for hospitals and prisons; others released information only in-
termittently. It is therefore more than fortunate that Henry Heylyn
Hayter, Victoria's government statist from 1874 to 1895, chose to
investigate the incidence of phthisis with all his great skill and vigour.
One of Hayter's major tasks was the publication of reliable comparative data gleaned from regular communications with his counterparts
elsewhere in Australia and New Zealand. In 1874 he instituted the
Victorian Year Book as an official inventory and authoritative annual
guide. The potential utility of the 'Vital Statistics' section of that
compendium obviously attracted him. While he strove to accumulate
relevant material for the local professionals, he also grasped the need to
communicate with a broader audience. His succinct statements on the
incidence of consumption, in particular, showed a solid understanding
of its nature and provided good material for the press. Like Thomson,
he was inclined to iconoclasm. Above all, he ridiculed the repeated folly
of crude comparisons between Great Britain and Victoria and
recommended the equally simple but vastly more significant correlation between Melbourne alone and the whole of England, in order
to avoid the obvious errors associated with the different degrees of
crowding, occupational structure and so on, between the colony and
homeland.[52]

In any bustling young colony, a statistician would have complex
problems in attempting to isolate the essential characteristics of a
disease over which even the medical fraternity was becoming deeply
divided. Hayter's decison to produce separate tables for Melbourne was
valuable for those who favoured the contagion theory; in Greater
Melbourne and its suburbs the mean death rate from phthisis between
1873 and 1875 was shown to be 21.4 per 10,000, compared with 22.1 in
England and Wales. But he also indicated that the large numbers of
consumptive immigrants, for whom no special data were gathered,
might swell the Melbourne total inordinately. The early *Victorian Year
Books* continued to display comparisons between Victoria and England
and Wales but always distinguished the unfavourable ratio for the
Victorian capital. Later, Hayter's statistical correlations between
nativity and mortality finally rejected the 'native immunity' hypothesis
and greatly strengthened the anti-Bird faction.[53]

The Image in Exile, 1880–1901

Victoria's image as a resort for consumptives declined in the last two
decades of the nineteenth century, but fresh waves of medical
promotion emanating from Great Britain offered a useful smoke screen,

which allowed the image to reappear in disguise and to seek refuge in less controversial and less accessible locations. The new period of confusion was heralded by the publication of Dr. William S. Wilson's *The Ocean as Health Resort* (London, 1880). This offered a comprehensive and attractive guide for voyages to all parts of the globe and celebrated once more, in an immensely popular and practical fashion, the curative influence of comfortable sea travel upon all sorts of diseases, tuberculosis included. The book breathed new life into that part of Bird's theory which emphasized the voyage, and like the Californian promotion, resuscitated the flagging concern with medical climatology. Directly and indirectly, it also rekindled the notion of therapeutic emigration.

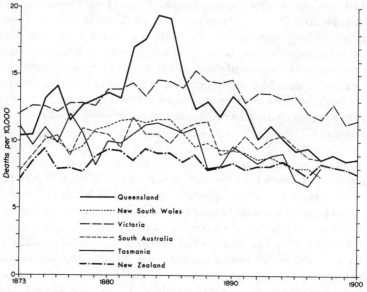

Fig 13   Death rates from tuberculosis, 1873–1900. (Sources: *Victorian Year Books*, relevant dates) Earlier rates for Victoria, not displayed here, were calculated differently: in the 1850s and 1860s the range was probably between 12.0 and 15.0 deaths per 10,000 population. Blanks on the graph reflect the incomplete information in the later years for some colonies. The trend for Queensland is deceptive, in so far as it reflected a relatively small population characterized by large numbers of highly susceptible Pacific Islanders who were 'imported' to work on the sugar plantations.

Taking their lead from some European literature favouring those inland resorts which dated from Sir James Clark's earliest endeavours in the promotion field, descriptive writings on Australia in the 1880s and 1890s emphasized the potentials for new *sanitaria* in the higher altitudes.[54] The 'exhalations from our boundless eucalyptus forests' were said to effect marvellous cures, and the 'mountain air in Australia' was proclaimed a 'real miracle worker'. Established predilections for town life should be abandoned, and the harassed invalid should choose somewhere like the southern part of the Great Dividing Range, Queensland's Atherton Plateau, or the Blue Mountains west of Sydney.

> Away up on the tablelands of the interior . . . where there is an equable bracing atmosphere, the consumptive patient rallies rapidly, appetite and strength are restored and renewed, the hectic flush disappears, the hacking cough ceases, and the racking pain is quickly alleviated by the fine, temperate, bracing mountain air of Australia . . . 'Away, away, to the mountain's brow!' should be their cry.[55]

Koch's experimental proof of the specificity and transmissibility of tuberculosis was completed in 1882, but the full implications of his discovery were not widely diffused and accepted until the end of the decade. The varied forms of treatment that resulted from this work were reported in several issues of the *Australian Medical Journal* for 1891 and this led to the successful testing of the new model in the local situation. Sanitaria were then already established in various inland centres of Victoria, usually in the highlands. Most patients came from Melbourne, but Hayter still deemed it essential for the *Year Books* to continue to carry the message that the attributes of the local environment were incorrectly evaluated in Great Britain. An unequivocal denial of the elementary insistence on climatic therapy in the treatment of consumption was published in the 1890–1 *Year Book*, which accommodated an abridged version of the recent report on the prevention of the disease prepared by the pathologists of the Health Department of New York City. This forthright document, a landmark in the history of municipal public health, insisted that the principle on which all preventative measures should be based was that 'a living germ, called the tubercle bacillus, is the cause, and the only cause'.[56] During the early years of the present century, modern forms of treatment based upon isolation, rest and improved nutrition in well-administered *sanatoria* became established.[57] As the old image of the disease was abandoned, so too was the idea of therapeutic emigration and migration.

At no time were details kept of the actual number of consumptive immigrants who entered Victoria: accurate diagnosis of the disease was then quite impossible, and only the most cursory medical examination was ever required by immigration officials. No evidence of any considered move by the authorities to monitor the situation is known, but it was an exaggeration to claim that the immigrants were 'the exported victims of a theory'. Yet something much deeper is implicit here. Like all misconceptions about the Australian environment, Bird's simple hypothesis was most successfully challenged by the colonists' evaluation of their own experiences. Had it not been for Thomson, Hayter and other sympathetic thinkers, and for the opportunism of a crusading newspaper, the chances are that the government of Victoria might have added the full weight of its own successful promotional efforts to cast the net even wider among the consumptives of Europe. But the colony really did have a great deal to offer to *all* those who sought better futures, whatever their state of health, and it is perhaps only mildly disturbing to note that the good intentions of a small group of image-makers may have been marginally instrumental in making some of those new lives briefer than they might otherwise have been.

> Since the days of the cave man, the earth has never been a Garden of Eden, but a Valley of Decision where resilience is essential to survival. The earth is not a resting place. Man has elected to fight, not necessarily for himself, but for a process of emotional, intellectual and ethical growth that goes on forever.[58]

The boosting of both California and Victoria as unique bases for various types of 'climato-therapy' was closely associated with responses to urbanization and industrialization in the Western World. But the Victorian example exhibited strong international linkages of people and ideas in an imperial setting, whereas developments in California were always far more intimately connected with specific transformations in America's own national scene. California was regarded as a final frontier, 'of geography and of expectation'; it therefore became a 'symbol of renewal', urgently and variously employed by most sectors of American society.[59] The Victorian experience was quite different in its breadth and intensity. Yet in both examples, though more markedly so in the Californian case, the distinction between medical promotion *per se* and the broader evocation of the Arcadian ideal is difficult to draw: indeed, these two images were mutually dependent in the situations described here. Furthermore, crucial types of environmental appraisal for each region were similarly based on neo-classical explanations of the nature of disease, and in California as in Victoria it is possible to discern again the important contributions of key individuals and groups towards this influential debate over man's relationship with nature.

For the most part, the early conquest of endemic and epidemic diseases resulted from campaigns for pure water, pure food and pure air, and these campaigns were based as much on a philosophical faith as on scientific doctrine. In Britain and Western Europe, and subsequently in North America and Australasia, the nineteenth century saw the rise of humanitarian movements dedicated to the eradication of the social ills of the Industrial Revolution and a recapturing of the goodness of life in harmony with the ways of nature. Long before the arrival of the germ theory and the doctrine of specific etiology, earnest champions of 'Public Hygiene' achieved a phenomenal improvement in living conditions for the mass of the people and thereby drastically reduced the frightening toll exacted by Western man's most feared diseases.

The battle with disease is obviously a primary theme in man's continuing exploration of himself and his relationship with his evolving habitat. In this respect as in each of our other examples, the New World presented an unusually varied array of uncharted landscapes of threat and opportunity which radically altered the scale and complexity of the great Valley of Decision. As always, desperation, plain courage and blind optimism blazed the new trails, with vision, greed and compassion lending a hand. If resilience has been the essential ingredient of survival, then it is an acquired trait, and its analysis must be social and historical, as well as biological: 'To grow in the midst of dangers is the fate of the human race, because it is the law of the spirit.'[60]

6

Utopia, Millennium and the
Co-operative Ideal[1]

A map of the world that does not include Utopia is not worth even glancing
at, for it leaves out the one country at which Humanity is always landing.
And when Humanity lands there, it looks out, and, seeing a better country,
sets sail. Progress is the realisation of Utopias.[2]

Man, we have argued, is indeed the incomparable Amphibium,
possessing the unique capacity to act simultaneously upon a number of
worlds which are different, yet not really divided.[3] The recent spate of
behavioural and perception studies in human geography has produced
a much clearer picture of the several worlds which man inhabits, but the
evidence of our earlier chapters suggests that one basic point has still to
receive adequate emphasis: put simply, it could be said that the ideas,
ideals and institutions of society must be considered as indispensable
elements in the behavioural matrix which the geographer seeks to
reconstruct and evaluate; that the social milieu, like the natural
environment, is differentially perceived. This final set of case studies
deliberately seeks to sharpen the humanistic focus by drawing upon the
extraordinarily rich body of literature concerning two principal
motivating forces, utopianism and millenarism, which have had a
lasting and universal appeal in the processes of settlement evolution.

Utopia, the Impelling Vision

Since it was first coined by Thomas More in 1516, the term 'utopia' has
become utterly debased in the vernacular. It was intended to mean
'nowhere', simply that; but it is now commonly defined as 'an
impracticable scheme of social regeneration' and the utopian is seen as
an idealist, or even an incurable optimist. Indisputably, the utopia

represents one of man's noblest aspirations and one of his greatest reservoirs of experience.[4]

The writings of the utopists have had an amazing influence in stimulating men to dream of a better world, and in prodding them into action. The utopist is far more than a satirist, and he is not simply a reformer or a theorist; nor is he merely a dreamer. Utopia is a very special form of literary expression: a world of fiction, which if successful will capture the minds of millions — many of whom would never be so inspired by any other form of writing. But although it is fictional, the author's feet are firmly on the ground. For his readers, the faults in the utopist's own *real* society are highlighted by comparison with the better world he describes: the conjured vision is recognizable, as required, for utopia has a purpose. Utopias are therefore appropriate to their own historical period, but their authors give full reign to their imagination by choosing a fictional presentation, and some of the most effective of these writings incorporate an effort to escape from all the restraints of period and location. A few utopias, however, closely resemble some favoured society of the past, and in these cases at least, 'nowhere' was certainly 'somewhere'.[5]

The eternal appeal of utopia has varied in strength through the ages. The great revival of utopianism during the Renaissance, for example, reflected the rise in humanism and naturalism which accompanied the decline of the medieval ideal of a static, divinely-sanctioned international order. Utopia had been transplanted to the sky and called the Kingdom of Heaven, but the will to utopia remained as the idea itself lost much of its practical hold. The rise of the monastic systems and the attempts of the great Popes to establish a universal empire under the Church's dominion show that there was still a breach between valued mental images and the real facts of human existence and institutional compulsions.[6] The Kingdom of Heaven as a utopia of escape ceased to hold men's allegiance when they discovered other channels, alternative opportunities. More's worldly *Utopia* was in fact the first expression of the new age; together with a number of Italian writings, it commenced a tradition of humanist utopias linked to a renewed study of the classics.

Some of these works resembled Plato's *Republic*, in so far as they were mainly concerned with universal ideals of the philosophical and theoretical basis of a state. Others were more practical, offering 'model' constructions for national and local application, but as inputs into the ideological system the two types are not so easily separated. Some common themes which attracted utopists between the Renaissance and the seventeenth century were the value of military order, communism, the importance of scientific and technical education, the 'natural right' of every human being to the possession of the land and the consequent abolition of private property. More and others tempered their communistic views with a humanist stress on the natural virtues and the family homestead set within a pleasant agrarian-based society. A few writers collected the best of the contemporary ideas on environmental management, and they offered impressive word pictures of future landscapes with planned green belts and the separation of industrial and residential sectors—beautifully constructed verbal butterfly nets, which still caught the imagination of a more responsive readership generations later.[7]

From the seventeenth to the nineteenth centuries, communitarian ideals were specially favoured by the utopists. They described a decentralized society which would assist the achievement of what was called 'individual perfectibility', notably by discarding most of the institutions of orthodox religion, law, politics and economics. The nineteenth century was particularly significant in these respects. Compared with the early period of utopist activity, it was manifestly a new age in its own right, at least for Western societies: a technical, mechanized world was visibly being despoiled by man; it was an age of dismal realities and great possibilities, including a New World of vast resources in which it was quite possible to consider the production of a completely different order of things, without escaping to some remote corner. Utopia *could* therefore be imminent. It was not an impractical, impossible notion. Not surprisingly, about two-thirds of our utopias were written in that remarkable century, and before they changed in form they encouraged a spate of settlement mutations.

In Europe and especially in North America, hundreds of groups broke away to form 'experimental utopias', each group influenced by some favoured vision of the future. Utopian principles formed the structure of the drama, set the scene and drafted the dialogue; the inspired communities provided the actors. After the fashions of their separate guidelines most of the groups were self-sufficient and self-contained to a large degree, and they depended on the fundamental values of artisanship, co-operation or some form of communitarianism, the family base and natural piety. Yet the simple ideals expounded in the utopist writings could never be widely achieved in the increasing pace of industrialization and urbanization. The description of strange, remote and 'unknown' societies, perhaps on uncharted islands, was a frequent literary motif; but the elementary geographical isolation which was apparently essential for the preservation of the fictional communities had become far too unreal by the mid-point of that era of progress. Thereafter it could only be conceived as a fantastic literary device, and as a form of utopian expression it declined considerably in power.

Towards the end of the nineteenth century the utopists made a fresh assault. The new breed returned to the original emphasis upon institutional structures in a highly centralized complex. But, whereas the earliest writers had expected that either religion or science would provide the force and binding thread of centralized organization, the utopias of the late nineteenth and early twentieth centuries described the centralization of *economic activity* within society. In a period of unrestrained individualism and free enterprise, they were clearly anticipating nationalization and the welfare state. And, while the image-making of its antecedents had inspired the withdrawal of many groups who sought to build entirely new communities, the utopist literature of the late nineteenth century was almost non-fictional, for it was aimed more or less directly at reconstruction. Again, whereas the medieval thinkers seemed to believe that nothing could be done to rectify institutions while individuals themselves were so easily corrupted, their successors made the opposite error and forgot about the men, the primary actors in the drama. If we omit the machinery or institutionalization for the 'good life', too many of the utopias of this later period do seem to be quite inhuman. Our most recent satirical utopias attacked this type of process as it really emerged, and alerted us once more to the dangers.[8]

But related to these trends were the 'partisan utopias' which chose to espouse specific goals, rather than the rebuilding of society as a whole — prohibition, for instance, and proportional representation and several aspects of socialism.[9] One good example could be mentioned here. The numerous writings of Henry George, the 'prophet of San Francisco', together with the emotional appeal of his successful international lecture tours, captured the minds of working-class people and liberal politicians throughout the English-speaking world. His 'single tax' philosophy added articulation and direction to the emerging views on land settlement which dominated the life and times of the young democracies of Australia and New Zealand, and this assisted in accelerating the momentous decisions to substitute new principles of leasing for the consuming ideal of the small freehold.[10]

The less extreme forms of co-operation became increasingly institutionalized during this later period and may therefore be judged less significant as formal 'behavioural responses'. Geographers might look more carefully, however, into the rise of the Co-operative Wholesale Society as a global organization. The C.W.S. developed manufacturing, retailing and farming interests in scores of countries, supported by millions of predominantly working-class subscribers. At the national and regional levels there were other related innovations which transformed the cultural geography of their respective areas. The Canadian government permitted and encouraged the entry of certain co-operative and communistic groups from Europe, and Australia and New Zealand, those great 'laboratories of social experiment' in the latter half of the nineteenth century, passed special legislation to facilitate the settlement of religious and national groups. But in these latter countries State sponsorship and control quickly became the norm, and the spontaneity of genuine group settlement was far less common than in North America. On the other hand, it is an important characteristic of those two small democracies that attempts were made by their young parliaments to nurture the co-operative settlement of landless and jobless families from various backgrounds.[11] The international revival of co-operative settlement after each of the major wars in the twentieth century is also a particularly interesting response to the search for new values — and there is, of course, a wealth of literature on the form and special function of modern co-operative settlements in Israel.

The Millennial Dream

> There is little to choose between heavens above and heavens on earth. Both are intended to compensate the weak and oppressed for their present trials; and the one heaven is as elusive as the other.[12]

In terms of the circumstances which triggered the initial activity and also in the subsequent career of the group involved, millenarism may be political as well as religious in character, but the political ingredient derives most of its force from the millennial inspiration. The most common characteristic is the expectation of, and preparation for, imminent salvation; and it is this central idea which separates the millenarists from the utopians. Thrupp and others have emphasized the spatial and temporal universality of the millennial dream, and the idea of a perfect age is indeed a familiar element in the aesthetic perception of the cosmos which has been shared by all societies throughout time. Thus the writings of Ribeiro, van der Kroef and Eliade show that in many primitive or pre-industrial societies, millennial movements form a normal and major part of tradition, and it would obviously be foolish to dismiss them as mere eccentricities or brief spasms of insanity.[13] Similarly, Thrupp points out that our own 'historical' societies also possess the tradition, in a somewhat dormant form, and that its irregular call to action may be explained by looking beyond the aesthetic appeal 'to circumstances that are not present in the long periods when the tradition is latent or merely talked about'.[14] The 'perfect age' was possibly brought into action to serve a number of social purposes, one of which was undoubtedly social protest. But Thrupp cautions that, without strong supporting evidence, it would be dangerous to project our modern obsession with the themes of anxiety and insecurity into the interpretation of these movements.[15] The explanation of the triggering mechanism clearly requires further work by psychologists and social anthropologists, but the important implications for migration, resource-appraisal and settlement evolution should also concern the geographer.

Common manifestations of these movements involve the demands of some type of ordeal on the part of the faithful to make them 'worthy' — a difficult journey; the building of a settlement in some remote district; the performance of certain rituals and ascetic purifications. Another feature is the clear dominance of the visionary leader — messiah or prophet — who evokes the 'sense of time', and may even choose the 'perfect place'. The leader may be supported by an *alter ego*, or by a few practical lieutenants, who manage the organization of the movement.

A distinction is frequently made between pre-millennial and post-millennial movements, but this need not concern us greatly in this chapter. The pre-millennial groups held to the belief that the Second Coming, or the appearance of an equivalent 'deliverer', would take place before the millennial or transitional period of great preparation. This corresponds in the secular sphere to a revolutionary attitude towards social change, whereas the post-millennial movements are merely reformist in outlook, claiming that the millennium will come first, with the Second Coming or the delivering agent placed at the end of this process.[16] Post-millennial movements are usually set firmly within the normal Jewish–Christian tradition insofar as the millennium is to be brought about by orthodox human agencies, and their direct impact on settlement is more difficult to gauge. In its extreme form it may be quite as significant as the first type in justifying the withdrawal of the participants in the movement from the normal spheres of life, a removal which may be spatial as well as social. The millennial dream is acted out in the settlement behaviour of these various groups, but it also has a broader appeal, as will be shown.

The most obvious illustration of these processes is the oldest known form of millenarism, the messianic hope of the Jews. Under the Greek and Roman empires, militant apocalypses precipitated the wars leading to the annihilation of political nationality and the first dispersion of the Jewish people. The messianic hope changed its form accordingly: the messiah was no longer expected to lead Israel to military victory and the establishment of a world empire controlled by the Jews, but was simply to reassemble the scattered communities and reconstitute their national home in some Golden Age, when God's plan for the world would thereby find a consummation.[17] Whenever major disaster occurred, the coming of the messiah became a matter of tense expectancy. Thus, during the massacres of the eleventh to the fourteenth centuries European Jewry produced several pretenders to the role of messiah, and each time the result was a wave of millenarist enthusiasm, expressed in a sudden mass-emigration towards Palestine.

And, since it developed out of Judaism, Christianity inherited this expectation of the Golden Age — indeed, for many of its early adherents, Christianity was simply another millennial movement. Cohn suggests that to medieval Christians, Jerusalem was a symbol of that heavenly Jerusalem which was to replace it at the end of time; furthermore, the mass of the people could not easily distinguish between the celestial and the terrestrial city. So the fantasy of a miraculous realm played a major role in the bloody Crusades of the common people which were launched from Europe between A.D. 1000 and 1300 — the Christian counterparts, in a sense, of the great Jewish migrations. They were triggered by the emergence of ascetic, miracle-working preachers in times of mass insecurity, especially during periods of famine, drought and plague.[18] Their major hearth lay in the densely populated plains to the north of the Alps, where fanatical hordes of landless peasants were swept like so many lemmings to bizarre marches.

The New World was destined to play a special role in enriching this long tradition of millenarism. Mircea Eliade has demonstrated that the colonization of the Americas began under an eschatological sign — the time had come to renew the Christian world, to return to the Earthly Paradise, to begin again the Sacred History, and the manuscripts and literature of this period abound in paradisiacal and eschatological allusions.[19] For the first English settlers, the colonization of North America merely prolonged and perfected a Sacred History which was commenced at the onset of the Reformation, and so the drive of the pioneers towards the west continued the triumphal march of Wisdom and True Religion from the east. In Eliade's scenario, some Protestant theologians attempted to transfer the Ark of the Covenant of Abraham to the English, and were inclined to identify the West with spiritual and moral progress. An ancient solar symbolism became indeed the favoured motif, preserved forevermore in Bishop Berkeley's noted epigram, 'Westward the course of empire takes its way . . .'. Eliade extends the claim much further than this. The first English pioneers saw a sign from Providence in the fact that America had been hidden from the Europeans until the Reformation. The final drama of moral regeneration and universal salvation would surely begin with them, for they were the first to follow the sun in its course towards the Gardens of Paradise in the west — 'More than any other modern nation the United States was the product of the Protestant Reformation seeking an Earthly Paradise in which the reform of the Church was to be perfected.'[20]

An extravagant claim, perhaps; but it is not unsupported. It is significant that the millenarist urge was exceptionally strong immediately prior to the colonization of America. The most popular religious doctrines in the early colonies were that America had been chosen as the place of the Second Coming of Christ and that the millennium would be accompanied by a paradisiacal transformation of the earth 'as an outer sign of inner perfection'. The rivalry between the European powers was of course largely economic in character, 'but it was exacerbated by an almost manichean eschatology'—everything was reduced to a conflict between Good and Evil, with Catholic Europe usually presented as a 'fallen world'. The first North American colonists were the perfectionists and as such, they later found imperfections in the Reformation in England, which therefore replaced Rome to some extent in the apocalyptic imagery. The colonists proclaimed their break with, and moral superiority over, the English; and they announced their determination to return to a form of pure, early Christianity. And so for the Puritans, the major Christian virtue was simplicity: culture, luxury and learning were the Devil's own creations.[21] It has to be admitted that, seen in this light, Eliade's thesis is very persuasive.

These foundations have been discussed in some detail to facilitate an understanding of the general implications of this ideological setting. The metamorphosis of the millenarist views of so many of the original pioneers was actually hastened by the westward extension of the frontier and by the emergence of urban complexes in the north-east. The new cities were seen as infestations from urbanized Europe, and the ideal of rural life was presented as a contrast to the vices of the city. Thus the traditional criticisms voiced by the Puritans were gradually subsumed in a general assault on urban living as a despised, European product. Similarly, the stubborn resistance of the early American élites to industrialization has long perplexed both geographers and economic historians, partly because these decisions were made within a special set of inherited values which we no longer share, and their repeated exaltation of the virtues of farming (see Chapter 3) may possibly be ascribed in part to the same nostalgia for the Earthly Paradise. But Europe also experienced Arcadian idealism, in fact a veritable 'rage for the bucolic', especially in the eighteenth century, and we should at least dilute Eliade's heavy emphasis upon the American experience.[22]

Geographers cannot ignore the pervasive impact of such deeply rooted forces upon the transformation of the New World; until the wider implications are more thoroughly researched by other social scientists, however, some geographers might usefully concentrate upon those settlement mutations which are more or less directly attributable to utopian and millenarist motivations. In the brief outline which follows there is no attempt to rule a strict division between the two themes. For the present purposes such a division would be extremely difficult to establish and it is, in any case, not essential. Consider, for example, the pivotal role of evangelicalism in the formation of the American mind during the nineteenth century, and the special importance of revivalism on the western frontier, which has been frequently noted.[23] Even in Britain, where a traditional religious establishment was strongly entrenched, there was an industrial 'frontier' where similar forces were at work, and the central doctrines of perfectionism and disinterested benevolence characterized the evangelism of both countries.[24] Furthermore, the definite social implications of these doctrines committed many of their adherents to a deep sympathy for various aspects of social reform, and the reverse also applied: social reformers on both sides of the Atlantic, and to some extent in Australia and New Zealand, found a conceptual basis in the biblical doctrine of the millennium for their ideas of utopia, and a rhetoric with proven appeal which greatly assisted the transmission of their message. Throughout the period under review, these two themes were normally tightly interwoven.

Group Settlement in the New World

Since the days of F. J. Turner interpretations of the roles of ethnic minorities have constituted a major field of interest in American historical research, but there have been very few historical works which deal with the related spatial processes as more than a peripheral concern. The attention of geographers is frequently recalled to the various implications of ethnic heterogeneity as a principal impetus or controlling factor for many aspects of spatial change, and the ground has already been prepared for the pursuit of more specific analyses of significant inter-group differences in terms of their cultural, economic and technological approaches. One traditional focus favoured by geographers and agricultural historians alike is the examination of the supposed differences in farming methods practised by the immigrant groups, and inevitably, this type of enquiry must occasionally highlight the relatively compact forms of utopian and millenarist settlement set within that vast sea of regularly dispersed individual farmsteads which made up the 'fee-simple empire' (see Chapter 3). They were distinct 'islands' — marking, as it were, pronounced cultural-topographical breaks in the human geography of large regions. Other studies have identified the forces of social deprivation and charismatic or financial leadership in the migration and settlement of ethnic and religious groups, from the Highland Scots under their 'tacksmen' to the 'empresarios' of the Spanish empire.[25] Similarly, for Australia and New Zealand, the function of landed capitalists who were commissioned to settle their granted areas with people of their own choosing calls for further investigation, and the existing American works should serve as useful precedents.

But 'group settlement' resulting from the extreme utopian and millenarist motivations was obviously the most singular manifestation of that vital nexus which bound Europe and the New World together, an eloquent expression of the importance of group dynamics and of the function of deep-seated values and attitudes in the settlement process. The phenomenon merits far more detailed attention as a dominant element in the emerging geographical personality of each of the new territories.

Experimental Communities on the Old Frontier

During the sixteenth century, Europe's minority Christian groups were commonly persecuted for their social and economic radicalism as much as they were for their religious ideals. Thereafter, a decision was made by a number of these sects to concentrate upon the development of esoteric religious doctrines, but many of their members subsequently chose to emigrate to North America, where they profoundly influenced the development of democratic thought. This early connection of 'the left wing of the Reformation'[26] with the settlement of North America cannot be over-emphasized. Utopian modes of organization grew logically out of the values and attitudes of primitive Christianity, nourished by the opportunities presented by the *tabula rasa* of the frontier. Between about 1780 and 1860 over one hundred documented utopian communities were founded, with a peak of activity and membership during the final twenty years of that period, and a marked geographical concentration in the North-East and Middle West (Fig. 14).

Where religious beliefs supplied the prime motivation, the communities survived remarkably well. The *Shakers* — the 'United

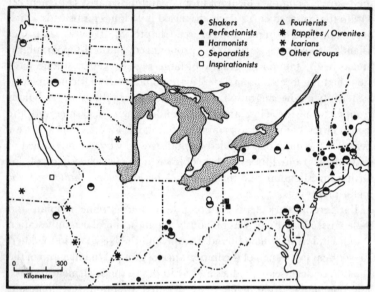

Fig 14   Distribution of selected communal settlements, USA. (Source: adapted from Nordhoff, 1966)

Society of Believers in Christ's Second Appearing' — originated in Manchester, England, as a Quaker sect under the leadership of the remarkable visionary Ann Lee. She died in 1784 after an astonishing missionary tour of America's North-Eastern states, and the first Shaker village was established a few years later by one of her successors, Joseph Meacham, an organizing genius. At its height during the 1830s this celibate, pacifist, communistic and extraordinarily industrious group had greatly improved its position, despite (or because of) the recurrent mob violence which was directed against its members. There were then some 6,000 Shakers in at least eighteen highly distinctive villages (Fig. 16, top), and the community is not yet extinct. Similarly, the *Harmony Society* of German separatists, under their leader George Rapp, escaped from Lutheran domination in the Wurtemburg area and formed communistic settlements first at Harmony, Pennsylvania, then at New Harmony, Indiana, and finally at Economy, Pennsylvania. Although the Society never boasted more than about 800 members, it was in existence from 1804 until 1904. The *Zoarists* also hailed from

Wurtemburg and emigrated to the Ohio wilderness under their sombre leader Joseph Baumeler (or 'Bimmeler', as he became known in the new country). Their Society survived from 1817 until 1898. Another German group, the *Society of True Inspiration,* was for a time very successful. In contrast to the energetic and practical Rapp and Baumeler, each of the founders of the 'Inspirationists' was regarded essentially as an 'instrument' of God's will. The irregular current of revelation managed to preserve this interesting group through the persecutions of the sixteenth and seventeenth centuries, and it returned with renewed vigour in the early nineteenth century to four individuals of markedly humble origin: a carpenter, a tailor, an illiterate serving-maid and a stocking weaver. They established strong co-operative settlements in Germany, but the insecurities resulting from their steadfast refusal to take oaths and to submit to military service finally persuaded the carpenter-leader Christian Metz, via some inspired message, to look to North America. He and his companions arrived in 1842, organized themselves under the name of the Eben-Ezer Society and purchased land in New York state near Buffalo. Within three years they had established about 800 immigrants in four communistic villages. As the group expanded and settlement around it intensified, a decision was made against competing in the rising local land market; instead, the leaders were inspired again, to sell up and move west to Iowa. Under the new name of the *Amana Society,* an estate of about 20,000 acres was purchased and eventually included seven villages. There were about 1,800 members in 1880 and the Society survived until 1932, when it was formally dissolved into two separate organizations, a church and a capitalistic business.

The 'future images' of several of the various secular groups were vigorously promoted in a language borrowed from revivalism; and in fact, most of these utopian groups were distinguished by aspirations, fears and needs which reflected those of the religious groups, and their social organization and modes of settlement expressed ideas for social and technological experiment which were also related. These similarities are very clearly displayed in Robert Owen's choice of media to communicate his *New Moral World,* and in his efforts at social reconstruction. Owenism was conceived and nurtured entirely within the great period of evangelism between 1800 and 1860. Its millenial strand increased, and was reinforced by the values and attitudes of sectarianism — the principles of community life practised by the Shakers and Rappites in America were indeed taken as useful models. Beginning in Britain with the industrial village of New Lanark, the Owenites turned to practical schemes of agricultural settlement based upon the idea of the 'Village of Co-operation'. There were seven Owenite communities in Britain, at least sixteen in America, and several projected settlements in each country which never materialized.[27] Owen's *Villages* and Francois Fourier's comparable *Phalansteries* were received enthusiastically in the United States, and together with scores of other ideas they were given their greatest trial as a simultaneous accompaniment to a number of dominant social themes.

> The deep religious interest of the age, the admiration of individual enterprise and pioneering endeavour, and that prosaic enthusiasm for practical application . . . Only when such generally acknowledged and approved notions were joined with the exigencies of actual experiment did the peculiarities of utopia appear. Then the communities seemed grotesque fantasies with scarcely a feature to represent the character of their age. Thus the better life might include communalism, celibacy, free love, greatest rewards for the least attractive work, intellectual exercise combined with physical toil, religious devotion, the free expression of natural passion, industry, education, intellectual isolation — a great store of ideas drawn upon in many different combinations by the earnest utopians.[28]

Hope and Refuge: Landscapes of the New Frontiers

Religious and socio-political motivations were also frequently combined in the creation of a number of distinctive settlements in the last quarter of the nineteenth century. In simple geographical terms some of these examples merely involved the expansion or relocation of old-established groups, but the special advantages of a few relatively undeveloped regions meant that they played a particularly important role in this settlement process. There is space here for only three brief case studies, from California, South-Eastern Australia and the Canadian West.

1. It has already been indicated that most of the American experimentation was concentrated upon the older frontiers of the North-East and parts of the Middle West (Fig. 14), but — as in so many other eccentricities—California presents a special case. Between 1850 and 1950, a greater number of specialized group settlements was accommodated there than in any other state in the union.[29] Some of the more flourishing movements of the early half of the nineteenth century were spent before California could participate, but the good climate and abundant land were well promoted by public and private agencies (*cf.* Chapters 3 and 5) and some of the older groups were encouraged to migrate to the new frontier. Members of the *Icaria Speranza* community, for example, had already failed in Texas and in their occupation of the former Mormon village of Nauvoo, in Illinois. They became reasonably

content in California, living out the principles expounded by Etienne Cabet in his *Voyage en Icarie*. There were also several locally-produced groups, whose emergence has been associated with the stress of rapid population growth and industrialization, combined with an unusually fluid and heterogeneous population, and supported directly and indirectly by trade union movements. The *Kaweah Co-operative Commonwealth*, the tangible manifestation of a socialist dream, was founded in 1884 by some lively unionists to emulate Gronlund's *Co-operative Commonwealth*. Gronlund himself became the resident secretary of the group for a time, but Edward Bellamy's *Looking Backward* almost supplanted his text as the very 'Bible of the Present' for this strange breed of bookworm pioneers.[30] Similarly, W. D. Howell's *A Traveller from Altruria* provided the spur for a committed troupe of Christians from the San Francisco Bay area to begin their quest for utopia at Fountain Grove near Santa Rosa, and a number of millenarist groups withdrew to their own refuges in the Californian hills.[31]

2. Utopian and millenarist groups were far less prominent in the settlement of Australia and New Zealand, partly because of the greater ethnic homogeneity of those countries but also because of their stricter controls over immigration and land disposal, their sheer isolation from Europe and their comparatively recent development, all of which meant that they were somewhat overshadowed by North America during the most adventurous episodes of community settlement. There were, however, significant millennial movements amongst the Maori people, and it is known that Moravians, Seventh Day Adventists, the Plymouth Brethren and other sects established small settlements throughout South-Eastern Australia.[32] These enterprises still require basic research. For comparative purposes, however, one important and characteristically Australian example might now be noted.

In the colony of Victoria during the depression of the 1890s, Edward Bellamy's utopian essay *Looking Backward*, Henry George's numerous quasi-messianic pronouncements on land ownership and 'the single tax', and Alfred Russel Wallace's appeal for land nationalization were immensely popular at all levels.[33] Quite as potent was the circulation of an amazing mixture of locally produced pamphlets which commented on the social ills of the day and prescribed their best remedies. For these smaller and cheaper works not only constructed the bridge in the communication process via imitation, paraphrase and discussion of the great international literature: frequently, they were also excellent pieces of invention in their own right. One of the Victorian groups which borrowed heavily from the leading British and American works

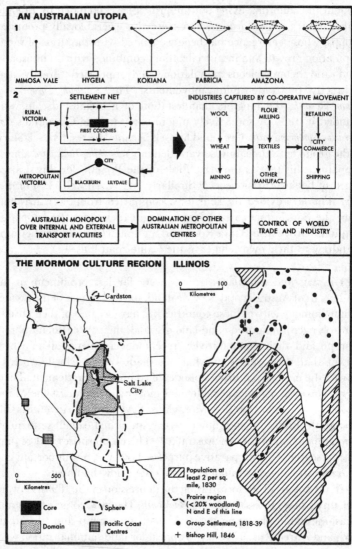

Fig 15 Examples of group settlement, I. *Top:* a reconstruction of the sequence of settlement outlined in H. F. Tucker's *New Arcadia* (1894), from Powell, 1971; *lower left:* the Mormon culture region today, after Meinig, 1965; *lower right:* group settlement in Illinois during the early nineteenth century, after Nelson, 1970 and Pooley, 1908.

was an enthusiastic band of 'Christian socialists'. Using their pulpits, broadsheets, letters to the press, public meetings and some enterprising literature, they urgently articulated an elementary theory of action to assist the unemployed throughout the colony. One of the leaders of this earnest group was the Rev. Horace Finn Tucker, whose hotch-potch novel *The New Arcadia* (1894) insisted that the continued general resignation to the spirit of competition had manifestly worked to the detriment of all classes, and that it should be replaced by a new philosophy of brotherhood which demanded the abandonment of all those revered notions of 'good business practice' and their substitution by 'honesty', 'unity', 'truth' and so on.[34] Despite its naive and frequently maudlin detail, the structural basis of the novel successfully prescribed an outline of a system of co-operative settlements based in the first instance upon Victoria and ultimately encompassing all of Australia, and beyond (Fig. 15, top). The 'Tucker Village Settlements Association' had in fact already introduced the system by launching a number of precarious ventures in the Victorian bush, and the novel served to publicize these activities and to provide useful rhetoric for Tucker's supporters. Although the 'village settlers' were soon in difficulties, the colonial government decided to bring most of them into a substantially similar but less pretentious programme for much wider use throughout Victoria (*cf.* Chapter 3).

3. A strong group of *Mennonite* colonies was established in Southern Manitoba during the 1870s. This was indeed the first large community of experienced agriculturalists to enter that newly created province, where there was abundant underdeveloped land to accommodate them after their flight from military conscription in Russia. A particularly interesting feature of their settlements is that they succeeded in reproducing their distinctive traditional field systems within the rigid framework of the rectangular survey. Groups of farmers, usually friends who had belonged to the same congregation in Russia, drew up a mutual agreement to select contiguous homestead blocks under the terms of the prevailing Canadian laws for land disposal. After the village site was chosen, the individual farmers made their own entries for adjoining quarter sections (160 acres) of the surrounding land.

The regular rectangular survey governed the future pattern of the landholding system only insofar as a simple and direct relationship was naturally maintained between the number of farmers in the village and the area of the *Flur* or village land, although the outer boundaries of the Flur were of course similarly determined, by the straight lines of the survey frame. Within the Flur the Mennonites used the traditional large fields or *Gewanne*, and each arable Gewanne was subdivided into so many strips or *Kagel* according to the number of landholders in the village. In addition, some effort was apparently made in a number of

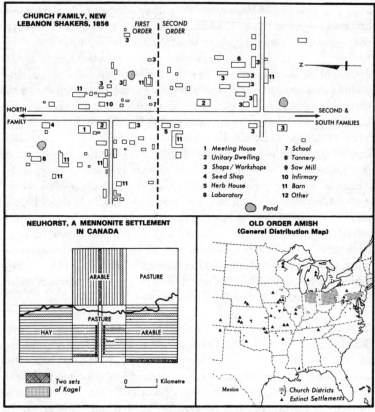

Fig 16 Examples of group settlement, II. *Top:* part of the Shaker village of New Lebanon, New York, in 1856, adapted from Andrews, 1963; *lower left:* the field plan of the Mennonite settlement of Neuhorst, Manitoba, in the late nineteenth and early twentieth centuries, after Warkentin, 1959; *lower right:* distribution of Old Order Amish communities, after Hostetler, 1968.

cases to apportion the fields equally between the landholders, and to ensure that there were no marked disparities in the distances travelled between the various individual strips and the house allotments in the village proper (Fig. 16, lower left). These methods actually contravened the established homesteading regulations (basically common throughout the New World) which amongst other things insisted on the personal residence of each settler on his selected allotment. In 1876, however, an amendment to the Dominion Lands Act recognized the special claims of the Mennonites and enabled them to continue the reconstitution of the Canadian landscape according to their own preferences. More than a hundred of these villages were established before the mid 1880s, after which the intricate system on which they were founded began to disintegrate as the community was seduced to Canadian ways, and the ultra-conservatives elected to move to Mexico. The colonies still survive in a greatly modified form, but the imported Old World patterns had been virtually obliterated from the landscape by the 1920s.[35]

Two other major European groups, the *Doukhobórs* and the *Hutterites*, established numerous settlements in the United States and Canada in the late nineteenth and early twentieth centuries, and they provide additional and striking examples of some of the triggering mechanisms which initiated group emigration from Europe. Their experiences offer further reminders, too, that the influence of the great magnet of the New World was frequently acting upon *established* traits of geographical mobility which were deeply ingrained in certain peasant societies in Europe. This was undoubtedly true of the Russian society in which each of these groups was based at the time of its decision to emigrate. Mobility had been fairly common throughout Russia from the thirteenth century, mainly as part of the attempt by the peasants to improve their social and economic status and to escape oppression: but during the nineteenth century, as many as six million peasants may have been on the move each year. The Doukhobórs and Hutterites are also notable for the fact that they have maintained a high degree of isolation and very rigorous codes of conduct, yet most of their settlements have endured and in some cases there has been remarkable expansion. Only the briefest of commentaries on these fascinating groups can be provided here.

The term 'Doukhobórs' has been translated as 'spirit-wrestlers' and certainly the name derives from their early characterization by the Russian Orthodox Church which denounced them as dangerous sectarians who were in conflict with the Holy Spirit.[36] The group itself preferred such titles as 'The Universal Community of Christian Brotherhood'. Its origins may be discovered in the activities of the *Hudaizers*, a fifteenth-century sect which combined certain Jewish beliefs with rationalism, rejecting both the divinity of Christ and the worship of icons, and in the arguments of the *Anabaptists* and those of other European Protestant groups which vigorously rejected the practice of infant baptism. The Doukhobórs' emphasis on the independence of individual judgement, underlining what they believed to be the supreme importance of the subjective consciousness in religion, was later extended to sustain their general refusal to express allegiance to those civil authorities which did not maintain social justice. Associated with these ideas of the group, a high value was (and is) placed upon the principle of individual inspiration — which may be compared with the 'inward voice' of the Quakers — and this provided excellent support in the early years, when illiteracy was normal. Finally, during the eighteenth century the Doukhobórs came to accept the principle of autocratic leadership, and this proved to be a crucial factor in their initial emigration and in their subsequent management decisions in the New World. When compulsory military service was introduced in the Caucasus in the late 1880s, the Doukhobórs were persuaded by their leader Peter Verigin to refuse to submit to conscription. They were permitted to emigrate in 1898 and by 1900 about 7,000 of these illiterate peasants, who united during Verigen's imprisonment in Siberia under Prince D. A. Hilkoff, settled on the Canadian prairies. Verigin had accepted Tolstoy's arguments against individual ownership, and after his release he moved to Canada in 1902 to organize the communistic management of the group's activities. The communal system did not survive and several divisions emerged within the group, yet the Doukhobórs still maintain a large number of distinctive settlements throughout Canada.[37]

The Hutterian Brethren or Hutterites also had their origins in the Protestant Reformation of the sixteenth century, as a small sect in the South Tyrol and Moravia. After surviving three hundred years of bitter persecution, in the late eighteenth century they accepted a Russian invitation to farm the raw frontier territory of the Ukraine. When their exemption from military service became threatened they moved again, this time to the Dakota territories in North America, where three small colonies were established in 1874. There are now about 200 distinct settlements in the United States and Canada, supporting a population of approximately 20,000. The Hutterite way of life reflects their essentially fundamentalist religious outlook on the world, and is best seen in their communal settlements, in their participation in society at large, and in their system of education.

The unusual success of this major communal society is largely due to the range of socialization patterns which has been adopted with some variation over the extensive territory it now commands. Above all, there is a progressive indoctrination from birth through each of the culturally-defined sex and age sets, and this procedure prepares the individual very well indeed for communal life.

> Every Hutterite is subservient to the colony at every stage of his life, and the goals for each stage are attainable by virtually all members. Individuals are thoroughly trained to meet clearly defined roles, and each member is rewarded by the awareness that his contribution is essential to the colony. There is minimal interaction with and dependency upon outsiders. The individual identifies ideologically and emotionally with the colony system.[38]

The very youngest child is indoctrinated by a system which minimizes individuality and maximizes his identity as a member of a group. As he grows into fuller participation in adult life in the colony, he usually finds that his own self-image positively requires colony identification: he becomes convinced that the collective unit is more important than the separate individuals comprising it; that they are nothing without each other.

These rigid controls may be quoted too readily in support of Kateb's famous attack on utopian communities.[39] Kateb insisted that society required conflict, change, tension and stimulation to give meaning to life; that the utopian groups were merely havens for eccentrics and neurotics, providing at best an unsatisfactory imitation of living. On the contrary, however, it has been shown that the Hutterite communities have developed a complex social system which effectively counters many of the traumatic features of modern life in North America: according to the most accepted indices of mental and physical health, the Hutterites have fared markedly better than their more 'competitive' and individualistic contemporaries. Their important secondary support is a viable economic base characterized by large scale management practices which have become well adapted to prairie farming. Their major areas of concentration in the 1970s are the Canadian Provinces of Alberta (91 colonies in 1974) and Manitoba (60 colonies), and the north-western states of the U.S.A., principally South Dakota and Montana (about 60 colonies).[40]

For the Hutterites the highest command of Christian love is the community of goods — which is, therefore, also argued to be a sign that their belief has resulted in their following the pattern of the New Testament Church. This interpretation clearly exhibits their origins in the radical Reformation, when one of the most contentious issues was the degree of separation between the Christian and the wider society: whereas the established churches hoped to influence society by including most of its members within their organizations, the radicals argued that only the complete separation of the two could allow the Christian to be uncompromising in his own faith. So the Hutterites' design for communal living is based on these deep convictions. Each member's needs must be provided equally and accordingly, personal indulgence of any type is effectively discouraged; food is nutritious but simple and dress is regarded as functional rather than as a form of personal expression; family dwellings are plain, are furnished only with basic necessities and do not possess an orthodox kitchen or dining room, since all meals are prepared and eaten in a central communal block. Traditionally, the Hutterites have chosen to be agriculturalists because

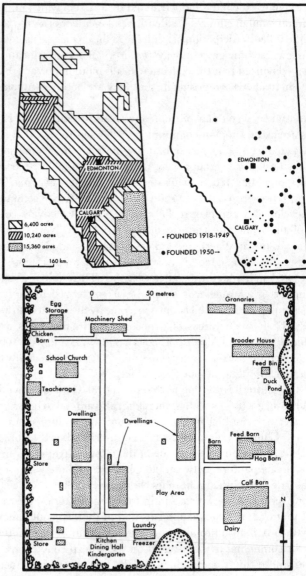

Fig 17 Hutterite settlement in Alberta. *Top:* limitations on colony size imposed under the Communal Property Act 1947 and its subsequent amendments, foundation periods of Hutterite colonies; *lower:* the Pincher Creek Hutterite colony, showing specialized functions of buildings in a mixed and balanced socio-economic structure. (Sources: adapted with permission from Laatsch, 1971, and checked against Evans, 1974 and personal field work.)

rural locations can better provide the kind of geographical separation they believe they require from the harmful influences of the 'outside', and the variety of tasks available in each isolated agricultural settlement ensures that every individual can contribute his or her labour and skill in a practical way.

The management of each communal economy is normally extremely carefully organized. It must be sufficiently successful to permit the accumulation of capital to finance the establishment of a new colony when the population of the existing settlement reaches some agreed critical threshold beyond which the land cannot support any increase and there will be insufficient work to engage all able hands. The choice of a new site is determined by general consensus and the daughter settlement is then laid out in the traditional manner, influenced throughout by the concept of order. Individual buildings and sets of buildings are squared to the main cardinal points wherever possible and frequently distinctive colours are employed to differentiate the various functions of each building. The result is a characteristically *Hutterite* plan for each settlement. The example illustrated above (Fig. 17, lower) is taken from Alberta, where the vigorous expansion of the Hutterite communities has been viewed with great concern by the Provincial Legislature — a concern which is, however, largely based on the exaggerated and misplaced fears of individual farmers and ranchers and small business interests in the rural townships. Since 1947, Hutterite expansion has been monitored and directed under the terms of the Communal Property Act and subsequent amending legislation. The principal geographical outcome of these attempts at control has been to diffuse the expansion more evenly throughout the Province, and to establish minimum 'rational' acreages for each new colony in accordance with a broad zonal soil classification (Fig. 17, top).

Group Dynamics and the Settlement Process

For the superficial observer many of the utopian and millennial groups may appear to offer abundant evidence to support the old notion of an historical event as 'the lengthened shadow of a man', in these cases the prophet or the original man of action. The idea is no longer favoured as a dominating practical hypothesis for general historical scholarship (although it continues to hold some attraction), and sociologists and social psychologists have always stressed the importance of working towards a more balanced and 'detached' viewpoint.[41] This is not to deny the special role of the 'isolated' individual, particularly in the religious groups. But — as Battis, for example, has shown in an admirable appraisal of the 'Hutchinson controversy' in Puritan Massachusetts — the independent and 'secular' motives of individuals and sub-groups other than the leading charismatic personality must also be assessed.[42] This latter study serves to illustrate the significance of group dynamics in the settlement process, a most important theme for the pursuit of humanistic perspectives in geography.

The scene was seventeenth-century America, a peculiar time and place in which religion was the mould which gave form and coherence to all other cultural values: for the Puritans, the term 'non-religious' had no meaning. Yet it cannot be denied that Luther's original repudiation of the papal claim to monopoly over the channels of divine grace also made it impossible for any other Church, including that of the Puritans, to set up the same claim and sustain it for any length of time.

> Thereafter, scarcely was a denomination freshly established before a process of amoebic replication brought forth another to challenge the pretensions of the parent body . . . insurgents had already made their way to New England's shore, some to protect the revolution they had already wrought, *others bearing the seed of revolt to come.*[43]

It is therefore surprising to see the Puritan mode of settlement displayed as such a semi-static phenomenon in Trewartha's otherwise commendable reconstructions, still widely quoted.[44] For a detailed analysis of the real, workaday business of moving and settling, and especially of the occasional process of 'fission' or 'hiving-off', the work of S. C. Powell offers modern human geographers a most readable alternative.[45] For the identification and elucidation of the complex conditions giving rise to the splintering of an original group and the movement of the discontents to a new settlement Battis's work does, however, offer a better model for detailed micro-studies of crucial psycho-social forces in settlement evolution. The background of cultural confusion and social heterogeneity is discussed by Battis as a prelude to the examination of the participants in the protest. These individuals and sub-groups are then ranged along an 'acceptance–rejection spectrum' according to their degree of sympathy and involvement, and analysed in depth to determine their motives. On this basis, the Hutchinson sect was characterized by three subdivisions, the core, support and peripheral groups: a familiar terminology for cultural geographers also, as will be shown.

There have been very few historical or geographical investigations which have approached this level of understanding of the dynamics of settlement evolution, and even fewer attempts have been made to examine the implications for agriculture and settlement *after* the foundation of the new communities. The investigation of their intricate 'commitment mechanisms' must remain the province of the sociologist and social psychologist,[46] but cultural-historical geographers should be especially concerned with the community settlements — at least as a collective phenomenon which is an important manifestation of the spirit of the age, and which provides at the same time special evidence of the work of man as a dominant environmental agent. The significance of sites and situations in influencing the livelihood and longevity of individual communities could be more clearly enunciated by the geographer's synthesizing skills, but these might also be applied to an analysis of the broader impact of the activities of the various groups upon the landscapes and economies of their surrounding regions.

These latter themes have certainly attracted a number of scholars, and particularly thesis-writers, over the years, but most of these investigations are not readily available for general student use. Some early publications now deserve a resuscitation in print. During the Second World War, for instance, Kollmorgen explained the existence of ethnic and religious 'cultural islands' in the settlement pattern of the southern States, and drew attention to their individual characteristics and their roles as innovators.[47] He also made the point that many of the new crops introduced by the group settlers were specifically developed through the establishment of a complex truck farming system, and that the large quantity of production demanded by this type of long distance marketing was maintained most effectively by the 'island' form of organization. Some years earlier, Dawson completed an extensive sociological study which was concerned with similar groups as sectarian forces within the pioneer society of Canada as a whole, and he clarified the range of advantages and disadvantages in their attitudes and modes of settlement.[48] Thus, formal institutional services sprang into existence very quickly, giving group members an immediate sense of security and permanency. Religious leadership, church buildings and various forms of organization were usually present at the outset, and schools were established almost as quickly. On the other hand, some of the ultra-conservative groups were continually hostile, erecting barriers to innovations from the outside and resisting the internal pressures for change. Also, whereas Kollmorgen's 'islands' were founded by later immigrants who were completely new to the American South, in the Canadian prairies the islands were frequently established in advance of 'newcomers' who were unsympathetic outsiders. This combination of factors caused a dilution of the exclusiveness of the Canadian groups, which persuaded Dawson to examine the associated processes of assimilation or 'secularization'.

The propensity for agricultural and industrial innovation attributed
to some of the communities is an important feature which has possibly
been overshadowed by the arguments derived from the observation of a
few highly conservative relict groups in modern times. This is naturally
a central issue in the analysis of the particular characteristics of these
settlements and in the general contribution they have made, and the
subject should therefore be approached from a variety of perspectives:
some studies will determine an emphasis on the positive aspects of
vigorous experimentation; others must demonstrate the negative effects
of the most extreme forms of voluntary isolation. Thus far the Shakers
have been credited with the invention of America's first circular saw;
they also designed their own printing press, a mowing and reaping
machine, revolving harrows, a metallic pen and machines for spinning
and planing — not to mention their ingenious pea-sheller and other
gadgets devised for their communal kitchens, and their highly successful
marketing of selected herbs. And similarly, the Amana colonies became
famous for their furniture and textile factories, and the *Oneida
Perfectionists* developed a wide repertoire of industrial projects with the
support of generous donations from wealthy members. But some of the
groups 'dropped out' so efficiently that they disintegrated completely
after a very brief and troubled interval, leaving only the slightest trace
of their work behind.[49]

It is axiomatic that the processes of innovation and adoption must be
examined within the context of the relevant social milieu. Geographical
analyses of these notable frontier developments must therefore require
the type of anthropocentric focus employed by Bjorklund in her
interpretation of the settlement of members of the Dutch Reformed
Church in Michigan.[50] Bjorklund's study lucidly restated the premise
that ideology may contain the primary bases from which decisions are
made or distinctive ways of organization and reorganization are
derived. Another geographical study, similarly anthropocentric but
more closely related to the present theme, is Landing's attempt to build
a dynamic regionalization of the areal occupance of the Old Order
Amish communities, now concentrated in Ohio, Pennsylvania, and
Indiana (Fig. 16, lower right). Landing has produced a predictive
model which also faithfully records the distinctive genesis of this very
large group.[51] Testing in detail by means of a survey of the diffusion of
selected innovations emanating from the surrounding non-Amish
population, he claims to have established the existence of three intra-
group divisions based upon family responses to change in a specific
settlement. These are the zone of innovation, where new procedures are
widely accepted; the zone of tradition, where customs are rigorously

maintained and change is strongly resisted; and a zone of acceptance between these two, deriving its traditions from the second area but modifying them through influences accepted from the first. The identification of this intermediate area was certainly an essential research objective, for it was shown to be vital to the diffusion of cultural traits. If innovations were successfully adopted there, the entire settlement would ultimately be engulfed; where resistance was too strong, families in the zone of innovation were forced to re-evaluate their course of action: the wave was turned back.

The Mormon movement dwarfs that of the other millennial groups as an agent of geographical change. In addition, it has been very thoroughly analysed by social scientists, and provides some useful models for research on other religious groups in the United States. Mormonism has been strengthened by four major social forces — leadership, ideology, conflict and co-operation — and each of these has been reflected in the evolution of a distinctive pattern of colonization.[52] It does, indeed, exemplify the chief characteristics of millenarism noted earlier in this Chapter. The movement was founded by the visionary leader Joseph Smith, who was killed in Illinois by an angry mob in 1844; it was then led by Brigham Young, a man of action who guided the westward migration. The Mormons also developed their own compact settlement form which contrasted markedly with the normal pattern of isolated farmsteads on the frontier, and it has been shown that this was for the most part a social invention, derived essentially from their religious beliefs. The American continent was 'choice above all other lands' according to the *Book of Mormon*, and the 'gathering place for the last days', the City of Zion, would therefore be located in America. The plan for the city had also been 'laid down', and as the group moved west the sacred plan was implemented in several small settlements. By the time the Mormons reached Utah and founded Salt Lake City the design was fully proven and entrenched. Thereafter they combined in a type of 'military co-operation', observing a very formal body of rules and strictly obeying the leaders, and this proved to be an excellent system to support the pioneer irrigation economy which had been decided upon—just as the compact village had also possessed the property of easy defence in frontier conditions, and fitted in remarkably well indeed with the secular rectangular grid.

Meinig has examined the history of colonization within the expanding and retreating Mormon 'empire' of *Deseret*. He pointed to the present existence of a complex culture region which has been built by changing settlement strategies during the last century, and distinguished three major internal zones — core, domain and sphere —

in descending order of importance, determined by the measurable degree of Mormon influence (Fig. 15, lower left).[53]

Communitarians and the Settlement Process

The settlements of utopian and millenarist communities, together with those of the less extreme ethnic and religious groups, differed from the orthodox North American pattern of dispersed, single family settlement in at least five major respects.

1. *Scale* This was the most obvious, and in many ways the most important contrast. Group membership varied from a few families to some thousands of individuals, requiring relatively large areas of land to be selected jointly in contiguous blocks. One consequence of this (though normally there were also other reasons for the decision) was that the group leaders were frequently persuaded to look beyond the settlement frontier, or to consider neglected areas in the older districts.

2. *Cultural homogeneity* The group settlements were usually characterized by a highly homogeneous population, especially in terms of ethnic backgrounds and social and religious beliefs. The various membership restrictions had the effect of maintaining this homogeneity, but the necessary corollary was the relative isolation of each group from the general field of communication and social interaction, particularly in the early pioneering years. They became, in a sense, worlds within worlds; but there were certainly numerous instances of vigorous interaction between the several constituent settlements of certain large groups.

3. *Stability* A high degree of instability was the norm over most of the frontiers of the New World, judged in spatial and temporal terms, but the group settlements were comparatively far more stable. Apart from the obvious factors which tended to bind the members together in specific locations, there was the fairly common factor of the early establishment of joint ownership which discouraged independent mobility or reduced it to a minimum. This is not to deny that some of the communities, especially the secular groups, may have maintained their locations and even their numerical strengths while their real membership or personnel accommodated to the individual enthusiasms and defections which must be expected in an age of intense experimentation. Similarly, there is abundant evidence of short- or long-term inter-group migration in which particular individuals or

family units sampled different locations and life-styles, and intra-group mobility of the type favoured by the surviving Amish, Doukhobórs, Hutterite and Mennonite groups, in which their members engage in social and economic activities in various kinship colonies over a wide geographical area — a process which unites the archipelago of cultural islands and helps to maintain each unit of these unusual spatial sub-systems.

4. *Planning* Community leaders indulged in a comparatively high degree of pre-settlement planning, including the selection and survey of village sites and farmlands, the construction of essential community buildings (mills and barns, churches or meeting houses, communal dwellings) and even the organization of the emigration or migration of the rest of the group, from Europe or from one of the older districts behind the frontier.

5. *Community services* The early establishment of a village nucleus, as Dawson emphasized for Canada, usually meant that the group settlements differed markedly from orthodox pioneer settlement in terms of their enjoyment of schools, churches, workshops and well-supported formal and informal sub-groups serving a variety of purposes.

The concentration of so many of these early community settlements on the prairie frontiers of the United States and Canada brings these five major features into sharp focus, and it suggests that in general, it was a particularly advantageous combination for pioneer settlement in those regions. The example of Illinois (Fig. 15, lower right), as useful as any other, demonstrates that the Scandinavian, German, Swiss, French, Mormon, Canadian, Scottish and English 'colonies' — together with a large number of organized Yankee communities, including many distinct church congregations continuing the Puritan tradition of group settlement — moved into the unoccupied prairie-woodland fringe of that state. Several of the Yankee settlements, however, were undoubtedly taken up for speculative purposes and did nothing to test out the virgin country.[54] Most of the other groups, while maintaining their island-like independence, soon demonstrated their main advantages over the individual families of prairie homesteaders. Above all, they could pool their labour and financial resources, and they benefited considerably from organized leadership and superior servicing and marketing capacities.

Significantly, one of the most successful of these latter Illinois groups was the Swedish communistic sect at Bishop Hill, originally led by the fanatical Eric Janson. The sect survived the flight to America, a cholera epidemic and the assassination of its prophet. Its efforts at self-sufficiency and its useful contacts with an established Shaker community in Kentucky resulted in the building of a highly diversified economy which promoted a certain amount of experimentation and advanced the group's adaptation to the prairie environment. Of equal relevance is the fact that Bishop Hill, like several of the other group settlements in North America, abandoned its communal organization when the rigours of the pioneering phase were more or less over.[55] Many other factors were involved in the decision, but it prompts the final reflection that at least some of these interesting communities positively required the special conditions of a frontier environment to preserve their chosen modes of settlement. They needed the kinds of problems and challenges which the frontier alone could provide, yet in reality their settlements were based upon forms of social organization which may have been peculiarly well suited to initiate the very processes of domestication which would transform the new territory.

So the plant devoured the soil. But it flowered brilliantly for a time in the new landscapes, and its seed remained, to yield again in our present age of discontent and cultural confusion.[56] The current feverish experimentation with rural and urban communes throughout the Western world is in some senses merely the most extreme expression of a widespread consuming search for new directions, new life styles, based on a rejection of dominant values and attitudes. It displays again man's precious gift of socio-geographical creativity. The new settlements may not have the staying power of those of the Amish, Hutterites and other long-established religious brethren, but they should be seen collectively as a 'sign of the times', pointing to a profoundly different future for us all.

7

Mirrors

Knowledge was never a matter of geography. Quite the reverse, it overflows all maps that exist. Perhaps true knowledge only comes of death by torture in the country of the mind.[1]

We can now paraphrase and extend one of those familiar statements so often restricted to the United States alone: the development of the English-speaking countries of the New World was a major part of the 'great explosion of intellectual and physical energy which transformed civilization' throughout the Western world; it cannot be understood in isolation from this international setting.[2] Above all, the astonishing changes which occurred in the eighteenth and nineteenth centuries were the products of a powerful rationalistic faith originating in the Old World — a faith which underlined the supremacy of man on the earth and was given wider opportunity in the New World, which on the one hand possessed bountiful resources, and on the other boasted its freedom from the continuing corruptions of Europe. The idea of the 'perfectibility of man' was made to support a wider repertoire of more practical meanings in the New World. Though it was displayed in different guises and with various accompaniments, this was the ultimate goal which directed New World settlement processes. It has been shown that the innumerable ways of achieving this end were reflected in the evolution of distinctive man/environment relationships and an exclusive range of novel landscapes, tangible and intangible, at every scale.

We have therefore encountered these young societies when they were engaged with varying degrees of success in gigantic transformations of their new territories — transformations which were obviously in-timately associated with their efforts to transform themselves as peoples, for in some measure they also represented explorations of their own potentials and limitations, and deeply-held desires to take greater command of their own destinies. In addition, from what we have seen thus far it is apparent that these same optimisms, together with the expectations of and predilections for change, were at least partly responsible for their frequent positive response to skilled promotional agents. Yet in the process hosts of ordinary people showed that they were extraordinarily creative geographical agents — and it does not detract from the argument, in its present context, to point to many of their actions which must now be judged destructive. The plain fact is that they brought about enormous changes by their individual and collective involvement. Only in the last quarter of the nineteenth century did they delegate the main control of this creative function to the politicians, bureaucrats and professional experts; and even then, some of our actors chose to remain more or less aloof and relatively independent of the influence of these remote authorities.

This last point is deliberately exaggerated, of course; such a romantic conclusion could only follow if this book had been intended as a comprehensive analysis of settlement evolution in the New World. But the emphasis throughout has certainly been placed for good reason on hopes, fears and aspirations, on *intentionality* in its many forms, simply to supply a necessary balance to more orthodox explanations of geographical change. Our journey through the changing geography of the New World illustrates sufficiently well that its landscapes have always mirrored the ideas and ideals of its inhabitants. We cannot attempt another tack in this erratic voyage on the vast ocean of Western man's experience with new environments, but this should not be necessary. This slender volume is intended for the students of today who seem to feel the need for engaging in independent exploration more urgently than most of their predecessors. The selected case studies on which the book is based may provide them with some useful guide and encouragement — and perhaps afford a justification, if one is needed. The opportunities for personal research in this approach are virtually limitless for any committed and imaginative student. Each of the major chapters was by no means exhaustive, for instance, and the notes and bibliography often suggest wider and different ranges of specialized case studies than space permitted in the present text; similarly, other issues, completely different from those selected for discussion here, would have sustained the approach equally well. For example, the 'identity' theme might be widened to embrace some of the traditional and continuing quests for regional autonomy — in the French-speaking areas of Canada and in the movement throughout the United States for black independence, and also in Australia, including several 'new state' movements and some pervasive fears of Asian domination which have influenced national and regional economic strategies. Again, the search for 'security' in the early experimentation with welfare state principles, especially in New Zealand, would be worthy of separate and detailed geographical investigation; and the development of modern ideas and ideals of urban and regional planning illustrates the Old World/New World interaction particularly well, and would amply repay further research.

The very humanity of our natures makes mental travellers of us all, and this is probably reason enough for the pursuit of any type of cultural–historical perspective. We discovered a mirror of mankind in our journey through these formative periods of New World settlement, and in it were images of ourselves as once we were, with so many of our blemishes and attractive features quite boldly delineated. The lesson in this for the study of human geography in general is simply that we should be more prepared to accept and employ the idea of the basic consonance of internal and external reality. For some reason we do not expect to identify ourselves so easily in the maelstroms of geographical change in the present chaotic age; perhaps we have indeed left too much of the creativity to others, or to the institutional machinery of modern, bureaucratized societies full of anonymous people. Yet the image of man is surely there too.

Notes and References

Chapter 1 *Introduction*

1 D. M. Potter, *People of Plenty* (Chicago, 1954; reprinted 1973); the quotation is on p. xiii.

2 H. Gerth and C. W. Mills, *Character and Social Structure* (New York, 1953).

3 Potter, *People of Plenty*, p. xiii.

4 A. Huxley, *Heaven and Hell* (New York, 1955), pp.1–3.

5 D. Lowenthal, 'Geography, experience and imagination: towards a geographical epistemology', *Annals, Association of American Geographers*, 51 (1961), 241–60; quotation is on p.252.

6 *ibid.*, p. 260.

7 See especially the volume of selected essays: J. K. Wright, *Human Nature in Geography. Fourteen Papers, 1925–1965* (Cambridge, Mass., 1966).

8 J. K. Wright, '*Terrae incognitae*: the place of the imagination in geography', *Annals, Association of American Geographers*, 37 (1947), 1–15.

9 For example, see D. Lowenthal and M. J. Bowden (eds), *Geographies of the Mind* (New York, 1976); H. Prince, 'Real, imagined and abstract worlds of the past', *Progress in Geography*, 3 (1971), 1–86; Y. F. Tuan, *Topophilia. A Study of Environmental Perception, Attitudes and Values* (Englewood Cliffs, N.J., 1974). And compare two recent statements by Guelke, which approach the central premises of this book very closely indeed—L. Guelke, 'An idealist alternative in human geography', *Annals, Association of American Geographers*, 64 (1974), 193–202, and 'On rethinking historical geography', *Area*, 7 (1975), 135–8.

10 D. O. Hebb, 'Concerning imagery', *Psychological Review*, 75 (1968), 466–77; R. R. Holt, 'Imagery: the return of the ostracized', *American Psychologist*, 12 (1964), 254–64.

11 K. Boulding, *The Image: Knowledge in Life and Society* (Ann Arbor, 1956).

12 W. Bell and J. A. Mau (eds), *The Sociology of the Future: Theory, Cases, and Annotated Bibliography* (New York, 1971); F. L. Polak, *The Image of the Future: Enlightening the Past, Orientating the Present, Forecasting the Future* (New York, 1961, 2 vols.). See also Bell and Mau, 'Images of the future: theory and research strategies', in J. C. McKinney and E. A. Tiryakian (eds),

Theoretical Sociology. Perspectives and Developments (New York, 1970), pp.205–34.

13 Bell and Mau, *Sociology of the Future*, p.19, quoting P. Bosserman, *Dialectical Sociology: An Analysis of the Sociology of Georges Gurvitch* (Boston, 1968).

14 *ibid.*

15 The common-sense relationship between the three components of the image — values, attitudes and information — may have been recognized implicitly in the works of Wright and those of the 'perception' school, but it has seldom been clearly enunciated or vigorously pursued in scholarly exposition. Similarly, there is some reason to believe that the information component — in terms of such basic details as the location, size and shape of specific areas, and the types, quantities and potentials of their environmental resources — was consciously or unconsciously preferred to the other components, which involved more complex dynamic processes. For a recent elucidation of these troublesome points, see Y. F. Tuan, 'Images and mental maps', *Annals, Association of American Geographers*, 65 (1975), 205–13. I have tried to avoid using the term 'perception' in any specialized sense; 'appraisal' appears to be far more useful for the purposes of this book.

16 See, for example, E. L. Brink and W. T. Kelley (eds), *The Management of Promotion. Consumer Behaviour and Demand Stimulation* (Englewood Cliffs, N.J., 1963), pp.15–48. For a general introduction to this important field, strangely neglected in geography, see B. Berelson and M. Janowitz (eds), *Reader in Public Opinion and Communication* (New York, 1966); C. Cherry, *On Human Communication: a Review, Survey, and a Criticism* (Cambridge, Mass., 1966): C. Mares, *Communication* (London, 1966); C. D. Mortensen, *Communication: the Study of Human Interaction* (New York, 1972).

17 *Cf.* Cherry, *On Human Communication*. p.3.

18 The adaptation of Becker's mosaic illustrated here is based on Mortensen, *Communication*, p.44; it originally appeared in his 'A conceptual model for communication research', *Journalism Quarterly*, 34 (1968), 31–8.

19 See the provocative remarks in Y. F. Tuan, 'Humanistic geography', *Annals, Association of American Geographers*, 66 (1976), 266–76.

Chapter 2   *Prelude: land and society in Europe*

1 This section draws on a variety of sources, especially H. S. Commager and E. Giordanetti, *Was America a Mistake?* (New York, 1967) and D. Echevarria, *Mirage in the West. A History of the French Image of American Society to 1815* (Princeton, 1957).

2 See, for example, C. O. Sauer, *Northern Mists* (Berkeley and Los Angeles, Calif., 1968), and C. J. Glacken's masterly humanistic treatise, *Traces on the Rhodian Shore* (Berkeley and Los Angeles, Calif., 1967), especially Chapters 13 and 14, pp.623–705.

3 Comte de Buffon, *National History, General and Particular*, trans. by William Smellie (London, 1812, 20 vols.), quoted in Commager and Giordanetti, *Was America a Mistake?*, p.64.

4 For a general discussion of the 'degeneration' theme, see Commager and Giordanetti, *Was America a Mistake?*, and Echevarria, *Mirage in the West*. For Peter Kalm, see A. B. Bensen (ed), *Peter Kalm's Travels in North America* (New York, 1937).

5   C. Chinard, 'Eighteenth century theories of America as a human habitat', *Proceedings, American Philosophical Society*, 91 (1947), 27–57.

6   For simplicity I have deliberately emphasized Franklin's role. Thomas Jefferson and John Adams also prepared excellent rebuttals of the works of Buffon and other French writers. Glacken, *Traces*, pp.681–5, offers a succinct account.

7   D. M. Potter, *People of Plenty*.

8   W. P. Webb, *The Great Frontier* (Boston, 1952), p.11.

9   For an appreciation of Turner's work and an excellent introduction to the hypothesis, see R. A. Billington, *America's Frontier Heritage* (New York, 1966). A good geographical interpretation is J. L. M. Gulley, 'The Turnerian frontier: a study in the migration of ideas', *Tijdschrift voor Economische en Sociale Geografie*, 50 (1959), 62–72, 81–91. For Webb, see G. M. Tobin, *The Making of a History: Walter Prescott Webb and 'The Great Plains'* (Austin, 1976).

10 A good general survey is available in C. T. Smith, *An Historical Geography of Western Europe before 1800* (London, 1967).

11 The most readable account of the connection is Echevarria, *Mirage in the West*.

12 *ibid.*, p.140.

13 *ibid.*, pp.148–9.

14 J. G. Gagliardo, 'Moralism, rural ideology and the German peasant in the late eighteenth century', *Agricultural History*, 42 (1968), 79–102; a fuller treatment by this author is *From Pariah to Patriot: the Changing Image of the German Peasant 1770–1840* (Lexington, Ky., 1969).

15 *ibid.*, p.81, footnote.

16 P. Taylor, *The Distant Magnet: European Emigration to the United States* (London, 1971) contains a very valuable survey of these influences. See also B. Thomas, *Migration and Economic Growth* (Cambridge, 1954).

17 This follows the oversimplified but generally acceptable classical division introduced in M. L. Hansen, *The Atlantic Migration 1607–1860* (Cambridge, Mass., 1940).

18 Scandinavian emigration is treated in more detail in Chapter 3.

19 C. Woodham-Smith, *The Great Hunger* (London, 1962). See also S. H. Cousens, 'The regional pattern of emigration during the great Irish famine, 1846–51'. *Transactions, Institute of British Geographers*, 28 (1960), 119–34.

20 T. Coleman, *Passage to America* (London, 1972); C. Erickson, *Invisible Immigrants: the Adaptation of English and Scottish Immigrants in 19th Century America* (London, 1972), and her earlier compressed statement in O. F. Ander (ed), *In the Trek of the Immigrants* (Rock Island, Ill., 1964), pp. 59–80.

21 Erickson, *Invisible Immigrants*.

22 *ibid.*, p. 25.

23 *ibid.*, p.29.

24 R. Boston, *British Chartists in America* (Manchester, 1971).

25 *ibid.*, pp.49–56.

26 W. H. G. Armytage, 'The Chartist land colonies, 1846–48', *Agricultural History*, 32 (1958), 87–96; J. Mackaskill, 'The Chartist land plan', in A. Briggs (ed), *Chartist Studies* (London, 1962), pp.304–41.

27 J. Locke, *Two Treatises of Civil Government* (Book 2, Chapter 5, par. 2); for an excellent standard appreciation see M. Curti, 'The great Mr. Locke.

America's philosopher, 1783–1861', *Huntington Library Bulletin*, 11 (1937), 101–51.

28 W. Ogilvie, *Birthright in Land: an Essay on the Right of Property in Land* (London, 1782; reprinted New York, 1970).
29 *ibid.,* p.19.
30 *ibid.,* p.23.
31 *ibid.,* pp.47–8.
32 *ibid.,* 48.

Chapter 3 *The 'yeoman farmer' and the quest for Arcady*

1 W. Whitman, *Song of the Broad-Axe.*
2 See, for example, Brink and Kelly, *Management of Promotion*, pp.1–14.
3 This section is based on H. R. Merrens, 'The physical environment of early America. Images and image-makers in colonial South Carolina', *Geographical Review*, 59 (1969), 530–56. For a general historical introduction, see H. M. Jones, 'The colonial impulse: an analysis of the "promotion" literature of colonization', *Proceedings, American Philosophical Society*, 90 (1946), 131–61.
4 J. P. Purry, *A Method for Determining the Best Climates of the World* (London, 1744).
5 Most of this section draws heavily on the works of J. M. R. Cameron, especially the following: 'Prelude to colonization: James Stirling's and Charles Fraser's examination of Swan River, March 1827', *Australian Geographer*, 12 (1973), 309–27; 'Distortions in pre-settlement land evaluation: the case of Swan River, Western Australia', *Professional Geographer*, 26 (1974), 393–8; 'Western Australia, 1616–1829: an antipodean paradise', *Geographical Journal*, 140 (1974), 373–85: 'Information distortion in colonial promotion: the case of Swan River colony', *Australian Geographical Studies*, 12 (1974), 57–76.
6 J. Barrow, in the April 1829 issue of the *Quarterly Review*, quoted in Cameron, 'Western Australia, 1616–1829', p.382.
7 Adapted from Cameron's model in 'Information distortion', p.72.
8 For good general guides to the topic of Scandinavian emigration to the United States, see the following selection. O. F. Ander, *The Cultural Heritage of the Swedish Immigrant: Selected References* (Rock Island, Ill., 1956); T. C. Blegen, *Norwegian Immigration to America, 1825–1860* (Northfield, Minn., 1931) and *Land of their Choice: the Immigrants Write Home* (Minneapolis, 1955); A. W. Hoglund, *Finnish Immigrants in America, 1880–1920* (Madison, 1960); F. E. Janson, *The Background of Swedish Immigration, 1840–1930* (New York, 1970; first published Chicago, 1931); L. Ljungmark, *For Sale — Minnesota: Organized Promotion of Scandinavian Immigration, 1866–1873* (Chicago, 1971); G. Nyblom (ed), *Americans of Swedish Descent* (Rock Island, Ill., 1948). Hansen, *Atlantic Migration*, pp. 146–71, discusses the general topic of emigrants' letters home; for British examples see A. Conway (ed), *The Welsh in America: Letters from the Immigrants* (Minneapolis, 1961), and C. Erickson, *Invisible Immigrants.*
9 Blegen, *Land of their Choice*, p.3.
10 G. Unonius, *Minnen af en Sjuttonarig Vistelse: Nordvestra Amerika*, 1 (Uppsala, 1862), 4ff.
11 Quoted in Blegen, *Land of their Choice*, p.180.

12　The classic exception is W. I. Thomas and F. Znaniecki, *The Polish Peasant in Europe and America* (Boston, Mass., 1918–20), 5 vols. Conway's *Welsh in America* does, however, give a number of examples of correspondents strongly disillusioned with America (e.g. on pp. 61, 129 and 130).

13　Quoted in Blegen, *Land of their Choice*, pp.436–7.

14　H. Mattson, *Reminiscences, The Story of an Emigrant* (St. Paul, 1891). For additional information see, for example, F. D. Scott, 'Sweden's constructive opposition to emigration', *Journal of Modern History*, 37 (1965), 307–35: A. A. Stomberg, 'Letters of an early emigration agent in the Scandinavian countries', *Swedish–American Historical Bulletin*, 3 (1930), 7–52.

15　For an early classic statement see J. B. Hedges, 'Promotion of immigration to the Pacific Northwest by the railroads', *Mississippi Valley Historical Review*, 15 (1928), 183–203. See also P. W. Gates, *The Illinois Central Railroad and its Colonization Work* (Cambridge, Mass., 1934; repr. New York, 1969); R. Ovington, *Burlington West: A Colonization History of the Burlington Railroad* (Cambridge, Mass., 1941).

16　R. K. Vedder and L. E. Galloway, 'The settlement preferences of Scandinavian emigrants to the United States, 1850–1960', *Scandinavian Economic History Review*, 18 (1970), 159–76.

17　T. Jefferson, *Writings* (New York, 1904; P. L. Ford, ed), Book 4, 95–6.

18　H. N. Smith, *Virgin Land: the American West as Symbol and Myth* (New York, 1950).

19　Quoted in Smith, *Virgin Land*, p.159.

20　*ibid.*

21　R. Hofstadter, *The Age of Reform* (New York, 1955). Note also that the New World conception of the 'yeoman' insisted upon the freehold principle: this was not originally an essential characteristic in Europe.

22　Horace Greeley, journalist and sometime land reformer, in *New York Daily Tribune*, 28 December 1849.

23　Galusha A. Grow, quoted in B. Hibbard, *A History of Public Land Policies* (New York, 1926; repr. 1965), p.369.

24　For a general introduction to land legislation in the United States, see A. G. Bogue, *From Prairie to Corn Belt. Farming on the Illinois and Iowa Prairies in the Nineteenth Century* (Chicago, 1963); V. Carstensen (ed), *The Public Lands. Studies in the History of the Public Domain* (Madison, 1963); D. M. Ellis (ed), *The Frontier in American Development: Essays in Honor of Paul Wallace Gates* (Ithaca, 1969); Hibbard, *Public Land Policies*; L. Lee, 'The Homestead Act: vision and reality', *Utah Historical Quarterly*, 30 (1962), 215–34; H. W. Ottoson (ed), *Land Use Policy and Problems in the United States* (Lincoln, Nebr., 1963); R. M. Robbins, *Our Landed Heritage, The Public Domain, 1776–1936* (Princeton, 1942, reprinted Lincoln, Nebr., 1964); F. A. Shannon, *The Farmer's Last Frontier: Agriculture, 1860–1897* (New York, 1945; repr. 1963). For a very significant geographical study see J. C. Hudson, 'Two Dakota homestead frontiers', *Annals, Association of American Geographers*, 63 (1973), 442–62, and 'Migration to an American frontier', *Annals, Association of American Geographers*, 66 (1976), 242–65.

25　G. McIntosh, 'Use and abuse of the Timber Culture Act', *Annals, Association of American Geographers*, 65 (1975), 347–62. For a general review see Robbins, *Landed Heritage*, pp.219–20, 292–7. A valuable related study is C. B. McIntosh, 'Forest Lieu selections in the Sand Hills of Nebraska', *Annals, Association of American Geographers*, 64 (1974), 87–99.

26 For the dominance of utilitarian values in the American landscape, see D. Lowenthal, 'The American scene', *Geographical Review*, 58 (1968), 61–88.

27 P. W. Gates, 'The Homestead law in an incongruous land system', *American Historical Review*, 41 (1936), 652–81; see his revision in Ottoson, *Land Use Policy*, pp.28–46. By 1935 over 505 million acres had been applied for under the Homestead Act and its amendments; 275 million acres of this total area had been given final proof and patent (title). It may never be possible to provide a reliable and comprehensive statistical account of 'successes' and 'failures'; perhaps the exercise itself should first be rigidly applied at local levels only, so that differences in the physical environment (especially soils and vegetation cover) as well as in the financial and occupational backgrounds, at various times, can be taken into account. For further information, the following references may assist. R. E. Ankli, 'Farm-making costs in the 1850s', *Agricultural History*, 48 (1974), 51–70; A. G. Bogue, *Money at Interest: the Farm Mortgage on the Middle Border* (Ithaca, 1955; repr. 1969); M. B. Bogue, *Patterns from the Sod: Land Use and Tenure in the Grand Prairie, 1850–1900* (Springfield, Ill., 1959); C. Danhof, *Change in Agriculture: the Northern United States, 1820–1870* (Cambridge, Mass., 1969); R. M. Finley, 'A budgeting approach to the question of homestead size on the plains', *Agricultural History*, 42 (1968), 109–14; J. C. Malin, 'The turnover of farm population in Kansas', *Kansas Historical Quarterly*, 4 (1935), 339–72; F. A. Shannon, 'The Homestead Act and the labor surplus', *American Historical Review*, 41 (1936), 637–51, reprinted in Carstensen, *Public Lands*, 297–313.

28 McIntosh, *Use and abuse;* Robbins, *Landed Heritage*.

29 This section is a modification of my earlier review article — J. M. Powell, 'Images of Australia', *Monash Publications in Geography*, 3 (1972), 21pp. See also R. L. Heathcote, *Australia* (London, 1975), pp.210–23; A. G. Serle, *From Deserts the Prophets Come. The Creative Spirit in Australia, 1788–1972* (Melbourne, 1973); I. Turner, *The Australian Dream* (Melbourne, 1964); R. B. Ward, *The Australian Legend* (Melbourne, 1958).

30 J. Philipp, *A Great View of Things: Edward Gibbon Wakefield* (Melbourne, 1971); see also M. F. Lloyd Prichard (ed), *The Collected Works of Edward Gibbon Wakefield* (Glasgow and London, 1968).

31 C. Lansbury, *Arcady in Australia: the Evocation of Australia in Nineteenth-Century English Literature* (Melbourne, 1970). For a much broader but simple anthology, see W. Friedrich, *Australia in Western Imaginative Prose Writings* (Chapel Hill, N.C., and Melbourne, 1967).

32 Lansbury, *Arcady,* p. 69.

33 S. Sidney, *The Three Colonies of Australia: New South Wales, Victoria, South Australia* (London, 1852), p.17.

34 D. Bidney, 'Myth, symbolism and truth', in J. B. Vickery (ed), *Myth and Literature* (Lincoln, Neb., 1966), pp.3–13; J. Campbell, '*Bios* and mythos; prolegomena to a science of mythology', *ibid.*, pp.15–23; N. Frye, L. C. Knights *et al.*, 'The developing imagination', in A. R. MacKinnon and N. Frye, *Learning in Language and Literature* (Cambridge, Mass., 1963), pp. 31–58; B. Slote (ed), *Myth and Symbol* (Lincoln, Neb., 1963).

35 Lansbury, *Arcady*, pp.121–2.

36 Ward, *Australian Legend*.

37 *Victorian Agricultural and Horticultural Gazette*, 21 May 1857.

38 J. M. Powell, 'The Victorian survey system, 1837–1860', *New Zealand*

Geographer, 26 (1970), 50–69; M. Williams, 'The parkland towns of Australia and New Zealand', *Geographical Review,* 56 (1966), 67–89.

39 *Geelong Advertiser,* 30 December 1856. The only general survey of Australian land legislation is S. H. Roberts, *History of Australian Land Settlement, 1788–1920* (Melbourne, 1924; repr. 1968); see also M. Williams, 'More and smaller is better: Australian rural settlement, 1788–1914' in J. M. Powell and M. Williams (eds), *Australian Space Australian Time* (Melbourne, 1975), pp.61–103.

40 *Victorian Parliamentary Debates,* 8 (1869), 956. For a detailed interpretation of the theme, see J. M. Powell, *The Public Lands of Australia Felix: Settlement and Land Appraisal in Victoria 1834–91 with Special Reference to the Western Plains* (Melbourne, 1970).

41 D. W. Meinig, *On the Margins of the Good Earth. The South Australian Wheat Frontier, 1869–1884* (Chicago, 1962; repr. Melbourne, 1976). pp. 78–92; for Victorian examples see J. M. Powell (ed), *Yeomen and Bureaucrats: the Victorian Crown Lands Commission, 1878–79* (Melbourne, 1974).

42 J. M. Powell, 'White collars and moleskin trousers. Politicians, administrators and settlers on the Cheviot estate, 1893–1914', *New Zealand Geographer,* 27 (1971), 151–74.

43 *Victorian Parliamentary Debates,* 21 (1875–6), 567.

44 J. M. Powell, 'The land debates in Victoria, 1872–1884', *Journal of the Royal Australian Historical Society,* 56 (1970), 263–80.

45 J. M. Powell, 'Arcadia and back: "Village Settlement" in Victoria, 1894–1913', *Australian Geographical Studies,* 11 (1973), 134–49, and 'An Australian utopia', *Australian Geographer,* 12 (1973), 328–33.

46 One very conservative estimate for Britain, Canada, Australia and New Zealand places the number of war veterans who received government assistance to establish themselves on farms as 75,000, at a total cost of about $A300 million. For a New Zealand example, see J. M. Powell, 'Soldier Settlement in New Zealand, 1915–1923', *Australian Geographical Studies,* 9 (1971), 144–60.

47 B. G. Reid, 'Agrarian opposition to Franklin K. Lane's proposal for soldier settlement, 1918–1921', *Agricultural History,* 41 (1967), 167–79.

48 Quoted in G. L. Fite, 'Daydreams and nightmares: the late nineteenth-century agricultural frontier', *Agricultural History,* 40 (1966), 285–93.

Chapter 4 *Refractions: identity, wilderness, illusion*

1 D. Lowenthal, 'Geography, experience, and imagination', *Annals, Association of American Geographers,* 51 (1961), 260.

2 E. S. Cahn and D. W. Hearne *et al.* (eds), *Our Brother's Keeper: the Indian in White America* (New York and Cleveland, 1972), p.68.

3 This section draws heavily on the following works: W. T. Hagan, *The Indian in American History* (New York, 1963); R. Horsman, *Expansion and American Indian Policy, 1783–1812* (East Lansing, Mich., 1967); W. R. Jacobs, *Dispossessing the American Indian: Indians and Whites on the Colonial Frontier* (New York, 1972); R. H. Pearce, *Savagism and Civilization: a Study of the Indian and the American Mind* (Baltimore, 1967); F. P. Prucha, *American Indian Policy in the Formative Years: the Indian Trade and Intercourse Acts, 1790–1834* (Cambridge, Mass., 1962); W. E. Washburn, *The Indian in America* (New York, 1975); A. T. Vaughan, *New England Frontier: Puritans*

and Indians, 1620–1675 (Boston, 1965). Most of these books contain good bibliographies.

4   Vaughan, *New England Frontier*, p.323.

5   J. M. McDonald, 'Treaties, territorial adjustments, and planned acculturation: negotiations and compensations in the evolution of the American Indian reservation pattern, 1778–1869', unpublished paper presented to the *Association of American Geographers* New York meeting, 1976. I am indebted to Dr. McDonald for this information.

6   Quoted in D. McNickle, 'Indian and European: Indian-White relations from discovery to 1887', in R. C. Owen, J. J. F. Deetz and A. D. Fisher (eds), *The North American Indians. A Sourcebook* (Toronto, 1967), pp.622–35, on p.634.

7   For more specialist interpretations of the Dawes Act and the general principle of allotment, see, for example, A. Debo, *And Still the Waters Run* (Princeton, N.J., 1940), concerning the Choctaws; R. W. Meyer, *History of the Santee Sioux: United States Indian Policy on Trial* (Lincoln, Neb., 1967); L. B. Priest, *Uncle Sam's Stepchildren: the Reformation of United States Indian Policy, 1865–1887* (New Brunswick, N.J., 1942).

8   Senator Pendleton of Ohio, arguing for the Dawes Act, quoted in McNickle, 'Indian and European', p.635.

9   This is not to say, however, that the American Indians did not transform their environment. Their use of fire, above all, profoundly influenced botanical succession on the western plains. The Australian Aborigines and the New Zealand Maoris were similarly highly significant ecological agents.

10 Based on McDonald, 'Treaties'.

11 This map has been adapted from the maps of S. B. Hilliard in *Map Supplement 16, Annals, Association of American Geographers*, 62 (1972). Compare the distribution with that shown on Fig. 5.

12 Horsman, *Expansion and American Indian Policy, 1783–1812*.

13 B. W. Sheehan, 'Indian-White relations in early America', in F. P. Prucha (ed), *The Indian in American History* (New York, 1971), pp.51–66, quotation on p.64.

14 T. R. Wessell, 'Agriculture, Indians, and American history', *Agricultural History*, 50 (1976), 9–20; the quotation appears on pp.19–20.

15 *ibid.*

16 This section draws on the following sources: B. J. Dalton, *War and Politics in New Zealand 1855–1870* (Sydney, 1967); B. J. Murton, 'Changing patterns of land ownership in Poverty Bay, 1869–88', *New Zealand Geographer*, 22 (1966), 166–76; J. G. A. Pocock (ed), *The Maori and New Zealand Politics* (Auckland and Hamilton, 1965); K. Sinclair, *The Origins of the Maori Wars* (Auckland, 1961); M. P. K. Sorrenson, 'Land purchase methods and the effect on Maori population, 1865–1901', *Journal of the Polynesian Society*, 65 (1956), 183–99. The most readable introductory text for geographers is K. B. Cumberland and J. S. Whitelaw, *New Zealand* (London, 1970). Other useful works include R. Chapman and K. Sinclair (eds), *Studies of a Small Democracy: Essays in Honour of Willis Airey* (Auckland, 1963); J. Miller, *Early Victorian New Zealand. A Study of Racial Tension and Social Attitudes 1839–1852* (Wellington, 1974; first published 1958).

17 For a good discussion see M. P. K. Sorrenson, 'The Maori King movement, 1858–1885', in Chapman and Sinclair, *Studies of a Small Democracy*, pp.33–55. For a more general exposition of the significance of

charismatic and other leaders, so important in the study of Maori affairs, see M. Winiata, *The Changing Role of the Leader in Maori Society: A Study in Social Change and Race Relations* (Auckland, 1967).

18   Quoted in M. P. K. Sorrenson, 'The politics of land', in Pocock, *The Maori and New Zealand Politics*, pp.21–45, on p.30.

19   For some useful perspectives, see H. C. M. Norris, *Armed Settlers: the Story of the Founding of Hamilton, New Zealand, 1864–74* (Hamilton, 1956).

20   The maps in Fig. 11 were compiled from the collection of more detailed official sources held in the Alexander Turnbull Library, Wellington, New Zealand.

21   Winiata, *Changing Role of the Leader*.

22   These aspects are best outlined in Pocock, *The Maori and New Zealand Politics*.

23   For further information, see R. C. Harris and J. Warkentin, *Canada before Confederation* (New York, 1974); D. Pryde, *Nunaga: My Land, My Country* (Edmonton, 1972); P. J. Usher, *The Banks Landers: Economy and Ecology of a Frontier Trapping Community* (Ottawa, 1971, 3 vols.).

24   The best guides are R. M. Berndt and C. H. Berndt (eds), *Aboriginal Man in Australia: Essays in Honour of A. P. Elkin* (Sydney, 1965); R. M. Berndt (ed), *Australian Aboriginal Anthropology* (Nedlands, W.A., 1970); G. Blainey, *The Triumph of the Nomads* (Melbourne, 1975); C. D. Rowley, *The Destruction of Aboriginal Society* (Canberra, 1970); J. Woolmington (ed), *Aborigines in Colonial Society: 1788–1850. From 'Noble Savage' to 'Rural Pest'* (Melbourne, 1973).

25   R. Nash, *Wilderness and the American Mind* (New Haven and London, 1967), p.2. This is an indispensable guide to the subject and has been drawn on heavily, with some reservations, in this section.

26   *ibid.*, p.4.

27   This interpretation has been influenced by Y. F. Tuan, 'Man and Nature', *Association of American Geographers, Commission on College Geography Resource Paper No. 10* (Washington, 1971).

28   See, for example, Smith, *Historical Geography of Western Europe*, pp.171–88; R. A. Donkin, 'The Cistercian Order in mediaeval England: some conclusions', *Transactions, Institute of British Geographers*, 33 (1963), 181–98. For a wider view of some of these themes, see G. H. Williams, *Wilderness and Paradise in Christian Thought* (New York, 1962).

29   Glacken, *Traces on the Rhodian Shore*, Part Two, 'The Christian Middle Ages', pp.171–351.

30   *ibid.*, pp.495–6.

31   M. H. Nicolson, *Mountain Gloom and Mountain Glory: the Development of the Aesthetics of the Infinite* (Ithaca, 1959).

32   H. N. Fairchild, *The Noble Savage: a Study in Romantic Naturalism* (New York, 1928); W. J. Hipple, *The Beautiful, the Sublime, and the Picturesque in Eighteenth Century British Aesthetics* (Carbondale, Ill., 1957); for some more specific examples, see B. Smith, *European Vision and the South Pacific, 1768–1850* (London, 1960).

33   Useful general works exploring these themes include E. von Erdberg, *Chinese Influence on European Garden Structures* (Cambridge, 1936); W. G. Hoskins, *The Making of the English Landscape* (London, 1965; first published 1955); C. Hussey, *The Picturesque: Studies in a Point of View* (London, 1967; first published 1927). And note the approach in G. A. Jellicoe and S.

Jellicoe, *The Landscape of Man* (London, 1975) which is closely related to that adopted in the present book. I have not mentioned the later Japanese influence, which was very important in the New World: for an example, see C. Lancaster, *The Japanese Influence in America* (New York, 1963).

34   Nash, *Wilderness*; S. P. Hays, *Conservation and the Gospel of Efficiency* (New York, 1959; reprinted 1972); H. Huth, *Nature and the American. Three Centuries of Changing Attitudes* (Berkeley, Calif., 1957; reprinted Lincoln, Neb., 1972).

35   R. Nash, 'American environmental history: a new teaching frontier', *Pacific Historical Review*, 41 (1972), 363–72.

36   See, for example, the works cited above in n.29, Chapter 3. For a general survey of wilderness ideas and the park movement in Australia, see J. M. Powell, *Environmental Management in Australia, 1788–1914: Guardians, Improvers and Profit* (Melbourne, 1976).

37   The most readable account of these developments is given in P. J. Schmitt, *Back to Nature: the Arcadian Myth in Urban America* (New York, 1969).

38   Tuan, 'Man and Nature'. The idea is treated in more detail in L. Marx, *The Machine in the Garden: Technology and the Pastoral Ideal in America* (New York, 1964).

39   A. Sutton and M. Sutton, *Yellowstone. A Century of the Wilderness Idea* (New York, 1972). The best general description of the early administrative history of the major national parks is given in J. Ise, *Our National Park Policy: a Critical History* (Baltimore, 1961); Yellowstone is discussed on pp.13–50.

40   *Statistical Abstract of the United States, 1974* (Washington, 1974), pp.205–6. In the same year, the National Forest Service recorded 188,175,000 'visitor-days' for the areas under its jurisdiction (the unit is reckoned on the basis of one person staying for 12 hours or 12 for one hour); in 1970 the 3,425 areas in the State Park systems comprised 8.5 million acres and attracted 50.5 million overnight stays.

41   Good introductions to their lives and works are given in a number of standard books. For Thoreau, see G. R. Anderson, *The Magic Circle of Walden* (New York, 1968); R. Rutland (ed), *Walden: a Collection of Critical Essays* (Englewood Cliffs, N.J., 1968), and especially W. J. Wolf, *Thoreau: Mystic, Prophet, Ecologist* (Philadelphia, 1974). For Muir, see H. B. Smith, *John Muir* (New York, 1965) and L. M. Wolfe, *Son of the Wilderness: the Life of John Muir* (New York, 1945). Muir is well-known to many geographers for his scientific writings as well as his proclamation of scenery: see the appreciation in J. Leighly, 'John Muir's image of the West', *Annals, Association of American Geographers* 48 (1958), 309–18.

42   Quoted in Nash, *Wilderness*, pp. 102–3.

43   H. R. Jones, *John Muir and the Sierra Club: the Battle for Yosemite* (San Francisco, 1965).

44   *ibid.*; see also Ise, *National Park Policy*, pp.85–96.

45   M. Williams, *The Making of the South Australian Landscape. A Study in the Historical Geography of Australia* (London and New York, 1974), pp.263–332.

46   Cited in W. Kollmorgen and J. Kollmorgen, 'Landscape meteorology in the Plains area', *Annals, Association of American Geographers*, 63 (1973), 424–41, on p.428. The authors also discuss the interesting contemporary notions of the 'modification of electrical influences' via the introduction of

the railroad and telegraph systems and the local and regional significance attached to the influence of water storages and irrigation schemes.

47   W. Kollmorgen, 'The woodsman's assaults on the domain of the cattleman', *Annals, Association of American Geographers*, 59 (1969), 215–39, on p.219.

48   Kollmorgen and Kollmorgen, 'Landscape meteorology'.

49   *Cf*. D. W. Meinig, *On the Margins of the Good Earth. The South Australian Wheat Frontier, 1869–1884* (Chicago, 1962, repr. Melbourne, 1970), pp.29–77 *passim*.

50   *ibid*. George Woodruffe Goyder, the Surveyor-General of South Australia, was a man of remarkable geographical and historical vision: *cf*. Powell, *Environmental Management in Australia*, pp.66–7, 86–9.

51   Quoted in Powell, *Environmental Management in Australia*, pp.69–70.

52   *ibid*.

53   This section is essentially a brief summary and critique of the following works: B. Blouet and M. Lawson (eds), *Images of the Plains. The Role of Human Nature in Settlement* (Lincoln, Neb., 1975); three papers by M. J. Bowden: 'The perception of the western interior of the United States, 1800–1870: a problem in historical geosophy', *Proceedings, Association of American Geographers*, 1 (1969), 16–21, 'The Great American Desert and the American frontier, 1800–1882: popular images of the plains and phases in the westward movement', in T. K. Harever (ed), *Anonymous Americans: Exploration in Nineteenth Century Social History* (Englewood Cliffs, N.J., 1971), pp.48–79, and especially 'The Great American Desert in the American mind: the historiography of a geographical notion', in Lowenthal and Bowden, *Geographies of the Mind*, pp.119–47; four papers by G. M. Lewis: 'Changing emphases in the descriptions of the natural environment of the American Great Plains area', *Transactions, Institute of British Geographers*, 30 (1962), 75–90, 'Three centuries of desert concepts of the cis-Rocky Mountain West', *Journal of the West*, 4 (1965), 457–68, 'William Gilpin and the concept of the Great Plains region', *Annals, Association of American Geographers*, 56 (1966), 33–51, 'Regional ideas and reality in the cis-Rocky Mountain West', *Transactions, Institute of British Geographers*, 38 (1966), 135–50; and the classical works on the subject: J. C. Malin, *The Grassland of North America: Prolegomena to its History* (Lawrence, Kan., 1947, reprinted with addenda Gloucester, Mass., 1967); W. P. Webb, *The Great Plains* (Boston, 1931, and several reprintings).

54   J. L. Allen, *Passage Through the Garden: Lewis and Clark and the Image of the American Northwest* (Urbana, Ill., 1975).

55   Quoted in D. M. Emmons, 'The influence of ideology on changing environmental images', in Blouet and Lawson, *Images of the Plains*, pp.125–36, on p.125. See also Emmons, *Garden in the Grasslands: Boomer Literature of the Central Great Plains* (Lincoln, Neb., 1971), for the promotional aspects.

56   Lewis, 'William Gilpin', p.45. Gilpin was a particularly impressive orator — ' a bardic seer . . . a mystic, burning with certainty, striving to convey to his audience the contagion of his own ecstatic vision', according to Smith, *Virgin Land*, p.37, quoted in this account by Lewis on p.46.

57   R. Bredeson, 'Landscape description in early American travel literature', *American Quarterly*, 20 (1968), 86–94; W. Goetzmann, *Exploration and Empire* (New York, 1966); Emmons, 'Influence of Ideology'.

58 Emmons, 'Influence of Ideology', p.128.
59 *ibid.*, p.129.
60 See note 53, above.
61 G. M. Tobin, *The Making of a History: Walter Prescott Webb and 'The Great Plains'* (Austin, 1976).
62 R. G. Bell, 'James C. Malin and the grasslands of North America', *Agricultural History*, 46 (1972), 412–24.
63 For a general interpretation of these Australian themes, and an introductory bibliography, see Powell, *Environmental Management in Australia*, and Williams, 'More and smaller is better'.

Chapter 5 *Elysium: the search for health*

1 R. Dubos, *Mirage of Health* (New York, 1959), pp.13–14.
2 This section draws heavily on W. G. Rothstein, *American Physicians in the Nineteenth Century: from Sects to Science* (Baltimore and London, 1972) and on the following works: D. J. Boorstin, 'New world medicine', in his *The Americans: the Colonial Experience* (Harmondsworth, 1965), pp.235–70 and bibliography, pp.442–7; R. H. Shryock, *The Development of Modern Medicine* (London, 1948; first published New York, 1936), and *Medicine in America: Historical Essays* (Baltimore, 1966), especially pp.71–89, 252–8, 307–32; F. Marti-Ibanez (ed), *H. E. Sigerist on the History of Medicine* (New York, 1960). Rothstein's analysis is particularly interesting in so far as it concentrates on the emergence of the occupational group itself rather than on the growth and diffusion of scientifically valid medical knowledge and the health of the populace.
3 Shryock, *Development of Modern Medicine*, pp.129–43.
4 Thomas Jefferson (1807), quoted in Boorstin, *The Americans*, pp.245–6.
5 See, for example, C. Bridenbaugh, 'Baths and watering places of colonial America', *William and Mary Quarterly*, 3 (1946), 151–81; H. Huth, *Nature and the American*, pp.105–28; H. E. Sigerist, 'American spas in historical perspective', *Bulletin of the History of Medicine*, 11 (1942), 133–47.
6 Shryock, *Development of Modern Medicine*, p.154.
7 See, for example, Rothstein, *American Physicians*, pp.125–74. Note that in this context, 'monistic' indicates that a single 'proximate cause' or underlying origin of all morbid phenomena was assumed. It might also be pointed out that the closest connection between environmental science and colonial medicine developed from detailed 'clinical' or field observations in botanical research, a field in which many of the early doctors excelled. The long-standing interest in 'herbal remedies' and the like was similarly based. For a guide to some Australian parallels see Powell, *Environmental Management in Australia*, pp.15–17.
8 The significance of the various religious and secular utopian communities in the search for health is touched upon in Chapter 6. Osteopathy, chiropractic and Mary Baker Eddy's Christian Science movement were also growing strongly at this time; the common feature distinguishing these later nineteenth-century cults from the earlier developments was their stringent espousal of drugless therapy. For an interpretation see L. S. Reed, *The Healing Cults* (Chicago, 1932).
9 For an appreciation see E. F. Horine, 'Daniel Drake and his medical classic', *Journal, Kentucky State Medical Association*, 50 (1952), 68–79.

10   J. E. Bauer, *Health Seekers of Southern California, 1870–1900* (San Marino, 1959); B. M. Jones, *Health-Seekers in the Southwest, 1817–1900* (Norman, 1967).

11   J. E. Vance, jr., 'California and the search for the ideal', *Annals, Association of American Geographers*, 62 (1972), 185–210; the quotation appears on p.197, my italics. It is also interesting to note that some modern theories argue that human physiological evolution in the tropics may be the ultimate basis for some climatic preferences. 'Thermal stress' may still be far more powerful than we care to admit in influencing migration patterns. See, for example, L. M. Svart, 'Environmental preference migration: a review', *Geographical Review*, 66 (1976), 314–30.

12   See the highly personalized but very stylish evocation of this and other themes in K. Starr, *Americans and the California Dream 1850–1915* (New York, 1973) and the treatment of the state's continuing attraction in modern times in W. J. Stein, *California and the Dust Bowl Migration* (Westport, Conn., 1968).

13   Starr, *California Dream*, p.370.

14   J. Blake (1852) and Hittel (1862), quoted in K. Thompson, 'Insalubrious California: perception and reality', *Annals, Association of American Geographers*, 59 (1969), 50–64, on pp.51–2.

15   C. Nordhoff, *California: for Health, Pleasure, and Residence. A Book for Travellers and Settlers* (New York, 1873), p.11.

16   R. J. Roske, *Everyman's Eden: a History of California* (New York, 1968), pp.413–24.

17   Bauer, *Health Seekers*, p.176.

18   See the maps in Thompson, 'Insalubrious California', p.54, and Vance, 'California', p.197. Note that 'sanitarium' derives from *sanitas* and simply implies healthy living in a comfortable and salubrious or hygienic environment; 'sanatorium' is, however, derived from *sanare* (to treat) and replaced the former term when more active forms of intervention or treatment based on the germ theory became normal.

19   K. Thompson, 'Irrigation as a menace to health in California. A nineteenth century view', *Geographical Review*, 59 (1969), 195–214.

20   *ibid.* Yellow fever, dysentery and typhoid were also frequently considered to be 'malarial' (literally 'of bad air') in origin. Malaria proper is transmitted by the bite of the anopheles mosquito; this was eventually established after the work of Laveran (1880), Ross (1897) and Grassi (1898).

21   T. M. Logan, 'General report to the Governor', *Third Biennial Report, State Board of Health of California for the Years 1874 and 1875*, cited in Thompson, 'Irrigation as a menace to health', p.204.

22   *Cf.* R. W. Kates, 'Natural hazard in human ecological perspective: hypotheses and models', *Economic Geography*, 47 (1971), 438–51.

23   K. Thompson, 'The Australian fever tree in California: eucalypts and malarial prophylaxis', *Annals, Association of American Geographers*, 60 (1970), 230–44.

24   Cited in Thompson, 'Irrigation as a menace to health', pp.212–13.

25   This case-study is a condensed version of J. M. Powell, 'Medical promotion and the consumptive immigrant to Australia', *Geographical Review*, 63 (1973), 449–76, by permission of the American Geographical Society.

26   J. Elliot (ed), *A Complete Collection of the Medical and Philosophical Works of*

John Fothergill (London, 1781); A. B. Granville, *The Spas of England and Principal Sea-Bathing Places* (London, 1841, 2 vols.); E. Gilchrist, *The Use of Sea-Voyages in Medicine, and Particularly in Consumption, with observations on that Disease* (London, 1771). Hippocrates himself, four centuries before Christ, indulged in deterministic views of climate control over human health; these ideas were to some extent resuscitated during the eighteenth century. See, for example, Glacken, *Traces on the Rhodian Shore*, pp.80–115, 429–60, 501–654, and E. H. Ackernecht, *History and Geography of the Most Important Diseases* (New York and London, 1965).

27   See, for example, J. Clark, *A Treatise on Pulmonary Consumption* (London, 1835) and *The Sanative Influence of Climate, with an Account of the Best Places of Resort for Invalids in England, the South of Europe, etc.* (3rd edition, London, 1841).

28   An excellent bibliography and technical discussion of these aspects appears in B. Thomas and B. Gandevia, 'Dr. Francis Workman, emigrant, and the history of taking the cure for consumption in the Australian colonies', *Medical Journal of Australia*, 2 (1959), 1–10. Dr. Gandevia is the leading authority on the history of medicine in Australia and his interpretation of the field as 'one facet of the story of man's adaptation to his environment' has particular appeal for the cultural-historical geographer — 'Complex interactions between man and the physical, cultural, religious and socio-economic components of his environment determine not only the medical problems encountered but also the medical practice': B. Gandevia, 'The medico-historical significance of young and developing countries, illustrated by Australian experience', in E. Clarke (ed), *Modern Methods in the History of Medicine* (London, 1971), pp.75–98.

29   *The Lancet*, 2 (1827–8), 480.

30   *ibid.*, 1 (1837–8), 716–17.

31   Wakefield's several works are reproduced in M. F. Lloyd-Prichard (ed), *The Collected Works of Edward Gibbon Wakefield* (Glasgow and London, 1968).

32   Wakefield, in Lloyd-Prichard, *Collected Works*, p.149.

33   *Historical Records of Australia*, Series 1, vol. 15, 377.

34   J. Kilgour, *Effect of the Climate of Australia upon the European Constitution in Health and Disease* (Geelong, 1855).

35   F. Lancelott, *Australia As It Is: Its Settlements, Farms, and Gold Fields* (2 vols., London, 1852), 1, 173–6.

36   J. Inglis ('Maori'), *Our Australian Cousins* (London, 1880). Several references to this situation appeared from time to time in the *Australasian Insurance and Banking Record*.

37   *The Lancet*, 1 (1854), 58–9.

38   S. D. Bird, *On Australasian Climates and Their Influence in the Prevention and Arrest of Pulmonary Consumption* (London, 1863).

39   *ibid.*, p.15.

40   *ibid.*, p.18.

41   Victoria became a separate colony in 1851; prior to that it was the Port Phillip District of New South Wales. Gold mining was very active in the 1850s and 1860s.

42   *The Lancet*, 2 (1863), 539–40; quotation on p.539.

43   I. B. Brown, *Australia for the Consumptive Invalid: the Voyage, Climates, and Prospects for Residence* (London, 1865).

44 The only reviews located appeared in the *Australian Medical Journal*, 2 (1866), 155, and the *British and Foreign Medico-Chirurgical Review*, 39 (1867), 89.

45 *The Lancet*, 2 (1869), 347–8.

46 For an example of this type of promotion, see Powell, *Public Lands of Australia Felix*, pp.99–102.

47 *ibid.*; see also G. J. Abbott and N. B. Nairn (eds), *Economic Growth of Australia, 1788–1892* (Melbourne, 1969).

48 *The Age* (Melbourne), 29 January 1870.

49 *ibid.*, 4 February 1870. Bird was described as 'an author absorbed with the grandeur of the notion of regulating the struma-saturated races of Europe, and renewing their types by "transplantation of masses to antipodal climates"'. Deaths from phthisis in both England and Victoria then comprised between 10 and 11 percent of all registered mortality. Some 40 or 50 percent of all deaths in the Melbourne Hospital were attributed to phthisis; between 1865 and 1870 there were said to be at least 2,143 deaths from tuberculosis in Victoria, and about 1,850 of these involved the consumptive immigrants. The information had very little effect in Britain, however: in the *British Medical Journal*, 2 (1871), 433–4, one J. C. Thorowgood proclaimed, 'It seems as if, while emigration is the remedy for a surplus population, it will also powerfully act if judicially used as a means of correcting *hereditary* tendency to disease, and so improving the breed of mankind' (my italics).

50 Thomson's special field of study was typhoid fever.

51 *Victorian Year Book, 1874* (Melbourne, 1875), p.198.

52 *Victorian Year Book, 1875* (Melbourne, 1876), p.136. Hayter was an honorary member of the Statistical Society of London and an active participant in colonial scientific and philosophical societies.

53 *Victorian Year Book, 1876–1877* (Melbourne, 1877), p.76.

54 *The Lancet*, 2 (1873), 474; J. Singleton, 'Phthisis in Victoria', *Australian Medical Journal*, 21 (1876), 278–86; B. J. Newmarch, 'New South Wales as a health resort in phthisis pulmonalis', *Journal and Proceedings, Royal Society of New South Wales*, 23 (1889), 503–10. But some traditional views were still being aired in Europe at this stage: see, for example, C. Faber, 'Australia and South Africa as Health resorts, especially for consumptive invalids', *Practitioner*, 20 (1878), 17–30 and R. Esler, 'Victoria as a health resort', *Dublin Journal of Medical Science*, 69 (1880), 225–60. And the authors of emigrants' guides were reluctant to abandon such a strong selling point — see, for example, G. Sutherland, *Australia or England in the South* (London, 1886): 'there are many men now living open-air lives in the Australian bush who in the English climate would not exist, even with the greatest care and caution. Probably there is no air or climate which can cure a case of far-gone consumption, but anything short of that is readily ameliorated, if not entirely removed, by the genial atmosphere of Australia' (p.48).

55 Inglis, *Our Australian Cousins*, p.335.

56 *Victorian Year Book, 1890–91* (Melbourne, 1891), pp.380–2.

57 See the summary graphs and tables for the period in Powell, 'Medical promotion and the consumptive immigrant', and the distinction between *sanitaria* and *sanatoria* in n. 18. above.

58 Dubos, *Mirage of Health*, p.230.

59 Starr, *California Dream*, p.vii.
60 Dubos, *Mirage of Health*, p.230.

Chapter 6 *Utopia, millenium and the co-operative ideal*

1 This chapter is a revised and greatly expanded version of J. M. Powell, 'Utopia, millennium and the co-operative ideal: a behavioural matrix in the settlement process', *Australian Geographer*, 11 (1971), 606–18.
2 O. Wilde, *The Soul of Man Under Socialism* (Boston, n.d.).
3 *Cf.* A. Huxley, *The Humanist Frame* (London, 1961).
4 See, for example, W. H. G. Armytage, *Heavens Below: Utopian Experiments in England, 1560–1960* (London, 1961); G. Kateb, *Utopia and its Enemies* (London, 1963); G. Negley and J. M. Patrick, *The Quest for Utopia: an Anthology of Imaginary Societies* (New York, 1952). For More, see B. R. Goodey, 'Mapping "utopia": a comment on the geography of Sir Thomas More', *Geographical Review*, 60 (1970), 15–30.
5 A. E. Morgan, *Nowhere was Somewhere: How History makes Utopias and How Utopias make History* (Chapel Hill, N.C., 1946).
6 L. Mumford, *The Story of Utopias* (New York, 1922).
7 *Cf.* J. H. Andreae, *Christianopolis: an Ideal State of the Seventeenth Century* (trans. F. E. Held, Oxford, 1916); C. Andrews (ed), *Ideal Empires and Republics* (New York and London, 1901).
8 Good examples are A. Huxley, *Brave New World: A Novel* (London, 1952) and G. Orwell, *Nineteen Eighty Four, A Novel* (London, 1949).
9 *Cf.* Mumford, *Utopias*.
10 Powell, 'The land debates in Victoria, 1872–1884', *Journal of the Royal Australian Historical Society*, 56 (1970), 263–80.
11 For general summaries, see W. P. Reeves, *State Experiments in Australia and New Zealand* (London, 1902, 2 vols.) and S. H. Roberts, *History of Australian Land Settlement, 1788–1920* (Melbourne, 1924; repr. 1968).
12 M. Holloway, *Heavens on Earth. Utopian Communities in America, 1680–1880* (New York, 1966), p.17.
13 S. L. Thrupp (ed), *Millennial Dreams in Action* (The Hague, 1962).
14 *ibid.*, p.22.
15 *ibid.*, p.17.
16 G. Shepperson, 'The comparative study of millenarian movements', in Thrupp, *Millennial Dreams*, pp.44–5.
17 N. Cohn, *The Pursuit of the Millennium* (London, 1957) and 'Mediaeval millenarism: its bearing on the comparative study of millenarian movements', in Thrupp, *Millennial Dreams*, pp.31–43.
18 *ibid.*
19 M. Eliade, 'Paradise and utopia: mythical geography and eschatology', in F. E. Manuel (ed), *Utopias and Utopian Thought* (Boston, 1967), pp.260–80.
20 M. Eliade, *Myth and Reality* (New York, 1963).
21 *ibid.*
22 *Cf.* P. H. Johnstone, 'In praise of husbandry', *Agricultural History*, 11 (1937), 80–95, and 'Turnips and romanticism', *Agricultural History*, 12 (1938), 224–55. See also Chapter 3 in this book.
23 A good discussion of this theme appears in P. Miller, *The Life of the Mind in America* (New York, 1965).
24 Armytage, *Heavens Below*.

25 *Cf.* H. E. Bolton, *Texas in the Middle Eighteenth Century* (Berkeley, 1915); D. Meyer, *The Highland Scots of North Carolina, 1732–1776* (Chapel Hill, N.C., 1961); D. W. Meinig, *Imperial Texas: an Interpretive Essay in Cultural Geography* (Austin, 1969); L. B. Simpson, *The Encomienda in New Spain: the Beginnings of Spanish Mexico* (Berkeley and Los Angeles, Calif., 1966). The 'cultural island' concept is very well discussed in these early articles by Walter Kollmorgen: 'A reconnaissance of some cultural-agricultural islands in the South', *Economic Geography*, 17 (1941), 409–30; 'Agricultural-cultural islands in the South: Part 2', *Economic Geography*, 19 (1943), 109–17; 'Immigrant settlements in southern agriculture: a commentary on the significance of cultural islands in agricultural history', *Agricultural History*, 19 (1945), 69–78.

26 Holloway, *Heavens on Earth*, p.29.

27 J. F. C. Harrison, *Robert Owen and the Owenites in Britain and America: the Quest for the New Moral World* (London, 1969).

28 M. Lockwood, 'The experimental utopia in America', in Manuel, *Utopias and Utopian Thought*, pp.183–200, quotation on pp.184–5.

29 *Cf.* J. H. Shideler, *A Preliminary List of References for the History of Agriculture in California* (Davis, Calif., 1967), pp.25–6.

30 E. Bellamy, *Looking Backward, 200–1887* (Boston, 1888).

31 R. V. Hine, *California's Utopian Communities* (San Marino, Calif., 1953). Compare the recent interesting discussion of utopia as a historical-geographical force, in P. W. Porter and F. E. Lukermann, 'The Geography of utopia', in Lowenthal and Bowden, *Geographies of the Mind*, pp.197–223, which also contains additional bibliographical information and an intriguing note on the utopist work of J. K. Wright's brother (Austin Tappan Wright), *Islandia*, published in 1942.

32 See, for example, L. J. Blake, 'Village settlements', *Educational Magazine*, 21 (1964), 425–32, 463–8, and 'Village settlement', *Victorian Historical Magazine*, 37 (1966), 189–201.

33 A. R. Wallace, *Land Nationalization, its Necessity and Aims* (London, 1882), and Powell, 'Land debates'.

34 Powell, 'An Australian utopia' and 'Arcadia and back'.

35 J. Warkentin, 'Mennonite agricultural settlements of southern Manitoba', *Geographical Review*, 49 (1959), 342–68.

36 A. Maude, *A Peculiar People: the Doukhobórs* (London, 1904).

37 There are between 7,000 and 8,000 Doukhobórs in Saskatchewan and Alberta and another 10–12,000 in West Kootenay, British Columbia. The fanatical wing of 3,000, the 'Sons of Freedom', is comprised of rigid fundamentalists who react bitterly to the Canadian authorities, regularly refusing to pay taxes, to be enumerated at the census, and to send their children to school; periodically they burn their own and others' property to express their condemnation of material wealth.

38 J. A. Hostetler and G. E. Huntington, 'Communal socialization patterns in Hutterite society', *Ethnology*, 7 (1968), 331–55; quotation is on p.353. See also J. A. Hostetler, *Hutterite Society* (Baltimore, 1974); J. W. Bennett, *Hutterian Brethren: the Agricultural Economy and Social Organization of a Communal People* (Stanford, Calif., 1967).

39 Kateb, *Utopia and its Enemies*.

40 K. Hoeppner and J. Gill, *Communal Property in Alberta* (Alberta Land Use Forum, Technical Report No. 60, Edmonton, 1974). See also W. G.

Laatsch, 'Hutterite colonization in Alberta', *Journal of Geography,* 70 (1971), 347–59; S. M. Evans, 'The spatial expression of cultural identity: the Hutterites in Alberta', in B. M. Barr (ed), *Kootenay Collection of Research Studies, Brit. Col. Geog. Series* No. 18 (Vancouver, 1974), pp.9–20.

41 See, for example, H. Cantril, *The Psychology of Social Movements* (New York, 1941); C. W. King, *Social Movements in the United States* (New York, 1958); N. F. Washbourne, *Interpreting Social Change in America* (New York, 1954). For a recent excellent social-psychological interpretation see R. M. Kanter, *Commitment and Community: Communes and Utopias in Sociological Perspective* (Cambridge, Mass., 1973).

42 E. Battis, *Saints and Sectaries: Anne Hutchinson and the Antinomian Controversy in the Massachusetts Bay Colony* (Chapel Hill, N.C., 1962).

43 *ibid.,* p.255.

44 G. T. Trewartha, 'Types of rural settlement in colonial America', *Geographical Review,* 36 (1946), 568–96.

45 S. C. Powell, *Puritan Village: the Formation of a New England Town* (New York, 1965). See also D. McManis, *Colonial New England. A Historical Geography* (New York, 1975) for a more modern geographical interpretation.

46 Kanter, *Commitment and Community.*

47 See n. 25 above.

48 G. A. Dawson, *Group Settlement: Ethnic Communities in Western Canada* (Toronto, 1936).

49 *Cf.* two works by E. D. Andrews: *The People Called Shakers. A Search for the Perfect Society* (New York, 1963, first published 1953) and *The Community Industries of the Shakers* (Philadelphia, 1972, first published 1932); A. E. Bestor, *Backwoods Utopias: the Sectarian and Owenite Phases of Communitarian Socialism in America, 1663–1829* (Philadelphia, 1950); C. Nordhoff, *The Communistic Societies of the United States* (London and New York, 1875, reprinted New York, 1966). See also D. H. Davis, 'Amana: a study of occupance', *Economic Geography,* 12 (1936), 217–30; R. Jones, *The Quakers in the American Colonies* (New York, 1966).

50 E. M. Bjorklund, 'Ideology and culture exemplified in South-western Michigan', *Annals, Association of American Geographers,* 54 (1964), 227–41.

51 J. E. Landing, 'Geographic models of Old Order Amish settlements', *Professional Geographer,* 21 (1969), 238–43. See also J. A. Hostetler, *Amish Society* (Baltimore, 1968).

52 J. Nelson, *The Mormon Village: a Pattern and Technique of Land Settlement* (Salt Lake City, 1952); N. Anderson, *Desert Saints: the Mormon Frontier in Utah* (Chicago, 1942, reprinted 1966).

53 D. W. Meinig, 'The Mormon culture region: strategies and patterns in the geography of the American West', *Annals, Association of American Geographers,* 55 (1965), 191–200. See also R. V. Francaviglia, 'The Mormon landscape: definition of an image in the American West', *Proceedings, Association of American Geographers,* 2 (1970), 59–61.

54 W. V. Pooley, *The Settlement of Illinois from 1830 to 1850* (Madison, 1908). The process is best described in R. E. Nelson, 'The Role of Colonies in the Pioneer Settlement of Henry County, Illinois', unpublished Ph.D. thesis, University of Nebraska, Lincoln, 1970.

55 Nelson, 'Role of Colonies', pp.120–88.

56 *Cf.* Kanter, *Commitment and Community.*

Chapter 7   *Mirrors*

1   P. White, *Voss* (Harmondsworth, 1963, first published 1957), p.446.
2   W. R. Brock, 'Americanism', in D. Welland (ed), *The United States. A Companion to American Studies* (London, 1974), pp.59–88; quoted section appears on p.66.

Select Bibliography

Allen, J.L., *Passage Though the Garden: Lewis and Clark and the Image of the American Northwest* (Urbana, Ill., 1975)

Ander, O.F. (ed), *In the Trek of the Immigrants* (Rock Island, Ill., 1964)

Anderson, N., *Desert Saints: the Mormon Frontier in Utah* (Chicago, 1942; repr. 1966)

Ankli, R.E., 'Farm-making costs in the 1850s', *Agricultural History*, 48 (1974), 51–70

Battis, E., *Saints and Sectaries: Anne Hutchinson and the Antinomian Controversy in the Massachusetts Bay Colony* (Chapel Hill, N.C., 1962)

Bauer, J.E., *Health Seekers of Southern California, 1870–1900* (San Marino, 1959)

Bell, R.G., 'James C. Malin and the grasslands of North America', *Agricultural History*, 46 (1972), 412–24

Bell, W. and Mau, J.A. (eds), *The Sociology of the Future: Theory, Cases, and Annotated Bibliography* (New York, 1971)

Bennett, J.W., *Hutterian Brethren: the Agricultural Economy and Social Organization of a Communal People* (Stanford, Calif., 1967)

Berndt, R.M. (ed), *Australian Aboriginal Anthropology* (Nedlands, Western Australia, 1970)

Bestor, A.E., *Backwoods Utopias: the Sectarian and Owenite Phases of Communitarian Socialism in America, 1663–1829* (Philadelphia, 1950)

Billington, R.A., *America's Frontier Heritage* (New York, 1966)

Bjorklund, E.M., 'Ideology and culture exemplified in South-western Michigan', *Annals, Association of American Geographers*, 54 (1964), 227–41

Blainey, G., *The Triumph of the Nomads* (Melbourne, 1975)

Blegen, T.C., *Land of their Choice: the Immigrants Write Home* (Minneapolis, 1955)

Blouet, B. and Lawson, M. (eds), *Images of the Plains. The Role of Human Nature in Settlement* (Lincoln, Neb., 1975)

Bogue, A.G., *From Prairie to Corn Belt. Farming on the Illinois and Iowa Prairies in the Nineteenth Century* (Chicago, 1963)

Bogue, M.B., *Patterns from the Sod: Land Use and Tenure in the Grand Prairie, 1850–1900* (Springfield, Ill., 1959)

Boorstin, D., *The Americans: the Colonial Experience* (Harmondsworth, 1965)

Boulding, K., *The Image: Knowledge in Life and Society* (Ann Arbor, 1956)

Bowden, M.J., 'The perception of the western interior of the United States, 1800–1870: a problem in historical geosophy', *Proceedings, Association of American Geographers*, 1 (1969), 16–21

Cameron, J.M.R., 'Prelude to colonization: James Stirling's and Charles Fraser's examination of Swan River, March 1827', *Australian Geographer*, 12 (1973), 309–27

Cameron, J.M.R., 'Information distortion in colonial promotion: the case of Swan River colony', *Australian Geographical Studies*, 12 (1974), 57–76

Cameron, J.M.R., 'Western Australia, 1616–1829: an antipodean paradise', *Geographical Journal*, 140 (1974), 373–85

Cameron, J.M.R., 'Distortions in pre-settlement land evaluation: the case of Swan River, Western Australia', *Professional Geographer*, 26 (1974), 393–8

Carstensen, V. (ed), *The Public Lands. Studies in the History of the Public Domain* (Madison, 1963)

Coleman, T., *Passage to America* (London, 1972)

Commager, H.S. and Giordanetti, E., *Was America a Mistake?* (New York, 1967)

Conway, A. (ed), *The Welsh in America: Letters from the Immigrants* (Minneapolis, 1961)

Dalton, B.J., *War and Politics in New Zealand 1855–1870* (Sydney, 1967)

Danhof, C., *Change in Agriculture: the Northern United States, 1820–1870* (Cambridge, Mass., 1969)

Dawson, C.A., *Group Settlement: Ethnic Communities in Western Canada* (Toronto, 1936)

Dubos, R., *Mirage of Health* (New York, 1959)

Echevarria, D., *Mirage in the West. A History of the French Image of American Society to 1815* (Princeton, 1957)

Emmons, D.M., *Garden in the Grasslands: Boomer Literature of the Central Great Plains* (Lincoln, Neb., 1971)

Erickson, C., *Invisible Immigrants: the Adaptation of English and Scottish Immigrants in 19th Century America* (London, 1972)

Evans, S.M., 'The spatial expression of cultural identity: the Hutterites in Alberta', in Barr, B.M. (ed), *Kootenay Collection of Research Studies, British Columbia Geographical Series* No. 18 (Vancouver, 1974), pp.9–20

Finley, R.M., 'A budgeting approach to the question of homestead size on the plains', *Agricultural History*, 42 (1968), 109–14

Fite, G.L., 'Daydreams and nightmares: the late nineteenth-century agricultural frontier', *Agricultural History*, 40 (1966), 285–93

Gates, P.W., *The Illinois Central Railroad and its Colonization Work* (Cambridge, Mass., 1934; repr. New York, 1969)

Glacken, C.J., *Traces on the Rhodian Shore. Nature and Culture in Western Thought from Ancient Times to the End of the Eighteenth Century* (Berkeley and Los Angeles, Calif., 1967)

Goetzmann, W., *Exploration and Empire* (New York, 1966)

Guelke, L., 'An idealist alternative in human geography', *Annals, Association of American Geographers*, 64 (1974), 193–202

Guelke, L., 'On rethinking historical geography', *Area*, 7 (1975), 135–8

Hagan, W.T., *The Indian in American History* (New York, 1963)

Hansen, M.L., *The Atlantic Migration 1607–1860* (Cambridge, Mass., 1940)

Hays, S.P., *Conservation and the Gospel of Efficiency* (New York, 1959; repr. 1972)

Heathcote, R.L., *Australia* (London, 1975)

Hedges, J.B., 'Promotion of immigration to the Pacific Northwest by the railroads', *Mississippi Valley Historical Review*, 15 (1928), 183–203

Hibbard, B., *A History of Public Land Policies* (New York, 1926; repr. 1965)

Holloway, M., *Heavens on Earth. Utopian Communities in America, 1680–1880* (New York, 1966)

Horsman, R., *Expansion and American Indian Policy, 1783–1812* (East Lansing, Mich., 1967)

Hostetler, J.A., *Amish Society* (Baltimore, 1968)

Hostetler, J.A., *Hutterite Society* (Baltimore, 1974)

Hudson, J.C., 'Two Dakota homestead frontiers', *Annals, Association of American Geographers*, 63 (1973), 442–62

Hudson, J.C., 'Migration to an American frontier', *Annals, Association of American Geographers*, 66 (1976), 242–65

Huth, H., *Nature and the American. Three Centuries of Changing Attitudes* (Berkeley, Calif., 1957; repr. Lincoln, Neb., 1972)

Ise, J., *Our National Park Policy: a Critical History* (Baltimore, 1961)

Jacobs, W.R., *Dispossessing the American Indian: Indians and Whites on the Colonial Frontier* (New York, 1972)

Janson, F.E., *The Background of Swedish Immigration, 1840–1930* (New York, 1970; first pub. Chicago, 1931)

Jones, H.M., 'The colonial impulse: an analysis of the "promotion" literature of colonization', *Proceedings, American Philosophical Society*, 90 (1946), 131–61

Jones, H.R., *John Muir and the Sierra Club: the Battle for Yosemite* (San Francisco, 1965)

Jones, R., *The Quakers in the American Colonies* (New York, 1966)

Kanter, R.M., *Commitment and Community: Communes and Utopias in Sociological Perspective* (Cambridge, Mass., 1973)

Kollmorgen, W. and Kollmorgen, J., 'Landscape meteorology in the Plains area', *Annals, Association of American Geographers*, 63 (1973), 424–41

Laatsch, W.G., 'Hutterite colonization in Alberta', *Journal of Geography*, 70 (1971), 347–59

Lansbury, C., *Arcady in Australia: the Evocation of Australia in Nineteenth-Century English Literature* (Melbourne, 1970)

Leighly, J., 'John Muir's image of the West', *Annals, Association of American Geographers*, 48 (1958), 309–18

Lewis, G.M., 'Changing emphases in the descriptions of the natural environment of the American Great Plains area', *Transactions, Institute of British Geographers*, 30 (1962), 75–90

Lewis, G.M., 'William Gilpin and the concept of the Great Plains region', *Annals, Association of American Geographers*, 56 (1966), 33–51

Lewis, G.M., 'Regional ideas and reality in the cis-Rocky Mountain West', *Transactions, Institute of British Geographers*, 38 (1966), 135–50

Ljungmark, L., *For Sale — Minnesota: Organized Promotion of Scandinavian Immigration, 1866–1873* (Chicago, 1971)

Lowenthal, D., 'Geography, experience, and imagination: towards a geographical epistemology', *Annals, Association of American Geographers*, 51 (1961), 241–60

Lowenthal, D., 'The American scene', *Geographical Review*, 58 (1968), 61–88

Lowenthal, D. and Bowden, M.J. (eds), *Geographies of the Mind* (New York, 1976)

McIntosh, C.B., 'Forest Lieu selections in the Sand Hills of Nebraska', *Annals, Association of American Geographers*, 64 (1974), 87–99

McIntosh, G., 'Use and abuse of the Timber Culture Act', *Annals, Association of American Geographers*, 65 (1975), 347–62

Malin, J.C., *The Grassland of North America: Prolegomena to its History* (Lawrence, Kan., 1947; repr. Gloucester, Mass., 1967)

Manuel, F.E. (ed), *Utopias and Utopian Thought* (Boston, 1967)

Maude, A., *A Peculiar People: the Doukhobórs* (London, 1904)

Meinig, D.W., *On the Margins of the Good Earth. The South Australian Wheat Frontier, 1869–1884* (Chicago, 1962, repr. Melbourne, 1970)

Meinig, D.W., 'The Mormon culture region: strategies and patterns in the geography of the American West', *Annals, Association of American Geographers*, 55 (1965), 191–200

Merrens, H.R., 'The physical environment of early America. Images and image-makers in colonial South Carolina', *Geographical Review*, 59 (1969), 530–56

Nash, R., *Wilderness and the American Mind* (New Haven and London, 1967)

Nash, R., 'American environmental history: a new teaching frontier', *Pacific Historical Review*, 41 (1972), 363–72

Nelson, J., *The Mormon Village: a Pattern and Technique of Land Settlement* (Salt Lake City, 1952)

Pearce, R.H., *Savagism and Civilization: a Study of the Indian and the American Mind* (Baltimore, 1967)

Pocock, J.G.A. (ed), *The Maori and New Zealand Politics* (Auckland and Hamilton, 1965)

Polak, F.L., *The Image of the Future: Enlightening the Past, Orientating the Present, Forecasting the Future* (New York, 1961, 2 vols.)

Potter, D.M., *People of Plenty* (Chicago, 1954; repr. 1973)

Powell, J.M., *The Public Lands of Australia Felix: Settlement and Land Appraisal in Victoria 1834–91* (Melbourne, 1970)

Powell, J.M., 'Utopia, millennium and the co-operative ideal: a behavioural matrix in the settlement process', *Australian Geographer*, 11 (1971), 606–18

Powell, J.M., 'Soldier Settlement in New Zealand, 1915–1923', *Australian Geographical Studies*, 9 (1971), 144–60

Powell, J.M., 'An Australian utopia', *Australian Geographer*, 12 (1973), 328–33

Powell, J.M., 'Arcadia and back: "Village Settlement" in Victoria, 1894–1913', *Australian Geographical Studies*, 11 (1973), 134–49

Powell, J.M., 'Medical promotion and the consumptive immigrant to Australia', *Geographical Review*, 63 (1973), 449–76

Powell, J.M. and Williams, M (eds), *Australian Space Australian Time* (Melbourne, 1975)

Powell, J.M., *Environmental Management in Australia, 1788–1914: Guardians, Improvers and Profit* (Melbourne, 1976)

Powell, S.C., *Puritan Village: the Formation of a New England Town* (New York, 1965)

Prince, H.C., 'Real, imagined and abstract worlds of the past', *Progress in Geography*, 3 (1971), 1–86

Prucha, F.P., *American Indian Policy in the Formative Years: the Indian Trade and Intercourse Acts, 1790–1834* (Cambridge, Mass., 1962)

Prucha, F.P. (ed), *The Indian in American History* (New York, 1971)

Robbins, R.M., *Our Landed Heritage. The Public Domain, 1776–1936* (Princeton, 1942; repr. Lincoln, Neb., 1964)

Roske, R.J., *Everyman's Eden: a History of California* (New York, 1968)

Rowley, C.D., *The Destruction of Aboriginal Society* (Canberra, 1970)

Schmitt, P.J., *Back to Nature: the Arcadian Myth in Urban America* (New York, 1969)

Shannon, F.A., *The Farmer's Last Frontier: Agriculture, 1860–1897* (New York, 1945)

Smith, C.T., *An Historical Geography of Western Europe before 1800* (London, 1967)

Smith, H.B., *John Muir* (New York, 1965)

Smith, H.N., *Virgin Land: the American West as Symbol and Myth* (New York, 1950)

Sorrenson, M.P.K., 'Land purchase methods and the affect on Maori population, 1865–1901', *Journal of the Polynesian Society*, 65 (1956), 183–99

Starr, K., *Americans and the California Dream 1850–1915* (New York, 1973)

Stein, W.J., *California and the Dust Bowl Migration* (Westport, Conn., 1973)

Taylor, P., *The Distant Magnet: European Emigration to the United States* (London, 1971)

Thomas, W.I. and Znaniecki, F., *The Polish Peasant in Europe and America* (Boston, Mass., 1918–20, 5 vols.)

Thompson, K., 'Insalubrious California: perception and reality', *Annals, Association of American Geographers*, 59 (1969), 50–64

Thompson, K., 'Irrigation as a menace to health in California. A nineteenth century view', *Geographical Review*, 59 (1969), 195–214

Thompson, K.,'The Australian fever tree in California: eucalypts and malarial prophylaxis', *Annals, Association of American Geographers*, 60 (1970), 230–44

Thrupp, S.L. (ed), *Millennial Dreams in Action* (The Hague, 1962)

Tobin, G.M., *The Making of a History: Walter Prescott Webb and 'The Great Plains'* (Austin, 1976)

Trewartha, G.T., 'Types of rural settlement in colonial America', *Geographical Review*, 36 (1946), 568–96

Tuan, Y.F., 'Man and Nature', *Association of American Geographers Resource Paper* No. 10 (Washington, 1971)

Tuan, Y.F., *Topophilia. A Study of Environmental Perception, Attitudes and Values* (Englewood Cliffs, N.J., 1974)

Tuan, Y.F., 'Images and mental maps', *Annals, Association of American Geographers*, 65 (1975), 205–13

Vance, J.E., 'California and the search for the ideal', *Annals, Association of American Geographers*, 62 (1972), 185–210

Warkentin, J., 'Mennonite agricultu.al settlements of southern Manitoba', *Geographical Review*, 49 (1959), 342–68

Washburn, W.E., *The Indian in America* (New York, 1975)

Webb, W.P., *The Great Plains* (Boston, 1931)

Webb, W.P., *The Great Frontier* (Boston, 1952)

Wessell, T.R., 'Agriculture, Indians, and American history', *Agricultural History*, 50 (1976), 9–20

Williams, M., *The Making of the South Australian Landscape. A Study in the Historical Geography of Australia* (London and New York, 1974)

Williams, M., 'The parkland towns of Australia and New Zealand', *Geographical Review*, 56 (1966), 67–89

Williams, M., 'More and smaller is better: Australian rural settlement, 1788–1914', in Powell and Williams, *Australian Space Australian Time* (1975), pp.61–103

Wolf, W.J., *Thoreau: Mystic, Prophet, Ecologist* (Philadelphia, 1974)

Wright, J.K., *'Terrae Incognitae:* the place of the imagination in geography', *Annals, Association of American Geographers*, 37 (1947), 1–15

Wright, J.K., *Human Nature in Geography. Fourteen Papers, 1925–1965* (Cambridge, Mass., 1966)

Index

Ioan. Stradanus in.